adobe ~

build it yourself

adobe~

build it yourself

REVISED EDITION

Paul Graham McHenry Jr.

The University of Arizona Press
Tucson & London

About the Author

PAUL GRAHAM McHENRY, JR., architect and builder in Albuquerque, New Mexico, has a perspective on earth architecture gained in years of building experience as well as international travel, research, writing, and lecturing. He is an international consultant for private industry and a number of foreign governments, and he teaches at the University of New Mexico School of Architecture and Planning. His other book on adobe construction, *Adobe and Rammed Earth Buildings,* is also available from the University of Arizona Press.

All photographs and drawings are the work
of the author unless otherwise credited.

Revised Edition 1985
Third Printing 1992

THE UNIVERSITY OF ARIZONA PRESS

Manufactured in the U.S.A.
♾ This book is printed on acid-free, archival-quality paper.

Library of Congress Cataloging-in-Publication Data

McHenry, Paul Graham.
Adobe: build it yourself.
Bibliography: p.
Includes index.
1. Adobe houses. 2. Building, Adobe. I. Title.
TH4818.A3M32 1985 690′.8 85-8432

ISBN 0-8165-0948-4 (pbk.)

Contents

Preface To The Revised Edition

THE CHANGES that have been made in this edition were brought about by changing environmental attitudes, a re-evaluation of our priorities, and increasing energy costs. The "easy," "undisciplined," "unconcerned," "wasteful" ways (the reader may pick the adjective) of the early 1970s have become a cause of great concern to most of us, both on environmental and economic levels. In an interval of fifteen years, basic housing costs have risen 500 percent or more. Energy costs for heating, air conditioning, and general use have been multiplied, in some areas at least, by a similar factor.

In addition, awareness of spending unrenewable resources has gone public and is not limited to the environmental alarmists who were the target of many jokes in years past. Researchers have explored the whys and wherefores of old ideas that worked in other times and have searched for scientific documentation of these successes. The net result of such research, when untainted by commercial motives or personal preconceptions, seems to be that most of the old ideas were valid. Energy awareness surfaced in the 1970s. The normal indoor heating level at that time was 72°F, but a shortage of energy supplies, with resultant higher costs, have brought this standard down to 68°F and a willingness to wear sweaters indoors. A general modification of priorities and acceptance of different standards have also taken place.

Most research projects are funded by private business, or by institutions supported by grants, or motivated by pressures generated by the business community. Adobe suffers in this regard because its use mainly benefits the homeowner or small business, there being few ways that big business can benefit directly. Manufacturers' associations such as the Portland Cement Association and the Brick Institute sponsor research projects funded by companies that promote increased use of the types of materials they manufacture. Adobe has no such champion so research efforts are limited by lack of funds and interest. Would-be homeowners, the most likely beneficiaries of such research, have no lobbies or funding sources.

Adobe-Build it Yourself was originally written in 1970 from class outlines and notes used as a text for a course at the University of New Mexico. By 1976, more than 1500 persons (few of them with experience in building) had taken the course. The result was more than 50 adobe homes and major projects in the Albuquerque/Santa Fe area—proof that such building can be done by the unskilled person. Frequently the out-of-pocket cost for these homes was half of what it would have been on the open market.

Since the publication of the book in 1973, more than 29,000 copies have been sold. The book is used in nearly every state and many foreign countries, with many hundreds of successful projects as a result.

In revising and updating the book after fourteen years, I found nearly all the ideas and techniques still valid and pertinent. The basic techniques of building with earth have changed little in more than a millennium. What has changed are attitudes, standards, and priorities.

These changes have been brought about by new materials and their incorporation into our technology. Often the most promising of these innovations are found wanting with the test of time. We must evaluate these, keeping new ideas that are effective, and modifying or discarding the rest.

Building with adobe involves a great deal of hard physical work. This has not changed. Various machines and labor-saving devices can lessen the physical labor to some degree, but not diminish the sweat by very much. We speed production by using mechanical mixers to mix mud for bricks and mortar, and tractors to haul larger quantities of mud to the brick forms. But at some point, each blob of mud or each brick must be moved and placed by hand. A new development in the adobe industry is the hydraulic pressing machine which will make bricks at the rate of five to ten per minute, ready for use without further curing. This type of device, while logical and cost-effective for a brick manufacturer, may not be so for the homeowner.

Most of the labor-saving devices that homebuilders can employ reasonably will be suitable for corollary tasks such as carpentry, rather than for working the adobe itself. We would not think of cutting boards with a hatchet, or even with a handsaw, if a low-cost electric circular saw was available. We might employ a pneumatic nail gun for increased speed and efficiency, but what sense would it make to invest $1000 in a device to speed up our nailing if the whole cost was little more than that? Sheets of plywood require less labor to put up than do individual boards. New types of insulation make adobe walls perform better while still retaining their uniquely desirable qualities. The modern homebuilder has much from which to choose.

Earthen roofs, providing both waterproofing and insulation, were used successfully for centuries when nothing else was available or within the economic reach of ordinary home builders. An incredible amount of labor was expended in the use of this material. The roof for a small house might require weeks of labor to shovel and compact 50 to 75 yards of earth (five to ten truckloads). More often than not, such a roof would have to be repaired after each rain. By contrast, modern insulation and asphalt roll roofing can be applied in a few days and may not require attention for ten years. Another point of interest: we have been wedded to the concept of steel-reinforced concrete foundations as the only acceptable base. Foundation designs now have been revised in the light of historical foundations ranging from complex to none at all. Nearly all of them worked, so now we may logically re-evaluate our standards.

The fundamental concepts and problems of building one's own shelter of adobe have remained unchanged for the most part. It is a trying but rewarding experience, both in personal satisfaction and in monetary consideration. It has been and remains a practical idea.

PAUL GRAHAM McHENRY, JR.

Introduction

ADOBE is the ideal material for the beginner. It is a warm, kind material that is forgiving of mistakes, and amenable to change. If you don't like what you have wrought, it is a simple matter to take it down and try again. The adobe bricks may get a little battered in the process, but it won't matter a bit. Adobe is a tough plastic material that will stand almost any sort of misuse. Most other materials are not this way. Lumber, when cut, can't be lengthened, although the too-short piece may possibly be used somewhere else later in the job. An adobe wall offers a place for nearly all the bits and pieces that might normally be thrown away.

The purpose of this book is to enable you to plan and build your own home intelligently and realistically. Primary emphasis is placed on adobe construction, but as you will find in pursuing the project, there are many other materials and problems with which you must deal, and many principles are discussed at length which would apply to building a home from many materials. This book cannot make you a skilled architect, contractor, or craftsman, and it cannot possibly answer all the myriad problems and questions that will arise during the job. I do hope, however, that it will give you a clue as to where to seek the answers, and perhaps even more importantly, to know what questions to ask. It should help you evaluate the problems and work of all the material suppliers and craftsmen with whom you must deal.

The prospective builder must be prepared for a long period of frustration, doubt, worry, and plain hard work. You must be willing to devote a great deal of time. If you are not able to do this, it is still possible to participate in the role of contractor, hiring skilled people to do most of the actual work, and thus effect a sizeable savings in money, while gaining a lot of personal satisfaction. Planning your home is one of the fun parts, and one on which you can really make your ideas influential. You should, because this is your home, and it should be designed and built the way you want it.

As an amateur architect you may be prone to overlook certain necessary portions of the plan, or omit things that are important. It is a tremendous puzzle, for which you must create and arrange all the pieces, and then live with the result. This portion of the project and all subsequent portions will offer you a choice of the amount of participation which you may want to do. It takes perhaps two to three thousand skilled man hours to build a home, more if unskilled. How many hours can you devote to this each week? The overall prospect is staggering, but actually is only a large number of very small tasks. If you break this down into small enough pieces, it becomes quite simple. The tasks must then be arranged in their proper order.

Looking back over the creation of this manuscript, I can't help but wonder whether enough information has been included. It does not pretend to be a complete work, since volumes have been written, and lifetimes devoted to the study of each phase of the subjects covered. Those of you who may be more expert than I am, please understand my purpose. The average layman is either bored or intimidated by most technical works, or lacks the patience to extract the useful information from the more formal presentation. It is hoped that this book will help bridge the gap between architects, builders, craftsmen, and the unskilled but determined individual who wants to build his own home. The book is the result of many years experience in what will work.

It would be impossible here to acknowledge all the help that I have received during more than twenty years in learning the basics of many phases of construction. Many architects, plumbers, brickmasons, craftsmen, and other contractors have patiently answered the questions I've asked, and taken pride in showing me the right way to do a given job. Pride of craftsmanship, in spite of many cries to the contrary, is very much alive.

Many other people have helped in the preparation of this effort, some even by being silent. My wife Carol, and the family, provided limitless encouragement, and sympathetic sounds during the early mornings, absent weekends, and midnight oil. My daughter Lynn typed the manuscript. My lawn and yard suffered too. Dr. Bainbridge Bunting of the University of New Mexico, with his fine collation of "Measured Drawings" done over the years by the UNM Department of Architecture under the Historic Buildings Survey of the National Park Service, provided valuable historic background. Dr. Bernard Fontana of the Arizona State Museum was most helpful with photographs of buildings from prestatehood Arizona and enjoyable conversations about the Southwest and its denizens. Kit Applegate, my editor, helped broaden the scope by pointing out some of the living differences between the "hot desert" and the "cold desert," correcting spelling, punctuation, and grammar in the process. Joe Tibbets, of the University of Arizona Press, provided a vital "in-house" enthusiasm, offering sound suggestions for a better book. Last but not least, the students of my classes over the years have provided enthusiasm, and countless questions which I have tried to answer here.

Whatever your participation, actual or just dreams, good luck on your project. Welcome to the fraternity of people who have had a part in creating something.

PAUL GRAHAM McHENRY, JR.

History of Adobe

ADOBE IS A WORD with several meanings. The first, and most common, is sun-dried mud brick; the second a general term for the basic earth that forms the mud; and the third a term for a building or structure made of these mud bricks. Adobe bricks are perhaps the oldest manufactured building material. The word itself is Spanish, but comes from several similar sounding words in Arabic, meaning to mix, or smooth.

Adobe has unique advantages that we will deal with in detail in subsequent chapters, but the main one is that it is readily available at *almost* any building site in the world Obviously, it wouldn't be feasible to use it at the South Pole, or the top of Mount Everest, but the basic material occurs at almost any point where there is dirt. All of the dirt on earth is the product of the breakdown of rock by the elements, but the resulting material has varying percentages of clay, sand, and fine particles, depending on the location. More on this is given in the chapter dealing with the making of adobe bricks.

Many references are made in the Bible (Exodus 5:7–19) and other ancient documents to the word "brick"; however, archaeological evidence leads us to the conclusion that this was not the brick material we think of today, but sun-dried mud brick. Excavations at the site of the smelters for King Solomon's mines at Aquaba in North Africa revealed the use of adobe bricks in construction. The idea of using adobe for brick is very logical, and was undoubtedly arrived at independently in several different parts of the world.

Mud has been and is still being used as a building material in many global regions. Some of the earliest forms of dwellings in the southwestern United States were "pit houses." The builders of these dug a pit, piling up the material to make a wall, and then roofed over the entire pit with timbers and brush, and then piled more earth on top. The builders must have noticed how durable and hard the mud became upon drying after a rain.

Wattle or *jacal* (hah-kahl′) construction is a refinement on the pit house, in that rather than a great quantity of dirt being moved, posts and brush were embedded in the ground, woven to some degree, and plastered with mud that became hard on drying. This technique required a great deal of continuing work, but was more satisfactory than the pit house. (Figure 1.3)

Solid mud-wall construction must have been thought of by some enterprising individual who reasoned that if the wall was of thick, solid mud, it wouldn't have to be repaired so often. This construction technique seems to have been done by packing damp mud into a wall shape, allowing it to dry, and then placing another layer. This process was improved on by the pre-forming of mud balls or roughly molded shapes that could be stacked on top of each other, thus speeding up the process of wall building. The construction of Casa Grande, a famous prehistoric ruin in Arizona, seems to have been accomplished in somewhat this manner. It appears that baskets of mud, perhaps semi-dried, called "turtles," were used.

Arizona State Museum, The University of Arizona. Helga Teiwes-French photograph.

Fig. 1.1 Papago Indian Reservation today. Standing adobes vertically speeds the curing process. Later, these will be moved to homesite in background.

Adobe pre-formed bricks of relatively uniform size in the more exact sense that we think of them today have long been thought to have been introduced into the Southwest by the Spaniards, but more recent discoveries and research indicate that this may not be the case. Many of the Pueblo and other primitive cultures that were in existence at the time of the arrival of the Spaniards used natural stone where available, chinked up with mud for mortar, and sometimes plastered over with more mud. All primitive construction must make use of the material that is most readily available. Where forests were at hand, timber was used; in some areas where such was not available, but a quantity of adobe was, domed igloo-type construction was conceived that required no roof beams. One unusual example occurs at Lake Titicaca in Peru, where a conical shape was evolved, rather than a dome, accomplishing the same purpose. Many examples of primitive construction can be seen today at the Hopi Indian villages in northeastern Arizona, at Acoma Pueblo in New Mexico, and in many other villages.

Pre-Spanish Indian stone masonry reached a remarkable degree of skill, where stone was the predominant available material. It is often possible to date structures by the type of stone work that was done. The Indians' skill, availability of materials, and additional refinements introduced by the Spanish settlers and priests resulted in magnificent examples of stone construction. The missions at Abo, Quarai, and Gran Quivira —all in New Mexico—are but a few. (Fig. 1.6)

Pre-molded (either with forms or by hand) bricks predating the Spanish conquest have been found in certain areas of the Western Hemisphere. Mexico, South America, and the

Fig. 1.2 Pueblo Grande, Arizona. Occupied prior to the Spanish conquest, 1200–1400 A.D. Background shows rubble-rock construction, foreground the later puddled adobe.

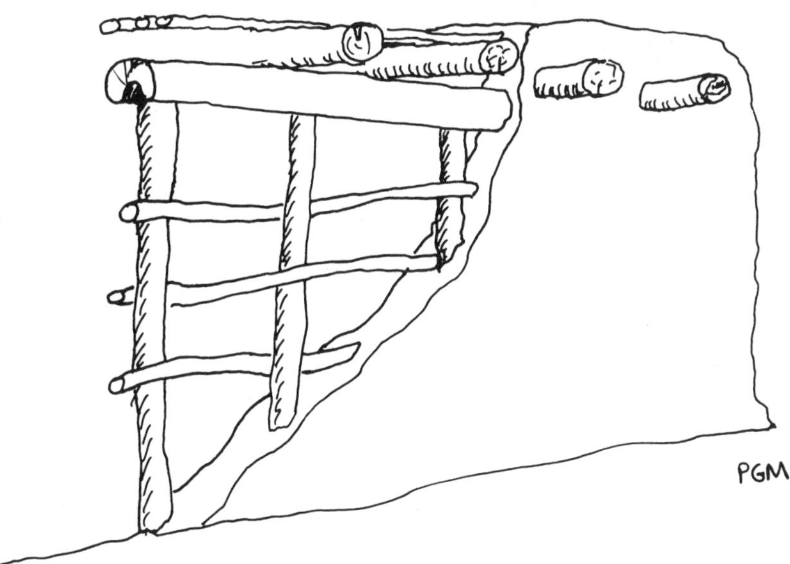

Fig. 1.3 Traditional wattle-and-daub or *jacal* construction. Posts set in ground, topped by grooved beam. Interwoven brush, finally plastered with mud. Many mountain adobe structures are mud-plastered timber or *jacal* rather than true adobe brick construction.

southwestern United States also have Precolumbian exampled of molded shapes that were laid up in regular courses to form a wall. Sod was also cut with shovels in a brick shape, dried in the sun, and laid up in walls. These are called *"terrones"* in New Mexico.

Rammed earth or *pisé* wall construction utilizes the same basic mud material but here the mud is packed into forms, shaping the wall. This method was used with considerable success in more humid climates where rainfall delayed or prevented the sun drying of adobe bricks. Fine old examples are in existence today in Washington, D.C., and along the eastern coast of the United States. (The use of sun-dried adobe brick as we will deal with it here is limited to the more arid climates where rainfall is limited.)

Burnt-adobe brick is a further refinement of the sun-dried variety. Here the mud bricks are fired in a kiln. The bricks are stacked loosely over a firepit, covered over, and baked by intense heat for several days. The resulting product is considerably harder and more durable than the mud adobes. This method of firing is used a great deal in Mexico, and burnt adobe is a common building material not only in Mexico, but also in areas of the southwest United States that are near the border. The city of Juárez, Mexico, has a fine example of a burnt-adobe brick factory.

The manufacture of regular brick (as we commonly think of it today) is a specialized process. In earlier times, brick plants sprang up in many cities where clay deposits were located. As quality control increased and public demand became more sophisticated, the poorer clay deposits were abandoned, and the manufacturers who couldn't keep up with the demand for quality and variety went out of business. Regular brick is *not* what we will be concerned with in the balance of this book.

Today there are some loyal supporters who still make sun-dried mud bricks. If you can't find someone, make them yourself.

Fig. 1.6 Quarai Mission, near Mountainaire, New Mexico. A Spanish Franciscan mission built in 1629, abandoned in 1670 due to drought and Indian depredations. Multiple corners and thickened lower walls provide strength for this traditional cathedral plan with its extremely high walls. Construction is of interlocking rubble-rock and mud mortar. Imagine trying to build this without modern tools and scaffolding. Inset: decorative treatment of hand-hewn lintel beam over doorway.

Fig. 1.4 Chaco Canyon National Monument, New Mexico. Multistory stone construction, more than one thousand years old.

Fig. 1.5 Chaco Canyon National Monument, New Mexico. Progressive improvement in stone building techniques helps date the large number of structures. Notice the bonding course of larger stones at intervals.

2

Planning Your Home

MANY CONFLICTING FACTORS enter into the design of a home, all of which must be recognized and integrated into a compatible whole, and none of which can be completely ignored. These must be resolved with a series of compromises by placing a greater importance on one or more of the factors. The main factors are:

- Site selection
- Site orientation
- Family habits
- Climate
- Style
- Selection of materials
- Budget

The owner must decide which of the above will dominate the other considerations. There is no such thing as a perfect plan, or an impossible site, and thoughtful consideration will yield some surprising results.

SITE SELECTION

Site selection is, of course, the first order of business. A cold-blooded analysis should be made before purchasing any particular parcel of real estate. The following is a brief checklist of points to be considered, with comments that I feel are pertinent.

SIZE: A site can be too small or too large. If the site is small, a more rigid discipline in room layout and possibilities must prevail. If the site is too large, what will be done with the part not needed for your purposes? It must be lived with, taken care of, or possibly may be sold sometime in the future to help recapture some of the purchase outlay.

SURROUNDINGS: Check all four sides, remembering that this is what you must look at for many years. What is the general appearance of the whole area with which your home will be associated? Are the logical traffic patterns to the property pleasant and generally desirable? Are there unsightly areas or neighboring houses that may detract from your standards? In my experience, people frequently tend to feel that some of these are only temporary, but it generally takes years for a neighborhood to change its trend. The way an area looks now is most likely the way it will continue to look.

TOPOGRAPHY: Will it be difficult or expensive to construct a road for vehicular access to the site? Arroyo bottoms, even if dry for years, can be a serious hazard. A church-school site in Bernalillo, New Mexico, was built many years ago in a "dead" arroyo — one that hadn't run in any living person's memory — and was destroyed when natural drainage resumed its course. Obviously to be avoided are swampy, marshy and low areas.

RESTRICTIONS: These are legal obligations that go with the property and are binding on all owners. They may change the whole character of the parcel affecting its usability. They usually spell out easements for utilities, roadways, minimum sizes for buildings, required distances from property lines, whether television aerials must be hidden, and the like. Certain uses for the land may be prohibited. Local zoning ordinances may also restrict the use you have in mind, and require that buildings be set back a certain distance from the property lines.

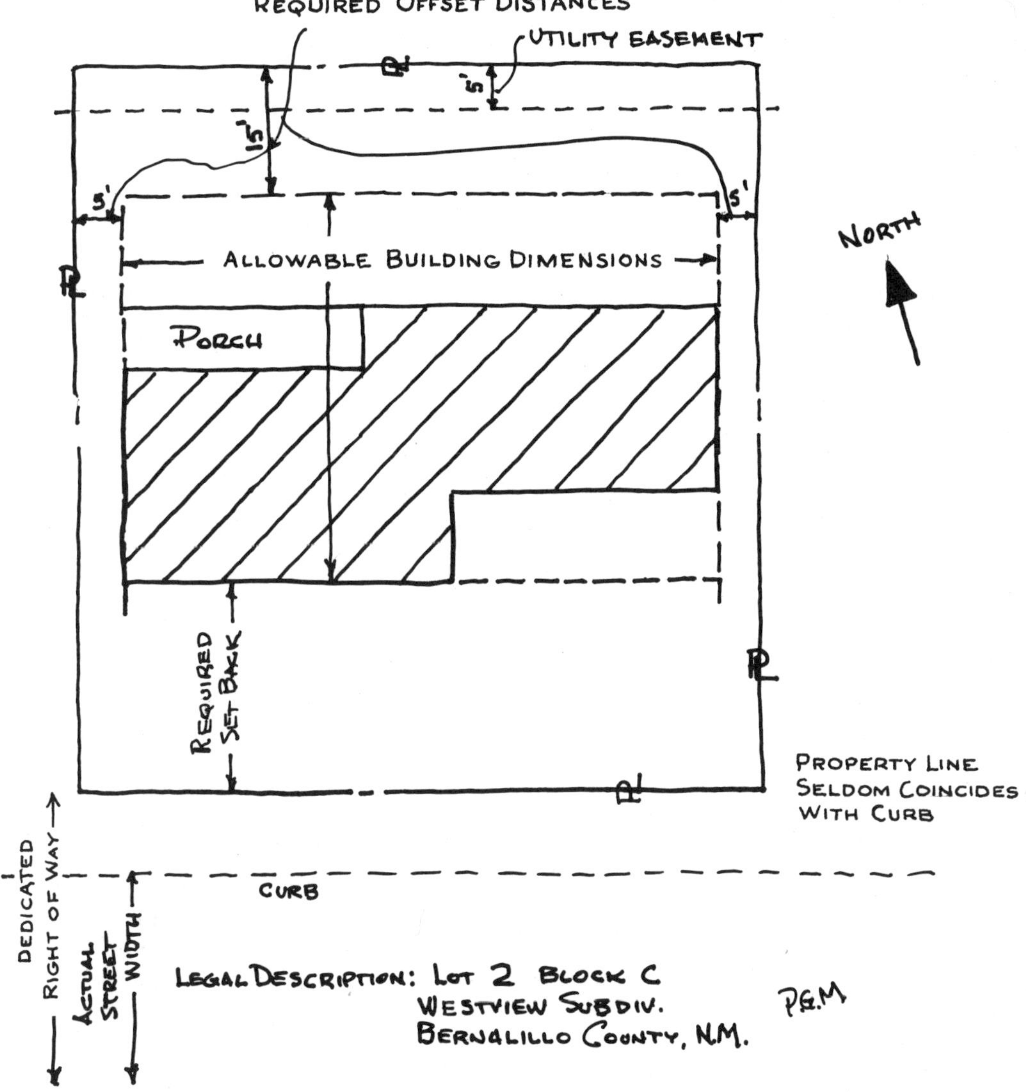

You must determine precisely what these are before even planning your construction. There are ways under which you may void these, or alter them, but it is a legal problem, and may require a long time to accomplish. The seller of the property, real estate broker, or attorney should supply this information. Insist on it, in writing, before you buy.

If you do not have this information with the deed and documents on a piece of land that you presently own, it may be obtained from the county offices, or from a title company. Seldom will the deed itself spell out the restrictions (restrictive covenants), but may only state "subject to restrictions and easements of record." Figure 2.1 shows a typical parcel.

LEGAL REQUIREMENTS: There are precise legal steps that must be taken when purchasing a piece of real estate. These are the result of hundreds of years of arguments as to who owns exactly what. Nearly every piece of real estate has a precise legal description. This is more than a street address, and must appear on each document dealing with it. Deal with a reputable real estate broker, or employ an attorney. The few dollars this will cost can save a great amount of worry and expense later.

In purchasing a property for construction, it may be useful to take an option until you are able to determine that you will be able to do what you want. It buys time for investigating the planning. Laws vary from state to state, but most insist that any real estate transaction must be in writing to be valid. I had one unfortunate experience in the beginning, where I located a specific lot at what I thought was a fair price. I spent several weeks drawing plans and checking financing. When I went back to close the deal, the property had already been sold to someone else. Wasted time!

Require the seller to furnish a "clear" title, plat, and legal description that shows the exact layout of the property, including line dimensions and bearings (compass directions). The plat should have been signed by a registered land surveyor, and recorded in the county offices of the county in which the property is located. If stakes cannot be located on the property, it may be necessary to have it resurveyed.

Determination of a "clear" title may be made in one of two ways. The older, in use in many parts of the United States, is the abstract of title. This is a collection of recorded documents showing sales, transfers, and other recorded occurrences that might give some third party a claim against that particular piece of real estate. The "abstract" should be examined by an attorney who will give you an "opinion of title." If the title is free of problems, the property will then have what is known as a "merchantable title." If there are "clouds" on the title, there are ways that these can be cleared through legal procedures, but it is certainly better to have the seller provide you with a clear title to begin with.

An alternate method now popular in many states is the use of title insurance. This is an insurance policy that reimburses you for a specific amount—usually the purchase price or loan—in the event the title becomes "cloudy" after you purchase it. It is customary for the seller to furnish the title insurance or current abstract.

UTILITIES: Water and electric power are not conveniences, but necessities. Determine that these are readily available. The absence of a supply of water from whatever source may make the property unsuitable for building. The extension of electric lines can cost thousands of dollars. Make sure you know about both before purchasing. Gas (natural or LPG) should also be available at reasonable cost.

SITE ORIENTATION

Site orientation is the blending of your ideas with a rigidly defined set of conditions. Since every site will have certain desirable features, and certain undesirable ones, you must figure out how to enhance the good, and either use, hide, or disguise the bad.

The slope and physical features (topography) of the lot must be identified and incorporated into the plan. I've seen many unfortunate examples of an excellent floor plan plunked down on a beautiful lot, with no relation between the two. One particular instance that comes to mind is situated on a mountain site, the spectacular view being lined up with the blind side of the garage, and a small high window in one bedroom. It doesn't have to be this way! An uneven sloping topography on the lot can be used to create a spectacular, unusual home. It takes more imagination in planning, and may be more expensive to deal with, but the result can be well worth the extra trouble and expense.

Compass orientation is the placing of your plan to take the best advantage of local climate. The north side (in the Northern Hemisphere) gets no sun, so it will be the coldest and darkest, and may be best for bedrooms or closets. Local conditions, like prevailing winds and hot late afternoon sun, may make the west side unsuitable for living rooms and patios. The wide temperature ranges each day in the Southwest make outdoor living possible even in midwinter if you have an area that is protected from the prevailing southwest wind, and is exposed to the midday sun on the south. The sun can be used to penetrate into a room with large glass areas during the winter months, with a wide overhang keeping the sun off the glass during the summer. Morning sunlight at any season of the year is pleasant illumination for a kitchen or breakfast room. Thoughtful placement of south windows for direct solar gain in the winter months can reduce heating costs by 50 percent or more.

Obviously you will not be able to arrange all the rooms to exactly the above considerations, but you must be prepared to make a series of compromises, selecting the factors most important to you. It is impossible to outline a specific set of do's and don'ts in this regard, because of personal preferences, views, and many other considerations. *Do* consider where the sun will be when the rooms will be used.

A home should look at peace with its surroundings, as if it belonged there. Nothing is more attractive to me than a snug home draped smoothly over a rugged site. It takes a great deal of planning to accomplish this. What is sometimes done, unfortunately, is the heavy-handed use of bulldozers to convert pleasant landscape to a city-type lot.

FAMILY HABITS

Your family's habits and likes will govern the general concept of what sort of home will suit your family best. A careful bit of honest examination of these habits will yield the answer. Do you enjoy entertaining? Or are close family projects more to your liking? Does any member of the family like to garden? Include one in your plan. Is yard work a chore? Why not then eliminate much of this with native-type plantings and a less formal theme. How old are your children? Or is this to be an adult home? What will the children need in five years? . . . in ten years?

You must take into account the fact that your requirements change over the years. What is precisely needed today may be unnecessary or even undesirable in five years. You must face the probability (actually, almost a certainty) that your home will be sold at some future date. If you depart too far from the normal range of what most people want or expect in a home, the sale may be made more difficult, or the value decreased.

One builder I know hates bathtubs. He feels that they are unsanitary, and that anyone in his right mind would prefer a shower. Undoubtedly, there are many people who will agree with him. However, perhaps an even larger number prefer bathtubs, so when he builds a home without a tub he has a problem selling to anyone in this group. The mortgage-lending people can frequently be helpful in this area. Their preferences seem to lean towards "plain vanilla" housing — houses without much personality that are a blend of what the average person wants. Build what you want, but within reason!

Zoning of your home is a logical approach to a continuing problem. You must recognize that when a home is lived in, particularly with children, a certain amount of clutter results. Most wives, and husbands too in some cases, are embarrassed at the sudden appearance of guests into a messy home. The most logical answer is zoning. The front or entry area can be separated from the area where most of the messier activities take place by a hall, closable doors, or some such device. I don't suggest that you retreat to the Victorian idea of a formal parlor that is opened only on special occasions, but merely a logical separation of activity areas. Most wives like to have one area that can be kept clear of children's clutter, and immediately available for receiving and entertaining guests without too much preparation. If this is ideally accomplished, the grownups can entertain guests, while the children are able to play in their usual areas, without being driven to their rooms. As the children grow older, the position reverses itself, and they should be able to entertain without banishing mom and dad to their room, disrupting routine severely.

Make a list of minimum requirements that you cannot do without. Then make a further list of the features that you would like (but perhaps won't be able to afford), in the order of their importance. Design for the minimum as a start and it will be much more pleasant to add than to delete, as the budget develops.

CLIMATE

One of the major considerations is climate. In the Southwest we experience almost a total range from sandy "hot" desert to semi-arid "cold" desert, and even Arctic conditions at higher elevations in the mountains. The building site selected will determine largely what materials you must use. The temperatures expected will determine what emphasis must be placed on shade, sun control, insulation, heating, and air conditioning. In the mountains of northern New Mexico and Arizona, air conditioning is something that is usually not required. Care must be used in the planning to deal with ice and snow problems. Heating is of vital importance. In the "hot" desert, heating arrangements may be minimal, or even nonexistent, and great emphasis must be placed on a satisfactory air-conditioning system. Your planning

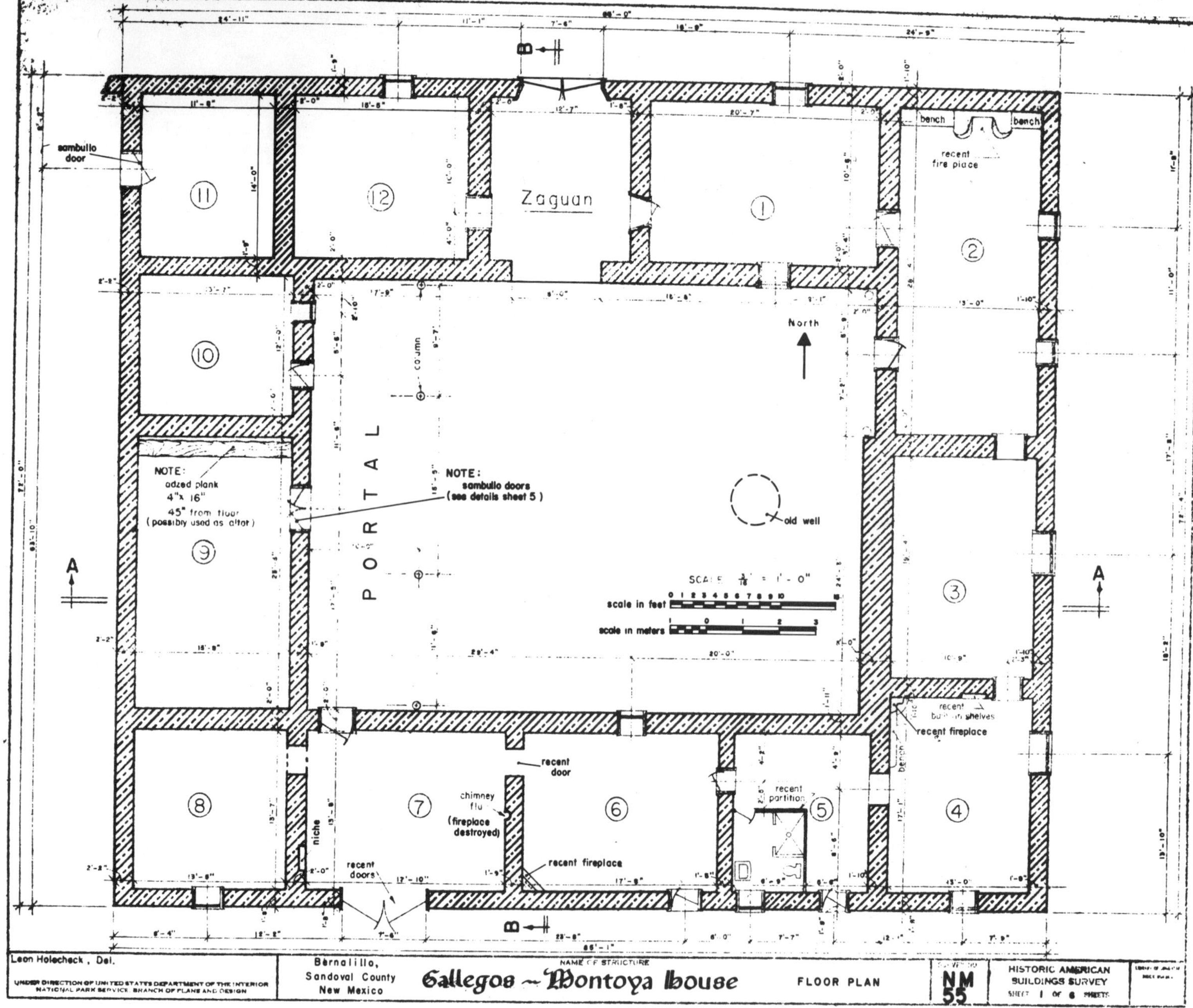

Courtesy Bainbridge Bunting. Fine Arts Library, University of New Mexico.

Fig. 2.2 Gallegos-Montoya House, Bernalillo, New Mexico. Fortress-like design, with well contained in the patio and large *zaguán* for entry of livestock and vehicles.

must reflect these factors. More specific examples will be given in the following chapters.

STYLE

Style is a matter of personal taste. Your home can follow the traditional patterns or it can be completely your own. The main consideration is that, whatever the design it should be at home with its surroundings. This is an area where it is difficult to make specific recommendations because so much personal taste and preference go into the selection. My own personal preferences lean to the easy informality that typifies the West. Some people are uncomfortable with this, and feel they must present to the world an appearance of rigid order and specific style. If this is your preference, indulge it! In my experience, however, most people who love adobe and are attracted to it in the first place don't fall into this category.

The front elevation and entry to your home are most important. They should be pleasing to the eye, and tend to invite the beholder to enter into a warm, pleasant interior. Inasmuch as personal preference is involved, it is difficult if not impossible to spell out what makes a pleasant, inviting appearance. The only solution I have found is to draw a scale elevation of what

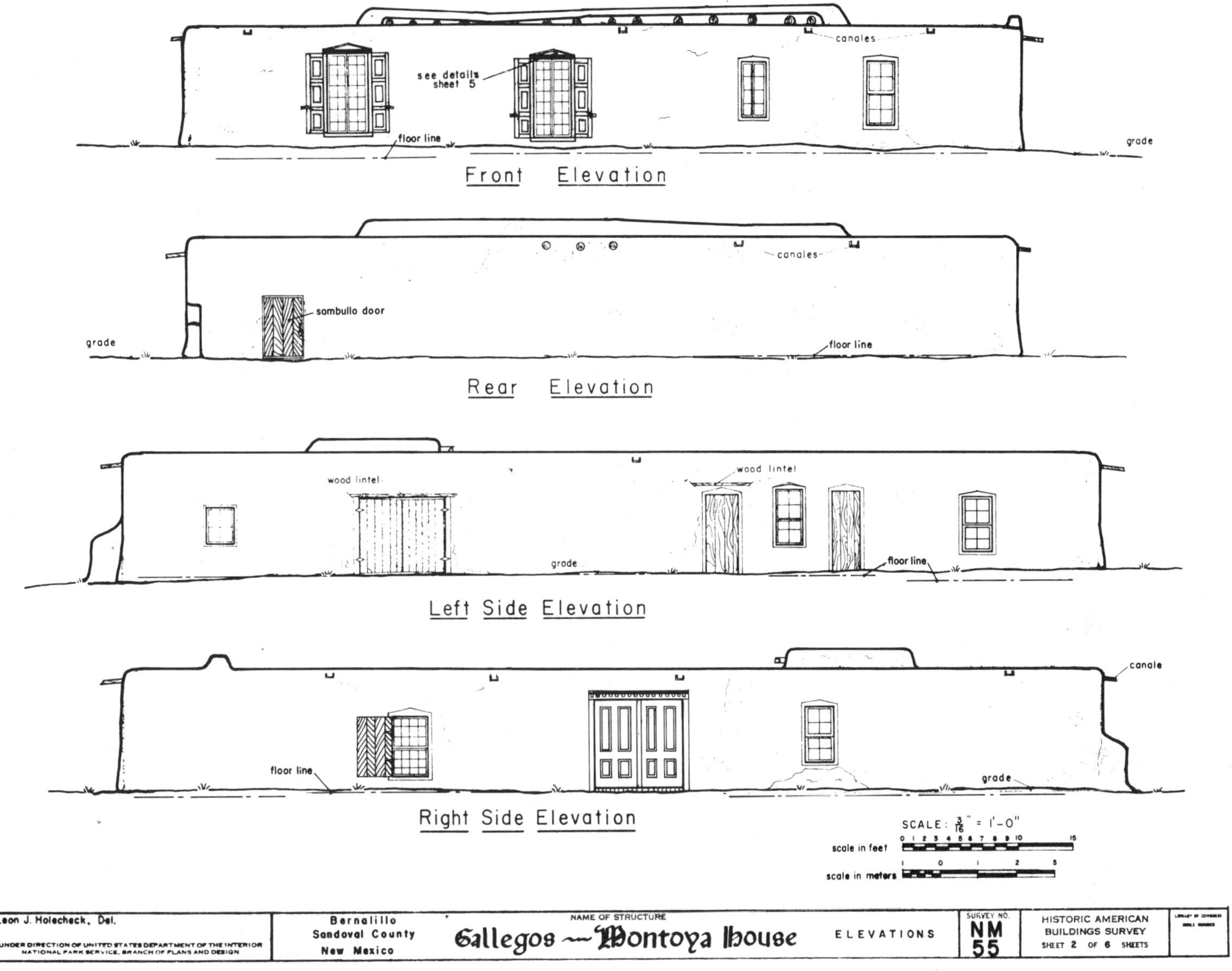

Courtesy Bainbridge Bunting. Fine Arts Library, University of New Mexico.

Fig. 2.3 Gallegos-Montoya House, Bernalillo, New Mexico.

the floor plan yields in terms of arrangement, windows, and so forth, and rearrange if necessary, or provide ornamentation and special effects to create this warmth and attractiveness. Project yourself into the plan. Give your imagination free rein.

Traditional style can be best explained by example. A Cape Cod cottage looks great in Connecticut or on the eastern seashore. I think it looks out of place in the Southwest. The design, proportions, and artistic merits may be above reproach, and the house can still look out of place. Perhaps the key lies in the selection of materials.

TRADITIONAL ADOBE STYLES, and I doubt they can be accurately separated, seem to fall into several general categories. Each of these tends to overlap but was mainly determined by the materials available, and the background and desires of the builder. Pure original examples are probably nonexistent. People in the past enjoyed modernizing their homes as we do today. Homes that were neglected disappeared. These are my classifications.

Spanish Colonial, Pueblo, or *Santa Fe* styles were undoubtedly the most functional. I suspect that little time was available for the creation of contrived beauty.

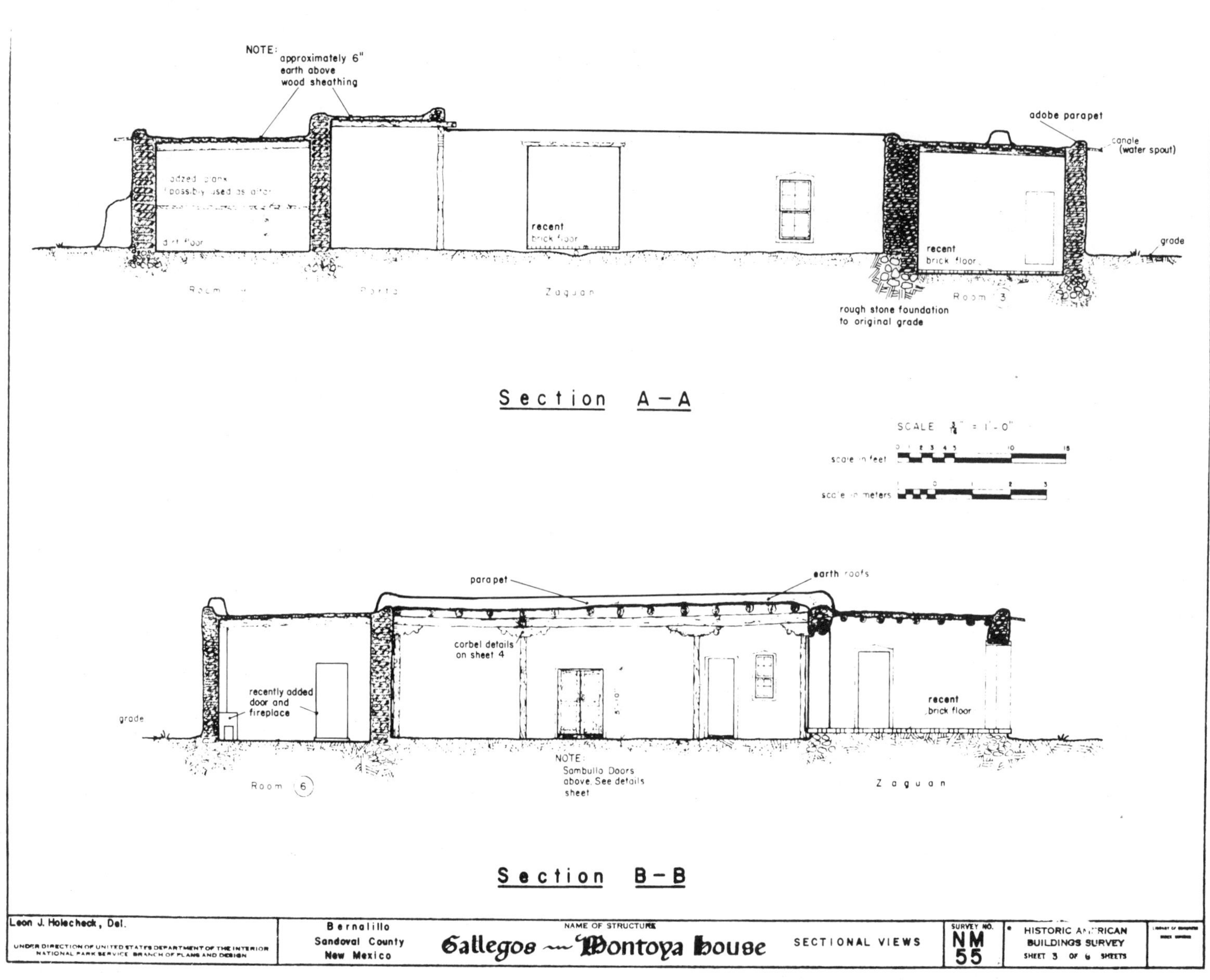

Courtesy Bainbridge Bunting. Fine Arts Library, University of New Mexico.

Fig. 2.4 Gallegos-Montoya House, Bernalillo, New Mexico.

It must have been almost a full-time job to keep from starving, freezing, or being molested by hostile Indians or lawless elements. What little manufactured material that was available must have been costly, and took years to accumulate. Many old wills on record show bequests of not only personal belongings and furniture, but also of doors and building materials such as beams and windows.

The absence of law and order, as we know it today, left the homeowner to his own resources, and he had to protect them as best he could. The resulting design was more fortress than anything else. The house generally had few if any outside windows, and only one entrance, which had to be large enough to accommodate livestock, carts, and anything else that might be stolen or destroyed if left outside. The lack of more durable building materials resulted in a large maintenance problem, such as replastering walls, repairing leaky roofs, and constant fighting with the elements to keep the place from coming down around one's ears. (Figs. 2.2–2.4)

Territorial style is perhaps best typified by the use of a burnt-brick coping at the top of parapet walls on homes. Without this more durable material, it must have been a constant problem to repair rain erosion. The establishment of

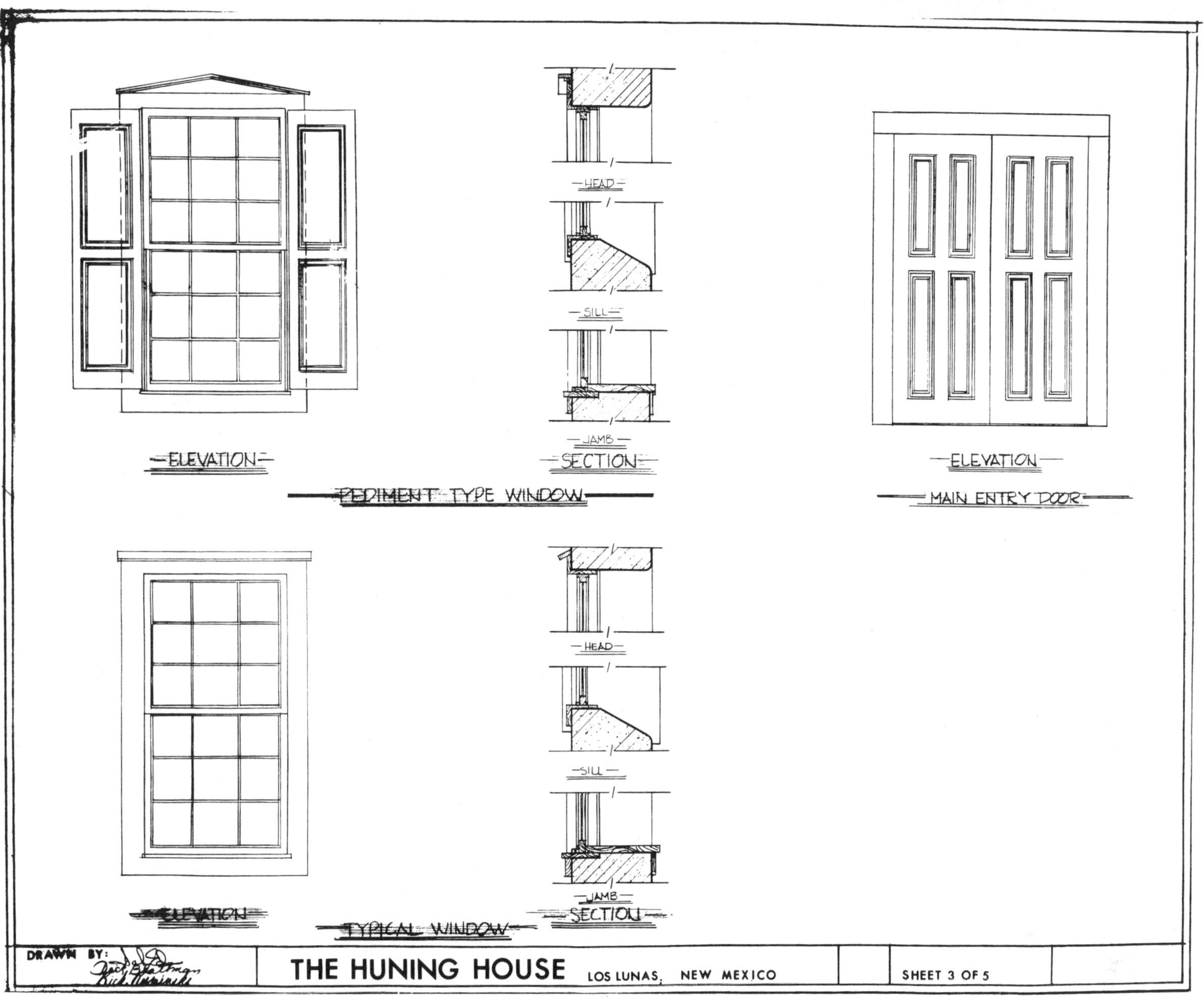

Courtesy Bainbridge Bunting. Fine Arts Library, University of New Mexico.

Fig. 2.5 Huning House, Los Lunas, New Mexico. Door and window detailing typical of the Territorial style, expressing desire for fancy ornamentation and availability of low-cost hand labor.

relative peace with hostile Indians, and of law and order, could lead to the setting up of manufacturing operations, and to more reliable trade and commerce with the East. The more affluent had time and money to indulge their tastes and comforts. Windows were cut in the outside walls, the panes of glass necessarily small because of cost and shipping difficulty. Hand labor was relatively inexpensive, and attention could be given to more formal decorative woodwork in the form of paneled doors, shutters, and ornate window and door casings. This style intensified and perhaps reached its peak near the turn of the century at the same time as the baroque gingerbread popular in the East. Today, in trying to recapture the more desirable aspects of handwork and careful attention to window and door detailing, one runs into the formidable obstacle of cost. Even with modern manufacturing methods and low cost materials, it becomes prohibitively expensive for most of us to achieve these effects. (Figs. 2.5–2.7)

Mountain-type adobe homes are prevalent in the northern part of New Mexico. They are typified by a pitched roof of galvanized iron, and double-hung windows with four lights—two up, two below. Traditional adobe construction methods are far from ideal in rainy, damp,

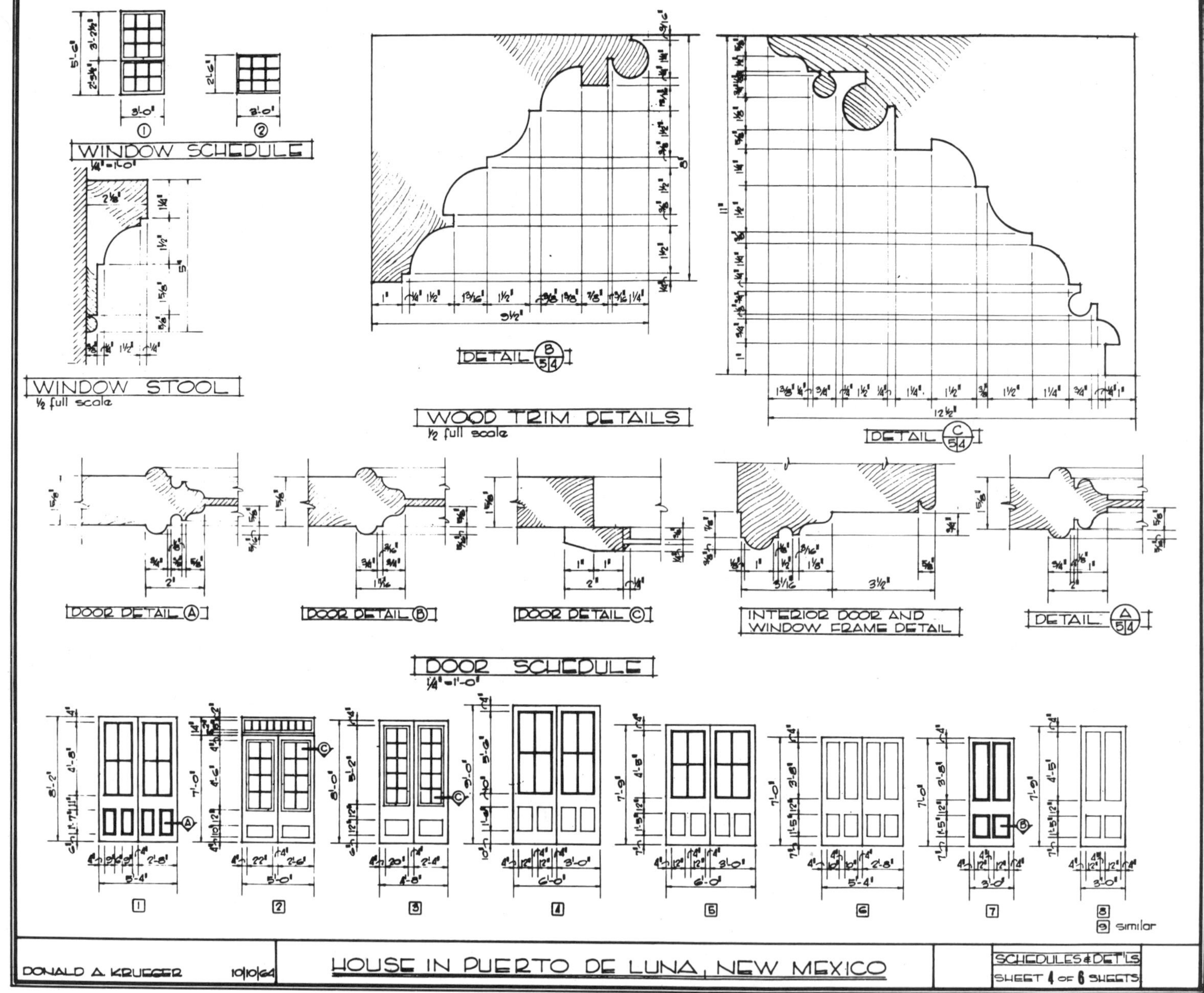

Courtesy Bainbridge Bunting. Fine Arts Library, University of New Mexico.

Fig. 2.6 House in Puerto de Luna, New Mexico. Typical Territorial style and detailing.

northern climates, and although these homes may appear to be of standard adobe construction, a close inspection may reveal that many are of log or timber construction that has been plastered with adobe. With the advent of corrugated galvanized iron, the hand-split shingle roofs were replaced. A few examples of this style are found outside mountain areas where remodeling was accomplished to use modern, up-to-date materials. The sound of rain on a metal roof is most charming and helps intensify the feeling of snug shelter.

Pueblo style is what the name implies. It is an attempt to copy the general building forms and details seen in the Pueblo Indian villages. In practice, it has been corrupted somewhat by the addition of many details from other styles. This style can have a tremendous amount of charm if tastefully handled. (See Fig. 2.8)

Tract builders have discovered that this style can be built economically by the use of frame-stucco construction. Relatively little ornamentation need be used beyond a few dummy poles protruding from the walls in different places, sometimes on all four sides. Actually, this construction method is quite sound and it is economical. If more attention could be given to the esthetics and individuality of design, it

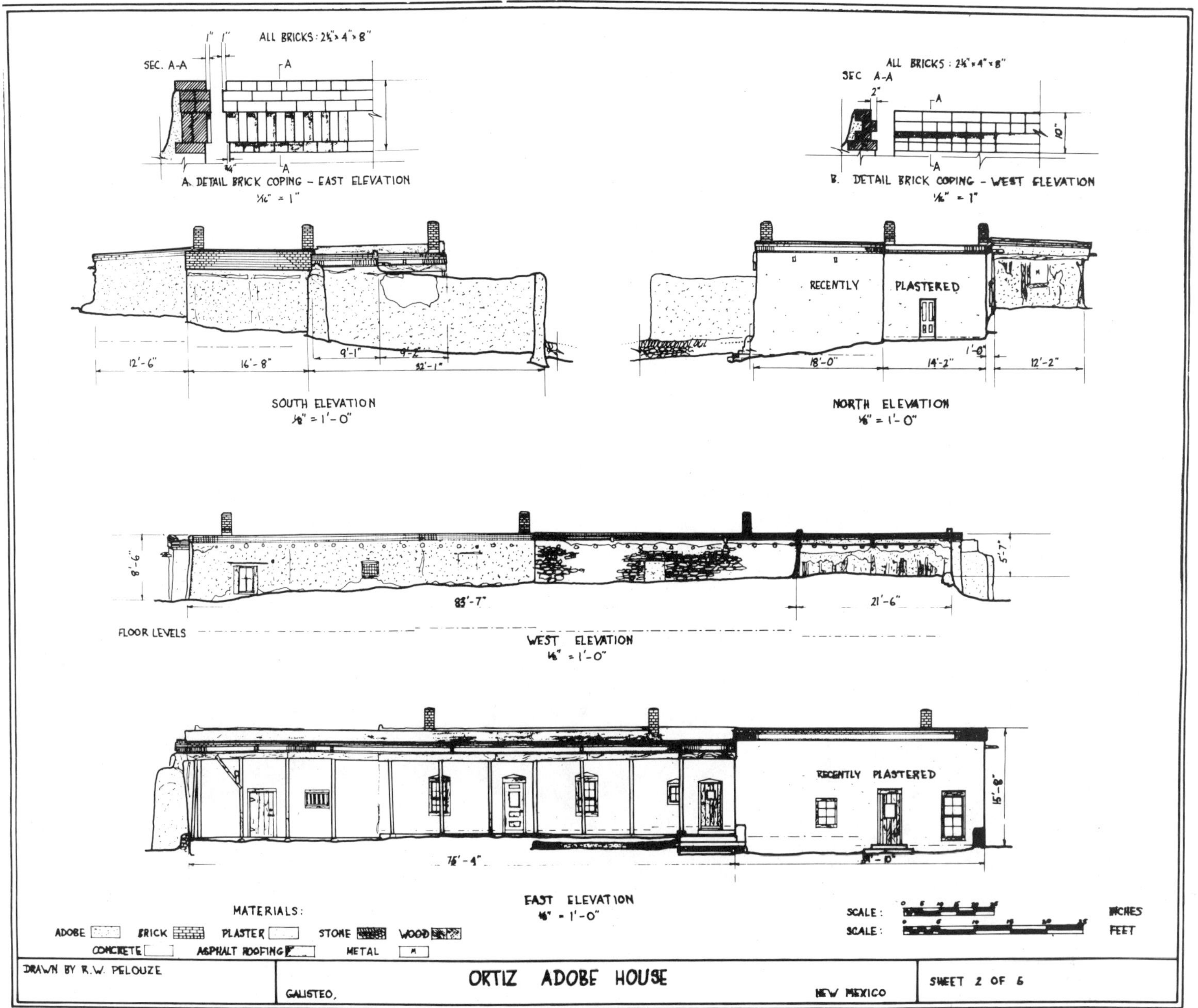

Courtesy Bainbridge Bunting. Fine Arts Library, University of New Mexico.

Fig. 2.7 Ortiz House, Galisteo, New Mexico. Early brick parapet wall coping.

wouldn't be nearly as objectionable as it seems to be. True adobe construction need not be a great deal more costly than frame stucco, but it does not lend itself to mass production. It requires a great amount of attention to handwork and detailing that most builders don't have the time or patience to put up with.

Contemporary adobe design can be magnificent, or it can be terrible. The better examples that I have seen present a front appearance of several large masses, pleasingly proportioned. These, to be effective, must have a boldness of line and a rather severe simplicity. This style does, of course, truly echo the earliest of the Spanish Colonial period with large windowless masses, generally with slightly tapered walls that represent a battered effect. A battered wall in adobe, incidentally, is a term describing a wall that is wider at the bottom than at the top, rather than one which has been abused.

It seems to me, however, that to deal with the front elevation before the floor-plan function puts the cart before the horse. Depending on the site aspects, it can limit the *floor-plan function* which I feel is more important. The contemporary type of treatment is very tricky to achieve without getting a feeling of artificiality and a deliberately contrived effect.

Fig. 2.8 Residence, Albuquerque, New Mexico. An excellent example of the Pueblo style. Note *canale* (roof drain) concealed in *viga*.

Fig. 2.9 Residence, Albuquerque, New Mexico, P. G. McHenry, Jr., architecture-builder. Modern adobe home detailed in typical Territorial style with coping at wall tops and ornate window and door trim.

Fig. 2.10 Tumacacori Mission, Arizona, about 1953. Built in the 1790s. Mixture of mud adobe (lower left) and kiln-fired adobes in higher construction at right. Hard-plastered facade provided a good medium for Franciscan style.

Spanish Mission style covers a wide variety of subclassifications. It would seem to be typified by the use of domed bell towers, arched openings, and sculptured plaster ornamentation. (See Fig. 2.12)

The Franciscan Fathers exercised great influence on these styles, by the innovations of more durable fired or baked bricks and more formal decoration, echoing church construction in Europe. The missions of New Mexico were much earlier and stayed with the simpler "pueblo" styles.

Baroque style is quite popular today in Mexico, where more economical hand labor can be utilized. This is reflected in tile roofing, hand-carved doors, ornamental iron work, and multiple details that must be handmade by master craftsmen. Occasionally, current construction in the Southwest will use carefully selected, and generally expensive, handmade details like this for sepctacular effects. (See Fig. 2.11)

SELECTION OF MATERIALS

Selecting the materials can be a complicated task. I have tried to present the idea that the most important aspect of pleasing design, whatever the style, is the feeling that the structure belongs to, grows out of, and is at peace with its surroundings. Perhaps the main key to this is in the selection of materials, textures, and colors. Except for a few carefully planned effects, materials that are out of harmony with their surroundings will inevitably have a garish, out-of-place appearance. After you have, tentatively at least, selected a particular style that pleases you, spend some time on the site and look carefully at the surroundings. What is the earth color at your site? It can range, depending on location, from an almost bright yellow to a deep red. Using the earth color is the most economical way to key the structure to its surroundings. Tree colors, both the leaves and bark, can be echoed in the trim. Rock formations near or

Fig. 2.11 St. Philip's in the Hills Episcopal Church, Tucson, Arizona. Josias T. Joesler, architect; John W. Murphey, builder, developer and contributor. Dedicated 1936. Multiple layer tile roof of handmade clay tiles. Careful, detailed handwork by master craftsmen is the predominating theme in this unusual example of Baroque style. Note arches and hand-carved stone columns. Current costs almost prohibit this style treatment.

Phil Stitt photograph.

Fig. 2.12 Casas Adobes Shopping Center, Tucson, Arizona. Top: Burnt adobe construction with multiple arch detail. Note that hard-fired brick was used at the arch and support points where the lower compressive strength of burnt adobe might fail. Center: Ornate rafter ornamentation. Bottom: Mission style belltower with ornate arches, mixed materials and styles.

Fig. 2.13 Downtown Tucson, southwest corner of Pennington and Pearl, circa 1883. Note Baroque and Victorian ornamentation done with locally available materials (adobe and plaster).

Courtesy Arizona Historical Society.

far, can be reflected in your color choices. The use of rock walls can be particularly effective if carefully considered. One particularly horrible example of this gone wrong is a home I saw that used darkly stained false wood members in a sort of Old English Tudor effect, with the resulting panels carefully filled in with a bright green rock. It was quite expensive, I'm certain, but the overall effect was startlingly unpleasant.

PLANS AND PLANNING

The architect's scale is perhaps the most useful tool you will use in planning your home (see Fig. 2.14). It enables you to project on paper, in reduced size, the exact size and arrangements of any detail of the construction or furnishings. By laying out your plan to exact scale, you can determine immediately whether there will be room for a door, window, refrigerator, or what have you. It is further useful in making possible the exact reproduction of any wall, cabinet, or elevation in order to determine its appearance. Most house plans are drawn to a scale of ¼″ = 1′. This means that you can draw a wall that is to be 8 feet long, and it will only take up 2 inches on the plans. Each foot of dimension on the plan will be represented by one-quarter of an inch on the plan. More detailed drawings of cabinets, wall sections, and the like, can be done in a larger scale (1″ = 1′ or even 3″ = 1′) more satisfactorily, showing more detail. These scales range in price from about $3 to $20. Buy a cheap one to begin with.

Complete plans are absolutely essential to the amateur builder. The professional should be aware (depending on his competence) of the various ramifications of any given situation. You should try to work it out on paper to make sure that you have room for beds, other furniture, the washer, dryer, refrigerator, and any special items you may want to include. The doors should be of sufficient size also to be able to move these items into the rooms. Every builder, amateur or professional, who has been faced with the problem of tearing out a door in a finished wall to make it larger — and I am one — will carefully consider this problem of door sizes.

Plans need only be clear. First let me say that it would take years for most of you to learn to draw a slick, professional-looking set of plans. It is *not necessary* for them to be polished looking, but only legible and clear, drawn to scale, and so that *you* understand them. The plans should have as few pages as possible, but be complete with every dimension and detail that you want to incorporate. If they are drawn so that others may easily understand them, it

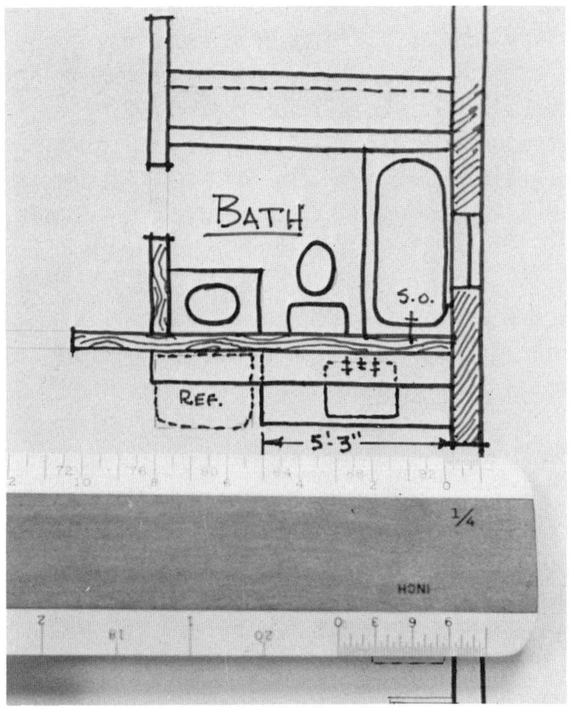

Fig. 2.14 Architect's scale. The most useful tool we have in planning.

will save a lot of verbal explanations, but bear in mind that many professional plans take a lot of explaining anyway.

Crafts that require great skill or a quantity of expensive tools are probably best left to competent professionals. The main ones are plumbing, heating, electrical, and perhaps finished carpentry. They (and you too) are governed by reasonably strict state and municipal codes. Sometimes these seem unnecessarily restrictive, but for the most part they are written for your safety. Adequate planning will enable you to anticipate and provide the spaces required for ducts, pipes, wires, and the like. Select contractors in these fields that you have confidence in, and pick their brains. They will be delighted to tell you how to build your house. They are (or should be) licensed professionals, and will be able to advise you on the best, cheapest, and most practical way to accomplish what you want. A note of caution here is in order, however. Each subcontractor feels that his particular field should receive first consideration. You cannot let the tail wag the dog. A specific example of this is back-to-back plumbing — where supply and drain-piping serve fixtures on both sides of a common wall. This is logical and efficient, but only if it does not destroy the esthetics or other practical aspects of the plan. It would be foolish to ruin the design of a home merely to save $200.

When you have the tentative plan laid out in the manner you like, ask each subcontractor what problems arise from the way you have arranged things. Don't worry about minor details — these are his business. If there are any major problems, he will discuss them with you. If you solve the major difficulties on paper before you start, it will save substantial amounts of time, money, and trouble. Chances are it will lower the bid of the subcontractor, too, if he knows exactly what he will encounter. A very few subcontractors may try to bend specifications to their own benefit, but the majority want to do a job you will be pleased with and that they can be proud of.

Negotiation with subcontractors you select is sometimes more beneficial than a straight competitive-bid basis. If you go the bid route you must specify and spell out everything completely or you may find yourself with a substantial bill for "extras" on completion. In the face of incomplete plans or specifications, the lowest bid may not be the best. There will always be two (or more) solutions to any given problem or set of circumstances. Examine first the best solution from a quality standpoint, then examine the cheapest. They probably won't coincide. Integrity is more valuable than price.

Standard sizes have been determined over the years for nearly all building materials. Lumber, for example, comes in increments of even feet in length and a number of different thicknesses, all of which are surprisingly precise. Plywood normally is supplied in 4′ x 8′ sheets, but can be purchased in some grades in a longer length. Doors are normally 6′8″ high and with a range of standard widths. Nonstandard materials can usually be obtained, but at considerably increased prices. Design around the standard sizes where possible. It usually is as easy, as satisfactory, and considerably more economical. The esthetics need not suffer from these considerations.

Standard measurements also prevail in most home construction. These refer to the height of electrical outlets from the floor, door-knob heights, hinge spacing on doors, cabinet countertop heights, and so on, ad infinitum. If there is a question regarding any of these, the best guide is to measure what is in your present home. Chances are about 95 percent that they will be standard. If you intend to depart from the standard in designing your home, and you may have excellent reasons for doing so, indicate this on the plans.

Furniture placement should be checked out after the tentative plan has been determined. Most furniture comes in relatively standard sizes also. Your furniture can be superimposed on the plan by the use of your architect's scale, or perhaps by making cardboard cutouts of your furniture to the same scale as your plan and trying out typical furniture arrangements to reveal any problems. This step may reveal some surprising conditions that hadn't been thought of previously. King-size beds can be particularly troublesome in smaller bedrooms. Sometimes not enough wall space has been provided. Location of windows and doors may need to be changed. Tables with chairs around them require a surprising amount of space. A normal dining-room chair is about 24″ deep. It requires another 24″ for it to be pushed back and used comfortably at a table. Thus, a dining room table of 3′6″ with chairs on each side will require a room width of at least 11′6″, with nothing left over for sideboards, serving tables, and so forth. It is much easier to correct this on paper than it is after the movers are trying to wedge things into a room that is too small.

BUDGET

The budget is the bugaboo of most building projects. We all have dreams of our perfect home. Unfortunately, by the time we are able to afford it, we sometimes no longer need what we have spent years dreaming about. You must start somewhere in your planning, and it must be governed by what you can realistically afford to spend, either in terms of cash outlay, mortgage payments, or both. You must also start with the realization that you will not be able to have everything you want in your home. This is a cold hard fact which will demand a series of compromises in lot size, site orientation, view, budget, and myriad other considerations.

Inasmuch as we have presumed that you won't be able to get everything you want, and that your requirements will be constantly changing, let us consider what will be necessary and desirable for the next ten years. Going back to your priority list, first try to buy space in terms of what is needed and most desirable. Basic considerations must be made for plumbing, heating, and electrical requirements. The more costly parts of a home are the doo-dads and frills; these can be added later. While it is true that it is more economical to incorporate things during the basic construction, they can be added later as you are able to afford them. Most people go through a short spell of insanity while building a home, and may become unreasonably enamored with the idea of hi-fi systems, gold doorknobs, or some other item that must be incorporated on the house. If it is really important, by all means indulge yourself; this is the thrill of building and pride in what you accomplish. But try to take an objective view. Many of the things that seem extremely important now will fade to their true perspective after living in your home for a short period. You might suppose that builders are immune to this sort of madness. We're not! I recall, in one home that I built for my family, insisting on some exquisite, hand-cast, brass tub fixtures for a sunken tub. These cost $100 more than standard tub trim which would have really been adequate. After only a few baths looking at the $100 knobs, I realized how unnecessary they had been.

You must set up a tentative budget for the project. Prices will vary from one locality to another, and often go up and down on a seasonal basis. I suggest that you contact local builders in your area to try and determine what current selling price is being asked on a square-foot basis. This will include a markup for overhead and profit which should approximate 15 to 25 percent, and which you may be able to save if you act as your own contractor. The price may be stated as a unit cost per square foot of building, including the thickness of the walls. It may or may not include carports, garages, portales, patios, and the like. It would be most prudent and conservative to use such a cost as your budget, in the event you are not able to complete the project yourself as planned. If all goes well, a considerable savings may result.

However, unit prices can be extremely misleading, because they are dependent on many variables. For example, the cost of heating, air conditioning, and plumbing a house will not change substantially, even though you double, or cut in half, the total footage of the house.

The unit price will vary with the prices of building material, the amount of work you plan to do yourself, labor rates, and all sorts of variables. I feel that the figure should be a reasonable average of what a contractor would charge.

COORDINATING AND SCHEDULING

Coordination of the trades is the main business of the general contractor. In your instance, *you* will be the general contractor and this will be your responsibility. It is merely a sorting out of the logical and necessary sequence of events that must occur in the correct order. For example: Concrete slab floors cannot be poured until any necessary plumbing has been installed beneath. However, the finished floor grade must have been determined prior to the plumbing installation so that the fixtures will come out at the right height. Electrical outlets and windows and door frames must be set before the wall is plastered, otherwise, cutting and patching must be done to accommodate these, resulting in extra trouble and expense. Don't let this frighten you, because the best plans sometimes go awry, and people who don't make mistakes don't do much. Anything can be cured, fixed, or rearranged at any stage of construction if you are willing to spend enough money. Ingenious solutions to correct boo-boos are a part of the fun of building.

Scheduling your entire job will yield a number of benefits. After your final plan has been determined, make a chronological list of what must be done in the order that seems most logical. By superimposing this list on a calendar, and noting the time required to do each of these steps, a completion schedule can be obtained. This will give time also to order special materials that can't be readily obtained and provide an orderly delivery schedule so that materials won't be in the way until you need them. (See Fig. 2.15)

If you plan to do portions of the work yourself, allow adequate time to enable you to do what must be done before the next required step.

WEEK 1 CLEAR SITE, SET STAKES, BATTER BOADS, FINISH FLOOR GRADE
DIG FOOTINGS, SET REINFORCING, INSPECTION
POUR FOOTINGS, SET STEM BLOCK, FILL W/CONCRETE

WK 2 SEWER LINES, INSPECTION
HEATING DUCTS
MAKE ROUGH BUCKS FOR WINDOWS & DOORS
WATER LINES, PRESSURE TEST
BALANCE OF CONCRETE FOOTINGS & PADS

WK 3 CONCRETE SLABS
ADOBE CORNERS
FRAME BEARING WALLS
SEPTIC TANK & FIELD

WK 4 ADOBES

WK 5 ADOBES
BOND BEAM
FIREPLACE ROUGHS

WK 6 BEAMS, POSTS, CORBELS
DECKING, DRY SHEET, PARAPETS, INSPECTION.
SPRAY STAIN, FRAME CURTAIN WALLS

WK 7 PLUMBING TOP OUT
ELECTRICAL ROUGH IN, INSPECTIONS
WINDOWS, FRAMES, GLAZING
DOOR FRAMES
LOCK UP
ROOF VENTS, TELEPHONE PREWIRE

WK 8 ROOFING
PRIME PAINTING
LATHING, PLASTER GROUNDS, INTERIOR
WINDOW SILLS
GAS LINES, YARD LINES

WK 9 CERAMIC TILE
BROWN PLASTER INTERIOR
HEATING START
STUCCO NET, EXTERIOR

WK 10 FINISH PLASTER · INTERIOR
PAINTING PREPARATION

WK 11 BRICK FLOORS
FLAT WALL PAINT
HANG DOORS
MEDICINE CABINETS
SCRATCH & BROWN PLASTER - EXTERIOR

WK 12 ENAMEL PAINTING
ELECTRICAL TRIMOUT
CABINETS

WK 13 COUNTERTOPS, TILE BACKSPLASH
PLUMBING TRIMOUT
APPLIANCES
STUCCO EXTERIOR
HANG ELECTRICAL FIXTURES, INSPECTIONS
TRASH HAUL
MIRRORS, BATH ACCESSORIES
WROUGHT IRON

WK 14 CLEAN WINDOWS
CLEAN UP JOBSITE
FINEGRADE EXTERIOR
BRICK FLOOR FINISH
PAINT TOUCH UP

NOTE: ADVANCE SCHEDULING HELPS DETERMINE THE TIME VARIOUS MATERIALS, EQUIPMENT & SUBCONTRACTORS WILL BE NEEDED AT THE JOBSITE, EVEN THOUGH IT MAY NEED BE CHANGED AS THE JOB PROGRESSES. NO TWO JOBS ARE COMPLETELY ALIKE. DELAYS FROM WEATHER, SUPPLIERS & SUBCONTRACTORS MUST BE EXPECTED & WILL CAUSE SERIOUS RE-ALIGNMENT OF THE SCHEDULE. ITS CAREFUL PREPARATION WILL PUT ALL ITEMS IN PERSPECTIVE AND MAKE CHANGES EASIER!

Fig. 2.15 Progress schedule.

3

Space and Room Considerations

ROOM REQUIREMENTS should be considered individually, and primarily from a size standpoint. These must then be fitted together like a giant jigsaw puzzle to provide the most pleasant and logical arrangement. I must point out that many of the following conclusions reflect my own personal observations and desires, and are ones that would seem to suit my family best. You are free to disagree.

ENTRY HALLS

An entry hall is the first thing to greet you as you enter a home. If there is room in the budget to waste a little space, this is the place for it. It is much more pleasant to step into a generous space than to come directly into a living room, or small utilitarian hallway. If the plan won't permit a separate hall, perhaps a little space can be borrowed from the living room, and a low divider, planter, or bookcase used for separation. By the use of some kind of a divider, you are able to maintain the impression of the full space in the room, while still establishing a division. A hall closet should also be incorporated into your plan, within or close to the entry. Many lenders insist that this be done as a part of the minimum standards.

LIVING ROOMS

Ideally, the usage of a living room should return somewhat to the old parlor concept, *if* your home is large enough to afford this luxury. The room would be used primarily for guests and be off limits for small fry most of the time except for special occasions. This means, however, that another area of the house, such as a family room or den, must carry most of the day-to-day activities. The standard smaller living room seems to average out at about 13 by 18 feet on many plans. You may select any size you require, bearing in mind that room widths can go to about 18 or 20 feet without any structural problems. It might be kept in mind, also, that many of the early Spanish homes had rooms of great length, but few were wider than about 14 feet. Presumably, this was due to the difficulty of obtaining longer and larger straight *vigas* (peeled logs), and the difficulty of handling the additional weight of these by hand when they could be found.

BEDROOMS

Planners of bedrooms seem to fall into two diametrically opposed groups. One is the functional school, whose followers believe that there only need be room to sleep; the other group feels that each bedroom should be a bed-sitting room. Both ideas have a certain amount of merit, and I suspect that the answer is in a combination. The key to how big a bedroom must be lies in the furniture arrangement, as well as size of the individual pieces. I feel that if the room is to be small, then make it only big enough to hold the required furniture. Additional space costs money, and unless some special effect is to be gained, additional space that can't be used is a waste of money.

Built-ins should be considered, because basically they are as economical as furniture, can be as attractive, and are extremely functional. I have seen fairly large bedrooms with door, window, and wall arrangements that made them very difficult to furnish. Personally, I feel that the bed-sitting room idea is more desirable if the budget will stand it. The room (particularly children's rooms) can be more economically sized if the furniture arrangement is carefully thought out. There should be space enough to read, study, and perhaps play. The master bedroom deserves some special consideration just because you are the master! Certainly there should be room for a desk, chaise lounge , easy chair, and perhaps a fireplace or a private patio. Measure the bedrooms where you now live.

KITCHENS

For most families with children, the kitchen is the heart of the home. More time will be spent in this room during the day than perhaps any other. Consequently, it makes sense to make the kitchen comfortable, attractive, and efficient. I must stress *efficient*. I knew one builder, gone to his just reward, who liked to brag about his big old-fashioned kitchens. They sure were. One I recall was about 18′ x 25′, with the range in one corner, the refrigerator in the other, and a table with chairs that you had to go around, in between. There is no reason that the essential parts of a kitchen can't be planned just as efficiently as an executive's desk or a factory assembly line. Look at efficiency first, and then by all means don't overlook appearances.

There are several essential items of equipment, with the range, refrigerator, and sink being the main three. You can further embellish your kitchen with dishwashers, wall ovens, grills and freezers, and an endless succession of goodies. You must also have storage space for dishes, cooking utensils, food, and work tops on which to prepare it. It seems to me that the sink should be between the range and refrigerator, with the work tops in between. Refrigerators can be bought with doors on either hand.

Bear one fact in mind. A countertop is 25″ wide. A passage between a blank wall and counter on one wall must be a minimum of 3′, giving a minimum kitchen width of 5′. If counters are to be on both walls, the passage must be at least 4′, giving a minimum kitchen width of 8′. This will suffice, but barely. Pantries are old-fashioned, but great, and are coming back into fashion. Pantry shelves can be cheaper than cabinets. Ideally, the kitchen should be at least 10′ wide. *You* figure out what will suit you — and the needs of your family — best. Why not solicit the help and advice of those who will use the kitchen most?

BATHROOMS

Bathrooms start with minimum sizes. A standard bathtub fits exactly into a 5′ space. Nonstandard tubs can be easily obtained 6″ longer or 6″ shorter, but they cost approximately double, whether larger or smaller. The physical dimensions of a toilet (water closet) are 20″ wide with a 27″ projection from the wall; but the space that one requires is larger, 36″ x 48″. A shower stall cannot be smaller than 30″ x 30″, and 32″ or 36″ is even better. Larger shower stalls are almost uncomfortably large and will cost considerably more because of the additional wall treatment. Lavatories are a minimum of about 18″ x 18″ for wall-hung units, while vanity tops must be at least 20″ deep from the wall and 24″ wide. In summary, the smallest full bath (tub, toilet, lavatory) size is 7′6″ long by 5′0″ wide.

If a shower is provided over a tub, the wall must be adequately protected from water damage. A shower stall must have an adequate waterproof pan incorporated into the construction or water leakage into walls and floors will require expensive repairs in a very short time. Ruined plaster, rotted studs, and ceramic tile are very expensive to replace. Luxury baths are fun to do but they seem to tax my imagination more than most phases of our planning. It has always seemed unreasonable to me that most master bedrooms have only a three-quarter bath adjacent, with the full bath somewhere down the hall. Why not create your own plan, a master bedroom suite with large bath, and dressing room incorporated with the closet area? It's fun.

FAMILY ROOMS AND DENS

In most cases the family room serves as the gathering place and entertainment center for the family. If this room can be designed as an integral part of the kitchen, perhaps separated by a counter, breakfast bar, or some such device, it allows the family to be "where the action is" without being underfoot in the kitchen. It makes an ideal place for many family meals unless there is space in the kitchen. In less formal situations, guests seem to gravitate to the kitchen, and the arrangement suggested above allows participation without everyone being in the way.

In recent years dens have frequently been added to existing homes, but in many cases this was a mistake. It may result in the abandonment of the living room, or worse yet, be a room that is seldom used. It is very difficult to integrate new traffic patterns into an already complete plan. The better a plan is to begin with, the more difficult it is to add on to.

PLAY AND HOBBY ROOMS

A play room for children or hobby room for adults makes sense. Shouldn't the children, or the adults, have a place where they can make a mess? If you don't provide one, the mess winds up in the living room or the den, with inconvenience and perhaps costly damage to floor and furnishings. Try to designate one room as the work, play, or hobby room, where sewing, painting, and other projects can be undertaken without the necessity of unpacking and packing everything away in the bottom of a closet. This room must be heated, cooled, and considered from a year-round comfort standpoint, as well as the floor finish, and so forth.

DINING ROOMS

A dining room as such is a luxury, pure and simple. If you can include one in your budget, it can be one of the most gracious and rewarding features of your home. It provides a place for truly elegant entertainment (if this appeals to you), and a showplace for prize possessions such as antiques, silver, and fine china. Many combinations of dining areas with living rooms and kitchens are quite charming, and they make great sense from an economy standpoint.

If you plan to incorporate a formal dining room in your plan, make it big enough. The biggest errors in dining rooms are ones of size. Absolute minimum size I feel is 11′ 6″ x 13′ 6″, to accommodate table and chairs. Sideboards, serving tables, and the like may require more. Most formal dining rooms are used infrequently, particularly when eating space has been set aside in the kitchen or family room. A dining room provides an ideal location for a combination room, if cleverly disguised. In the main, I personally dislike "combination"-type rooms that can wind up being unsatisfactory for both purposes for which they were designed. However, cupboards and built-ins can provide space for a desk, sewing room, and storage.

CLOSETS

Closets are the least romantic part of a house, but very important, in that the space they occupy costs the same as the living space, and you should use it as wisely as possible. Minimum inside depth for wardrobe-type closets is 24″. Any smaller than this will result in crushing the clothing. Any larger is a waste. If walk-in type closets are desired, they should be at least 6′ wide. This provides the 24″ on each side for rod and shelf with a 2′ passage. If 6′ is not available, a one-rod type (one side only) still requires 5′; thus you get quite a bonus by being able to hang rods on both sides if you can use the 6′ width.

Seasonal storage closets are great if you have a place for them. Try to plan for them, keeping in mind the special needs of your climate. A closet near the entry should not be overlooked, nor should some provision for linen storage. This can sometimes be accomplished by storage near the utility area, or perhaps a central hall closet. Most wardrobe closets can best be served by folding or sliding doors (bi-fold or bypass doors). These come in wider standard widths than swing doors at less cost, thus providing wall-length closets. Sometimes lower shelves for shoes, purses, and the like, are useful at one end or the center. Double-rodded closets, for a portion of the closet at least, increase available hanging space at very small cost. In most cases, at least half of the rod space used does not have clothes that hang all the way to the floor. Why not use this space with an additional rod to hang trousers, jackets, blouses, and skirts, or even for built-in dressers and storage cabinets.

UTILITY ROOMS

A utility room can take the place of the old-fashioned basement in adobe house plans. You must have a place for the washer (and dryer perhaps) that should be located somewhere

Fig. 3.1 Residence, Albuquerque, New Mexico. P. G. McHenry, Jr., architect-builder. Wide gallery provides a furnishable room in place of a long narrow hall. Change in floor levels may be easily made to fit uneven site (step in foreground).

near the source of the hot water, and not too far distant from the supply of dirty clothes. Take an objective look at what you do now. What is the exact path of dirty linen and clothing? How could it be made more convenient in your new plan? Ideally, for economy, the plumbing should be backed up to kitchen or bathroom plumbing, but this is not necessary. Would the utility room be more convenient in the main bedroom hall? Ask yourselves these questions and the answers will be easy. Provide a floor drain for leaky and overflowing washers. They all do at one time or another.

The location of your hot water heater is also important. They have a tendency to burst (usually immediately following the warranty expiration), doing considerable damage to floors and carpets. If the heater can be located in an exterior room, where little damage will be done to the house contents, you may even get a reduction on insurance costs.

HALLWAYS

Halls should be kept to a minimum. An imaginative arrangement of rooms can greatly reduce the number and length required. A certain amount of hallway is unavoidable, and as the number of bedrooms increases, the hall lengths also increase. In many cases, you may minimize the hallways required by using the end of one room, such as a living room or dining room, for a passage. This will yield the benefit of shorter (appearing) hallways, and larger (appearing) individual rooms. The eye sees the wall-to-wall dimensions of a room, and not the fact that one portion of the room is used as a passage.

Having wrung out the bedroom, bath, and closet arrangements to their highest efficiency, what shall you do with the hall width? The minimum usable passage space is 3′, is better with 3′6″, and better yet at 4′, depending on the length. If you go more than this, though, you start wasting space, *unless* you go wider than necessary and make a room that can be furnished. Five- and six-foot widths are more than necessary, and unfurnishable. Seven wide, or even better, eight, gives something usable for chests, chairs, and so forth. Assume a hall length of 15 feet. If you increase the width from 3′6″ to 7′0″, both minimums, you only add approximately 50 square feet to the total for the house, and have gained an extra room (see Fig. 3.1).

A hallway may yield other fringe benefits as well, depending on the width generated by other room arrangements. It can make an excellent

Fig. 3.2 Casas Adobes Shopping Center, Tucson, Arizona. Curving stairway with brick steps and ornamental iron railing provides tremendous charm if the budget permits.

area for the installation of shallow cabinets for card tables, folding chairs, and the like. It is also a fine place for bookshelves, or to hang pictures if adequate lighting is provided.

STAIRS

Stairways take a surprising amount of room. Although most adobe construction is single story, stairways and steps will be covered briefly here. An average step riser should be approximately 7½ inches. You may vary within limits of 6 inches minimum to 8 inches maximum, but much variance beyond this range will feel strange. Remember the courthouse steps that felt almost as though you might be able to take them two at a time, and couldn't quite? Those risers weren't high enough. Recall, also, the cellar steps that felt as though you were taking giant steps? Those risers were too high. The risers should also be of uniform height, or you will inevitably stumble on the step that is not.

The tread should also be at least 10 inches wide, and 12 inches is better. You may cheat a little here by overlapping one step over the other, but if the exposed tread is not wide enough, it feels very dangerous when one descends. You must plan the number of risers that will be required to raise you from one floor level to another, lay out the treads, and see how much room will be needed. Seldom will the total rise exactly equal even risers of 7½ inches, and if there is an odd distance left over, this may best be absorbed on the bottom riser. Also draw a cross section of the stairway so you can determine that there will be enough headroom to keep from bumping your head as you go up and down; most codes require a minimum headroom of 6 feet. (See Figures 3.2 and 3.3)

GARAGES, CARPORTS, AND RAMADAS

Garages have undergone quite a transformation since the early 1950s, as you may have noticed. This is due to two things. Cars generally are bigger, and there are more of them. In 1950, a single-car garage was standard, a two-car garage somewhat of a luxury. Now, most families have at least two cars, frequently three. I suspect that a three-car garage will be standard within a few years. The average car length is about 19′. The standard minimum for a double garage is 20′ x 20′. This is too small!! The absence of basement or attic in many new homes has thrown the burden of storage on the garage. My family hasn't been able to get our cars in the garage for years. I'm sure many others are in the same boat. Try to make the

Fig. 3.3 Residence, Albuquerque, New Mexico. P. G. McHenry, Jr., architect-builder. Stairways can be condensed into a small area when necessary. This corner (5′2″) was utilized to provide a stairway to a balcony, with a closet included.

garage at least 24′ deep. This will provide space for storage or workbench, and permit you to close the garage door comfortably with the car inside, without having to walk out over the hood. The ideal minimum width is 22′, although 20′ will handle it, since the average width of an automobile with the doors open is about 10′. Garage doors are usually 8′ or 16′ wide. I prefer the 16-foot width because it feels more comfortable to drive through, plus the fact that the cost of one 16′ door is usually less than for two 8′ doors.

Carports and ramadas (sun shades) make a lot of sense, perhaps more than garages, especially in warmer climates. They are more economical to build, and can also provide a shaded patio area if logically oriented with your home. Most garages seem to turn into storage areas rather than being used for their stated purpose, so why not build a more efficient storage area and park the car in a carport? The size requirements for carports approximate those given above for garages. A simple ramada can be constructed very easily and economically by using rustic posts and framing, with a roofing of poles, slats, or palm fronds. This type of construction will allow some air circulation and still provide a large amount of shade. This will not be as suitable in the colder desert areas that experience any quantity of snow, however, because the snow will collect on the roof, and may take a while to melt, resulting in a drippy carport for several days.

PATIOS

Patios that are usable all through the year are one of the big bonuses we get from living in the Southwest. They must be carefully located with regard to compass orientation and prevailing wind considerations. A west patio generally is a disaster. At the time you would expect to use it (late afternoon, early evening) it becomes extremely hot, or at least you have the sun in your eyes. If you wait until later when the sun is down, the concrete or stone areas may have absorbed so much heat that they will continue to generate this late into the evening. This problem can sometimes be dealt with using countermeasures such as trees, walls, and landscaping, but it is more logical to deal with it from the beginning. By incorporating outdoor living areas related to the indoor areas with large glass areas, you can create a feeling of additional space at relatively little cost. We frequently have warm sunny days in the middle of winter, where a sunny corner exposed to the south and protected from the wind can be most enjoyable. Perhaps you should consider seasonal patios, one for each season of the year.

Private patios for bedrooms offer a luxury touch at little cost. These can be ideal for sunning and privacy, using larger glass areas for the bedroom, and bringing the outside in, creating an apparently large bedroom from one that is actually quite small. New luxury innovations in the hot desert may include the air conditioning of patio areas, where summer nighttime temperatures stay high until quite late. "Sunset Books" have excellent volumes on planning and building patios (see Bibliography).

POOLS AND FOUNTAINS

Swimming pools are most welcome in hot desert areas. The cooling waters can make bearable an extremely hot climate. They also lend charm and space to the indoor-outdoor living trends. In many hot desert areas, a pool is almost a necessary part of the building project, and should be included, even if you don't particularly like to swim. It usually is more economical to install the pool with the initial construction than later.

Decorative pools and fountains always seem like a good idea at the time, but frequently are abandoned to the dead leaves and gook that seem to collect in them. They will present a daily upkeep chore that may not be worth the effort. Consider carefully before planning one, and try to make advance arrangements for ultimate conversion if it does not live up to your expectations.

OPTIONAL FEATURES

New products appear in the marketplace every year; many of them are desirable, and some are important to safety and changing life styles. These may include burglar, security, and fire protection alarms. Also important to you might be wiring and cables for intercom, stereo, television and computers, grills, central vacuum systems, electric garage door openers, etc. *Make a list,* estimate the costs, and include it in the budget.

4

Financing, Permits, and Insurance

NOW THAT YOU HAVE CONSIDERED all the factors discussed in the preceding chapters, have your plans carefully drawn, and have a pretty good idea of what the house will cost, it is time to think about where you are going to get the money with which to build. You must also arrange for the necessary permits, and for insurance coverage to protect yourself against liability.

FINANCING

Money to finance construction is a commodity, just like bricks, lumber, or anything else. You must have a sufficient amount to complete the project, and you should obtain it at the most favorable price and conditions. All mortgage loans have a certain quality, quantity, and price.

Two types of loans will be involved, regardless of the route you decide to take. The first is the permanent loan, which most of us are familiar with as the mortgage. The second is the interim or construction loan, which is actually used to construct the project. These will be dealt with individually.

Two documents will be involved in each loan: the note and the mortgage. The note is a promise to pay, setting out the terms. The mortgage pledges a particular parcel of real estate as collateral. Each parcel of real estate has a legal history of ownership called the "chain of title," or abstract. This is kept in the county offices. Any transaction that takes place concerning this parcel should be recorded, putting the public on notice. When a bank plans to loan money to you, secured by this parcel, it must ascertain that the title is clear and that they are next in line for any claims against it. To accomplish this, they have you sign the documents, inspect the property to make sure it has not changed, and then record the instruments. (See Fig. 4.2)

Foreclosure on mortgages is an unpleasant possibility that must be recognized. We sometimes hear the expression, "I can just walk away from it if I don't like it, cheaper than rent." In most cases, this is not true. The note may still be collectible after the property has been repossessed. If a deficiency results to the lender, from costs of sale, repair, or expenses, he may be able to recapture these from you in the form of a "deficiency judgment." Be sure you understand all the responsibilities of all parties to your loan. Laws vary from state to state, but most provide for a "redemption period." Even though someone might buy the property in foreclosure, the foreclosed party has a right to pay all charges and redeem it within a certain period of time. If you become involved in such a proceeding, on either side, have an attorney advise you.

PERMANENT FINANCING is almost what the name implies, unfortunately. It is a sum of money, representing a percentage of what the lender feels the total value of your property will be on completion. The loan is secured by a mortgage on the property, and by a note which is collectible, even in the event the property is destroyed or lost. The note is repaid, usually in level monthly payments, for a period of years, known as the "life" of the mortgage. The payments will include amounts for the interest, and the principal reduction, each of which change monthly, the exact amounts of each being shown on the amortization schedule. At the beginning, the main part of the payment is interest, with the principal reduction becoming larger each month until it is fully repaid. The payments may or may not include a sum to be put into a trust or escrow account that will provide funds to pay annual fire or homeowners' insurance premiums and yearly taxes on the property.

The amount that will be available for this mortgage will depend on two factors. The first is the total estimated value of the completed project—land plus proposed improvements—known as the appraisal, and the second is your ability to repay the loan. There are exceptions to this, since a government-insured loan provides a fixed maximum amount available, but the loan will not be issued if the lender feels you are not qualified to repay it.

The "price" you will have to pay for this commodity is actually governed by supply and demand. This price consists of several factors—the main two being the stated interest rate, and the discount or origination fee that will be charged. These, when combined, provide the effective yield to the person or firm providing the money. This price may vary from week to week depending on the supply of money available and the number of persons wanting to borrow it.

Determine in advance that an adequate supply of money will be available to finance your project. This is most important! If you desire to build in an outlying or less conventional location, it is wise to determine the availability of financing even before you purchase the property, if possible. It may be that lenders will not provide funds for certain locations, will charge a higher interest rate, or loan a smaller amount because of the risks they feel might be involved. You may determine this merely by making inquiry to the normal sources for this money. If it will be available, it will be indicated by a "commitment." A commitment is a promise to provide a specific sum of money at stated terms of repayment, on a particular project, by a certain date. It is customary to pay a percentage fee for this commitment, as the lender reserves this money for your project and must provide it when it is due, according to the terms of the commitment.

Two categories of permanent loans are generally available. The first is a government-insured loan, the money actually being put up by an individual or firm, the repayment of which is insured by the government. This is subject to many stringent regulations and red tape. The second is called a conventional loan, usually made by an insurance company, bank, or savings and loan association. They may differ greatly in price and conditions. It is wise to examine all the features of both very carefully.

Compare the following features:

Amount available: This may be larger in a conventional loan if the lender feels you are able to repay. The amount of a government-insured loan will be determined by more rigid appraisal standards.

Interest rate: The stated or "face" rate is generally lower on a government-insured loan, although the effective cost to the borrower may be higher because of the discounts involved.

Rapidly changing money supplies have created new "flexible-rate" loans in some areas. These may provide for a changed interest rate under certain conditions. The usual lower initial rate may be raised to meet money supply conditions. Be sure you understand all the conditions.

Life: This is the total number of years that will be required to repay the loan on a level-payment schedule. The longer the life, the smaller the payments, but the higher the total cost of repayment.

Discounts: These may not be called discounts, but may be referred to as "points," or "service" or "origination" fees. You must remember that the lender must receive an adequate return or yield or he will not be willing to lend his money. In the case of nominal low "face" interest rates, the discount may be large. This will vary weekly, but may reach 10 percent of the total loan. This means that if you sign a note for $10,000 the lender will actually supply only $9,000. This higher discount is usually prevalent in FHA or GI-type loans. If there is to be a new loan placed on a property that is to be sold, the seller must, by law, pay whatever discount is involved.

Closing costs: The total of such costs comes as a considerable surprise to many people. These costs will vary, depending on the lender and the amount of money involved. Ask the lender for a list of the items that will be included and an approximation of the amounts involved. They may include the following:

- Inspection fees
- Attorney's fees
- Title insurance
- Recording fees
- Escrow account for taxes and insurance

Other features: Conventional loans may include "bonus"-type features such as open-end borrowing, which allows you later to increase the loan back to its original amount without the formality of refinancing, or a freedom from the prepayment penalty that most government-insured loans include. (On many government-backed loans, if you decide to pay the loan off sooner than the payment schedule calls for, you must pay a penalty of some percentage of the outstanding balance.)

Letter of commitment: This is a written document that guarantees that the lender will provide a specific amount of funds for a specific project upon its completion. It will be valid for a specified period of time, during which your project must be completed. This must be considered in your completion schedule.

BANK LOAN STATEMENT

Branch ______ No. ______

Name of Borrower ______ Loan No. ______

Legal Description ______ Amount $ ______

Purchase Price $ ______

	DEBIT	CREDIT
Amount of Loan		
Funds Paid In:		
Bank, Service Fee ______ %		
Interest At ______ % From ______ To:		
Credit Report		
Appraisal ______ ☐ VA ☐ FHA ☐ Conventional		
Inspection Fee		
Extension of Commitment		
VA Funding Fee		
Recording Mortgage /Trust Deed		
Recording Release		
Recording		
Taxes: County ______ Parcel #		
Amount $ ______ Pay in Escrow ☐ ½ Yr ☐ Full Yr ☐		
Special Assessments: City ______ Series # ______ Assm't #		
County ______ Series # ______ Assm't #		
Fire Insurance: Agent		
Amount $ ______ Pay in Escrow ☐		
Salt River Valley Water Users' Association ______ Pay in Escrow ☐		
Title Fee		

Payment Breakdown	AMOUNT	Impoundments: NO. MONTHS REQUIRED	Impoundments: AMOUNT HELD
Principal & Interest			
Taxes			
Special assessments			
Mortgage Insurance			
Fire Insurance			
Home Protection Ins.			
Total			

Proceeds To ______

TOTAL

1st Payment Due ______ Closing Date ______

106-030 REV. 9-71

Fig. 4.1 A typical bank loan statement.

CONSTRUCTION FINANCING is sometimes called *interim financing,* and is used to actually build the project. You must remember that the permanent financing will not be available until the project is completed, so you need an interim loan of some sort to provide money until the job is finished. In some cases this may be provided in combination with the "permanent" financing, but is normally obtained through your bank, provided that it is backed up by a firm "commitment" from the permanent lender. The construction loan will have many of the same detailed costs and features that are listed in the "permanent financing" section. Find out exactly what the arrangements will be, in detail. One kind of financing is useless without the other, so be sure to arrange *both* before you

J. A. WOODS

REGISTERED PROFESSIONAL ENGINEER AND LAND SURVEYOR
1122-B SAN MATEO BLVD., S. E. ALBUQUERQUE, NEW MEXICO

CERTIFICATE OF SURVEY

I, J.A. Woods, a duly qualified Professional Engineer and Land Surveyor, licensed under the laws of the State of New Mexico, do hereby certify that, on the 25th day of June, 19 64, I did check the boundaries of that certain piece of property standing in the name of

P.G. and Carrol McHenry, Jr.

and more particularly described as follows to-wit:

SEE ATTACHED DESCRIPTION

That no encroachments exist on said property; and that the building_______thereon situate falls within the exterior boundaries thereof and in the manner set forth on the below inscribed plat, to-wit:

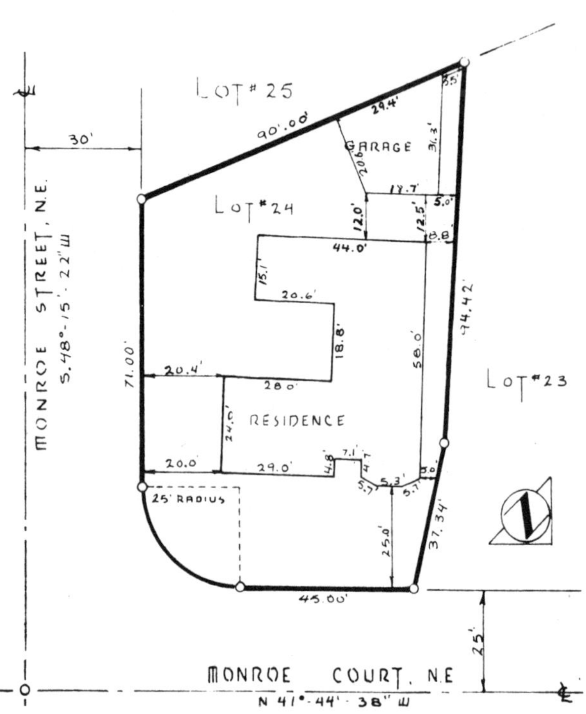

Certificate of Survey
for:
P.G. and Carrol M. McHenry, Jr.

27 June 1964

D E S C R I P T I O N

A certain tract of land, said tract being and comprising Lot numbered Twenty-four (24), and a portion of Lot numbered Twenty-three, of a Replat of Lots 1 thru 14 and Lot 17, Block "N" and all of Blocks "O" and "P", SMITH'S SANDIA HILLS Addition, in the City of Albuquerque, New Mexico, as the same are shown and designated on the Replat of said Addition, filed in the Office of County Clerk of Bernalillo County, New Mexico, on the 1st day of May, 1959, said tract being more particularly described as follows:

BEGINNING at the Northernmost corner of said tract, the identical Northernmost corner of Lot 24 of a Replat of Lots 1 thru 14 and Lot 17, Block "N" and all of Blocks "O" and "P". SMITH'S SANDIA HILLS Addition and running thence S 41 -44'-38"E, a distance of 45 feet, to a point on a curve, thence along said curve right, having a radius of 25 feet, a distance along arc of 39.27 feet, to a point of tangency with a straight line, thence S 48 -15'-22"W, a distance of 71.00 feet, along the Southeasterly boundary of said tract, to the Southernmost corner of said tract, the identical Southernmost corner of Lot 24, thence N 64 -22'-35"W, a distance of 90 feet, along the Southwesterly boundary of Lot 24, to the Westernmost corner of Lot 24, the identical Westernmost corner of the tract herein described, thence N 50 -56'-10"E, a distance of 94.42 feet, along the Northwesterly boundary of said tract, to a point, thence N 61 -39'E, a distance of 37.34 feet, to the Northernmost corner of the tract herein described, and point of beginning.

In witness whereof I have hereunto set my hand and seal this 27th day of June, 19 64.

J. A. WOODS
P.E. & L.S. #2367

Fig. 4.2 Typical certificate of survey and legal description, showing exactly how the building is situated on the lot, to indicate necessary setback requirements have been observed.

incur obligations. The "life" of the construction loan is important, since you must complete the project within the agreed length of time, to coincide with the final date of the commitment.

The lender may also specify that the bills incurred during construction must be "vouchered" or paid by "joint check," which merely insures that the funds set up are actually used for the purpose intended, and not dissipated or diverted for some other purpose. Progress payments, or "draws," may be made against the construction loan at various stages of completion. Plan these carefully, and make arrangements for payment of bills in accordance with your plan.

Make all financing arrangements firm *before* starting any construction activity, because the lender may decline the loan, or may penalize you the amount of the work already done, to protect his loan against prior lien rights of subcontractors or material suppliers.

A lien is a debt that has been recorded against a particular piece of property. It becomes a part of the permanent record or abstract, and must be removed before the property can be resold with a clear title. A lien can result from an unpaid claim for material or labor incurred by you or someone working for you, such as a general contractor or subcontractor. You may hire a contractor, who will order materials delivered to the jobsite, you pay him for it, and if he doesn't pay his bill, his supplier has a right to file a lien against your property. It is customary to obtain some evidence either in the form of a paid bill or release of lien, that any contractor you pay has paid the bill you are reimbursing him for. Another sound practice is to pay your contractor with a joint check, payable to the contractor and his supplier jointly. The possibility of the contractor using your money for other purposes is fairly remote if you deal with reputable people, but it is a possibility that must be recognized. You certainly don't want to have to pay the same bill twice!

In summary, we must conclude that the financing is as important as any other aspect of the construction. Not having sufficient funds to complete a project that has been started is a major disaster. Extra costs will occur, no matter how carefully you plan the project and estimate cost. The unforeseen *will* happen causing additional cost. Plan in advance for this. It is not even a probability, it is a *certainty*. When considering the term of the mortgage (perhaps 40 years), bear in mind the fact that according to a study undertaken several years ago, the average life of a mortgage is only eight to twelve years. Something will happen prior to the last payment that will require refinancing.

The advice of the lender may provide several fringe benefits, in that since he is so much more aware of the desires of the average homeowner, he may be able to provide useful suggestions in planning. Your home should reflect the real you, but within reason!

Owner-built financing may create additional problems. Most bankers shudder at the prospect unless the owner-builder demonstrates a working knowledge of his plans and has a detailed cost estimate. You must sell your ability to the banker if you plan to borrow money for construction.

PERMITS AND INSPECTIONS

PERMITS of one sort or another generally must be obtained from some governmental body. State and local laws vary greatly. If the project is within the limits of a municipality or incorporated village, a permit for the construction is usually required. This helps assure adequate standards for safe, sound construction (and revenues too!). In the past it was possible to build without permits outside of any recognized municipal area, with the possible exception of electrical and plumbing codes. Many states now require that any structure be built under permit, with the state assuming responsibility for inspections. In most cases, these permits and inspections are for the public protection, and if their standards are followed, minimums for sound construction will be obtained. In every case, the homeowner may request a "homeowner's" permit which will allow him to do any phase of the construction, without the help of a qualified, licensed contractor. This may or may not be advisable, depending on the ability of the homeowner, but you will find that most authorities will be most helpful in providing advice on the best way to accomplish this within the codes or

I. SEPARATE PERMITS

A. BUILDING construction, additions, alterations, repair or removal including installation of the following:

SIGNS	WALLS
CANOPYS	FENCES
TOWERS	SWIMMING POOLS

B. COMMERCIAL PARKING LOT subject to prior approval of the Traffic Engineer.

C. The installation, alteration or repair of the following:

PLUMBING & GAS	BOILER
AIR CONDITIONING	ELEVATOR
REFRIGERATION	ELECTRICAL

II. DRAWINGS (TWO COPIES)

A. LEGAL DESCRIPTION including street address, lot number, block number and subdivision.

B. PLOT PLAN: showing the location of all buildings and the distance from property lines; distance from other buildings located on the property; distance from any building located on adjacent property.

C. FOUNDATION PLAN: showing size, spacing and locations of all exterior footings, interior footings, piers, stem walls, grade beams, etc.

D. FLOOR FRAMING PLAN: showing spans, size, spacing, location and live loads for all floor and ceiling structure.

E. FLOOR PLANS: showing the location of all exterior and interior walls, room names, openings, plumbing and heating equipment, electrical outlets, service drop, equipment, exterior square footage for each floor of the structure.

F. ROOF FRAMING PLAN: showing spans, size, spacing and location of all roof and ceiling structure.

G. ELEVATIONS: showing main views, floor to floor dimensions, materials to be used, slope of roof, etc.

H. CROSS SECTIONS AND DETAILS to properly explain the plans listed above.

1. Footing details (depth, width, reinforcement, etc.)
2. Framing details showing size, spacing and material for floor, roof, and ceiling construction.
3. Wall sections showing construction of all exterior and interior walls.
4. Truss details and method of attachment to columns, walls, etc.
5. Stair details showing rise, tread, construction, handrails, etc.
6. Mechanical and electrical details.
7. Detail of commercial cooking hoods including filters, and fire dampers.
8. Utility Plot plans showing location and size of sewer, water, gas, fire lines, etc.
9. Information as to make, model, and B.T.U. Demand of Boilers.
10. Electrical Riser. Diagrams, showing size of conductors and meter location for all Commercial Buildings.

Fig. 4.3 Typical checklist for city or county requirements.

regulations. *When in doubt, ask!* Make sure that the lender has no objections to your doing all or part of the work. Separate permits may be required in addition to the general building permit. These may include permits for plumbing, electrical wiring, gas installation, a septic tank, etc. Determine for your location what these are, and make sure they have been secured. If building codes seem too unreasonable, get legal advice to ascertain your rights. (See Fig. 4.3)

INSPECTIONS by government agency code inspectors, or by the lender, may be required at various stages for:

Excavations and reinforcing for foundations (before pouring concrete)
Framing
Plumbing (rough in and pressure test)
Gas (if not a part of the plumbing inspection)
Electrical (rough in and final)
Lathing
Final

Inspection requirements vary widely in different areas; ask until you find out just what is needed.

Many of these inspections must be made before the next step is taken in the construction. For example, the electrical and plumbing rough-in inspections can be made later, but may also result in extra expense to you in having to remove wallboard, plaster, and so forth.

INSURANCE

Insurance coverage should be investigated ahead of time, to avoid exposing yourself to serious liability. If a person employed by you is injured on the job (accidents do happen!), you may be held liable for medical expenses, time lost from work, and serious disability or death — which can come to many times the total amount of the building budget. You may also be exposed to public liability from accidents to the public, particularly to children, who have been lured by an "attractive nuisance." Each state has different laws regarding public liability and workmen's compensation insurance. *Consult a qualified casualty insurance agent for the most economical adequate coverage.*

You should also get a "builder's risk" policy. It covers damage to the project from fire, wind, vandalism, and many other causes during construction. Its cost may be insigificant when included as a rider on your present policy. Get the "builder's risk" coverage as soon as construction work starts out of the ground (foundations are seldom damaged by vandals or wind). You will be charged for an annual premium, and then this will be pro-rated to the lesser period of time when the permanent insurance coverage is put in force, canceling out the builder's risk policy.

5

Plans, Setting Grades, and Staking

HERE ARE THE LOGICAL STEPS in developing a plan and preparing to start actual construction. It may be necessary to refer to later chapters to follow each step.

1. List your requirements in terms of rooms, in order of their importance.

2. Determine the maximum amount of money that you can afford to spend for your new home.

3. Make a scale plot plan of the lot, showing dimensions, easements, and set-back requirements, to determine usable space. Draw in approximate topographical grades (slope of lot), locations of trees and of permanent fixtures.

4. Walk the boundaries of the building site to see what each side looks out on. Get a comfortable chair and sit down in the middle of what seems to be the most logical place to build your home. *Think about it!*

5. Make a rough sketch plan of how you think the rooms should be arranged, starting with the one that is most important to you, or clearest in your imagination. Place yourself mentally in each room and see how it feels. Give your imagination a chance. Don't be bound by square corners or conventional considerations.

6. Make a scale drawing of your plan to see if everything will fit with your original ideas (chances are it won't quite!). Draw in wall thicknesses, door and window widths, then make what changes are necessary for the plan to work. You may find this very frustrating at first. The blank paper is intimidating. Start at one corner of one room and work outward from there, leaving space for necessary furniture, appliances, etc. Think of it as a big puzzle! YOU CAN DO IT!

7. Set markers at approximate locations of the corners on your building site, determine the ground levels (grades), and note these on the floor plans and elevations. Also check for physical obstacles that may occur within the building lines which might cause special problems.

8. Make an estimate of the cost; revise plan if necessary.

9. Prepare the following drawings, all to exact scale:

- Floor plan
- Elevations (scale pictures of each side).
- Foundation Plan
- Floor Framing Plan (if you have wood floors)
- Roof Framing Plan
- Wall sections (a vertical slice through each typical wall from the foundation up through the roof). If you have more than one floor level, it will be useful to draw a cross-section slice through the whole building.
- Electrical, mechanical plan (locations of electrical outlets, switches, ceiling fixtures, telephone and TV aerial jacks, furnaces, ductwork, etc.).
- Plot plan showing distances to property lines, etc.
- Door and window schedules.
- Interior elevations of cabinets, vanities, bookcases, etc.
- Additional details and sections you may need to clarify the actual construction.

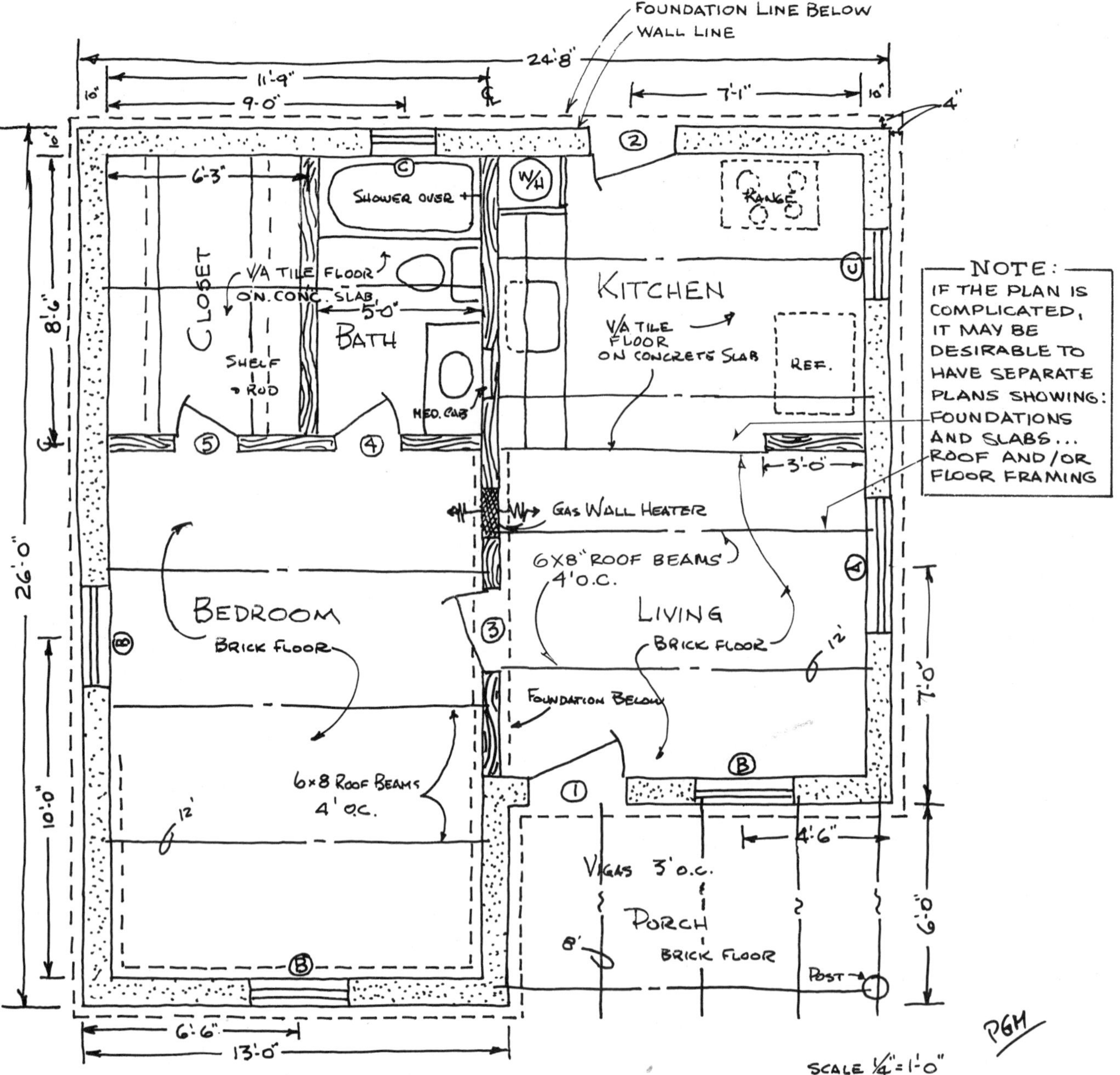

Fig. 5.1 Typical floor plan.

Try to combine as many of the above drawings on as few sheets as possible, but make them clear (Figs. 5.1 and 5.2).

10. Make the final cost estimate as carefully and as detailed as you can manage, then add a little (maybe 10 percent) for what you undoubtedly have forgotten.

11. Make a time progress schedule; allow for delays. See Fig. 2.15

12. Make absolute financing arrangements. Take out permits.

13. Set corner stakes (hubs) representing the corners and outline of your home. Recheck building dimensions and angles! Determine best finish-floor grade, set a reference marker where it won't be disturbed.

14. Erect batter boards from hubs.

Take a deep breath and start to work!

SETTING GRADES

Preparation of the final plan, clearing the site for building, and the determination of the final floor level are the last things to do before actually starting construction. We will assume at this point that you have worked out the plans in relatively complete detail and know exactly the shape and dimensions of the various rooms and the building outline. You will have determined the ground level (grade) at which each corner of your building corners will occur and noted the differences on your plan. You must then decide at what level the finished floor will occur. This is called the finish-floor grade. Bear in mind that you want to move as little dirt as possible, and yet you must have drainage away from all sides of the house, maintaining level floors inside.

The determination of the various grades (levels) of your lot at the building corners may seem like a complicated task. There are several ways to do this. The easiest is to use a builder's level on a tripod, or a transit (like surveyors use), which may be rented. If you use such an instrument, make sure that it is accurate and that you know how to use it properly. If you don't want to go to this sophisticated a procedure, there are simpler ways. One is to use a carpenter's level (at least 24″ long) or a "sight level." It should be set up level at a starting point slightly higher than where you think the finish-floor level will be set.

It takes two people to accomplish the grade determination. One sights with the transit or level, and the other acts as "rodman" to hold a stick, ruler, or some device that can be measured, to indicate how far up from the ground the sight-level line occurs (Fig. 5.3). Another economical instrument is the hand sight level that can be purchased in stores handling surveyors' and drafting supplies. It is a spyglass-type device that has cross-hairs of some sort and a mirror-reflected bubble level incorporated in the tube. By resting this against a support, reasonably accurate readings can be taken on the rod. If a large variance of grade is present in the lot, it may be necessary to take sights and measurements in several stages.

In deciding where to set the finish-floor level(s), you must consider the fact that if you choose the highest point, you must build up the lowest point to that level. If you choose the lowest point for the floor grade, you must then remove all the ground that is higher. In either extreme, a large amount of dirt must be purchased or hauled away. The best solution is to choose a mid-point, somewhere between the two extremes, and use the dirt you excavate to fill with. Each situation will be different and you must provide at least minimum drainage away from the house on all sides.

It may be to your advantage to do the major dirt work before starting any other foundation work, or even setting the final stakes indicating the corners. I neglected to do this on one of the first homes I built and found it necessary to excavate by hand two inches of dirt from inside

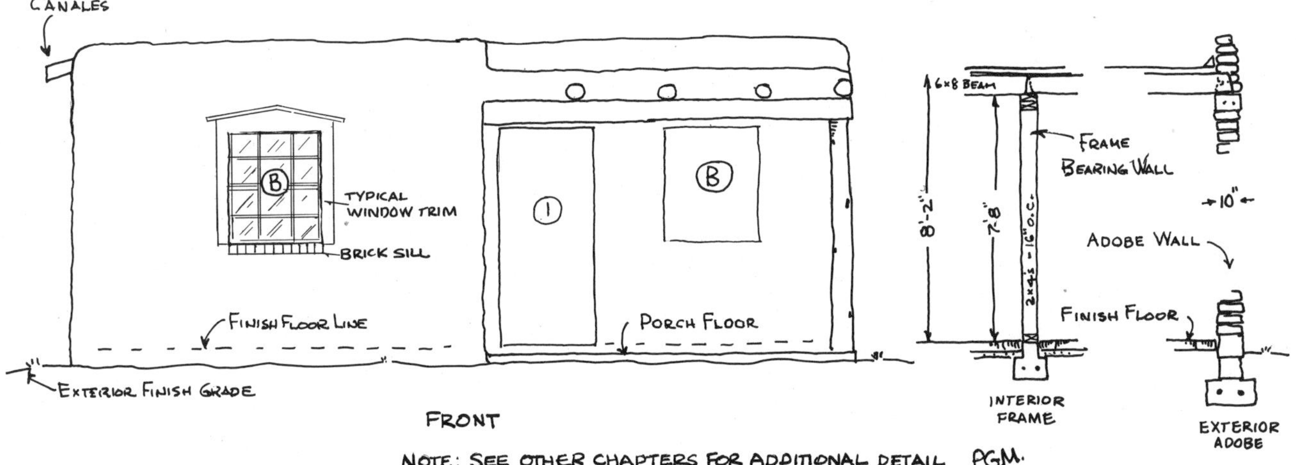

Fig. 5.2 Front elevation and wall sections.

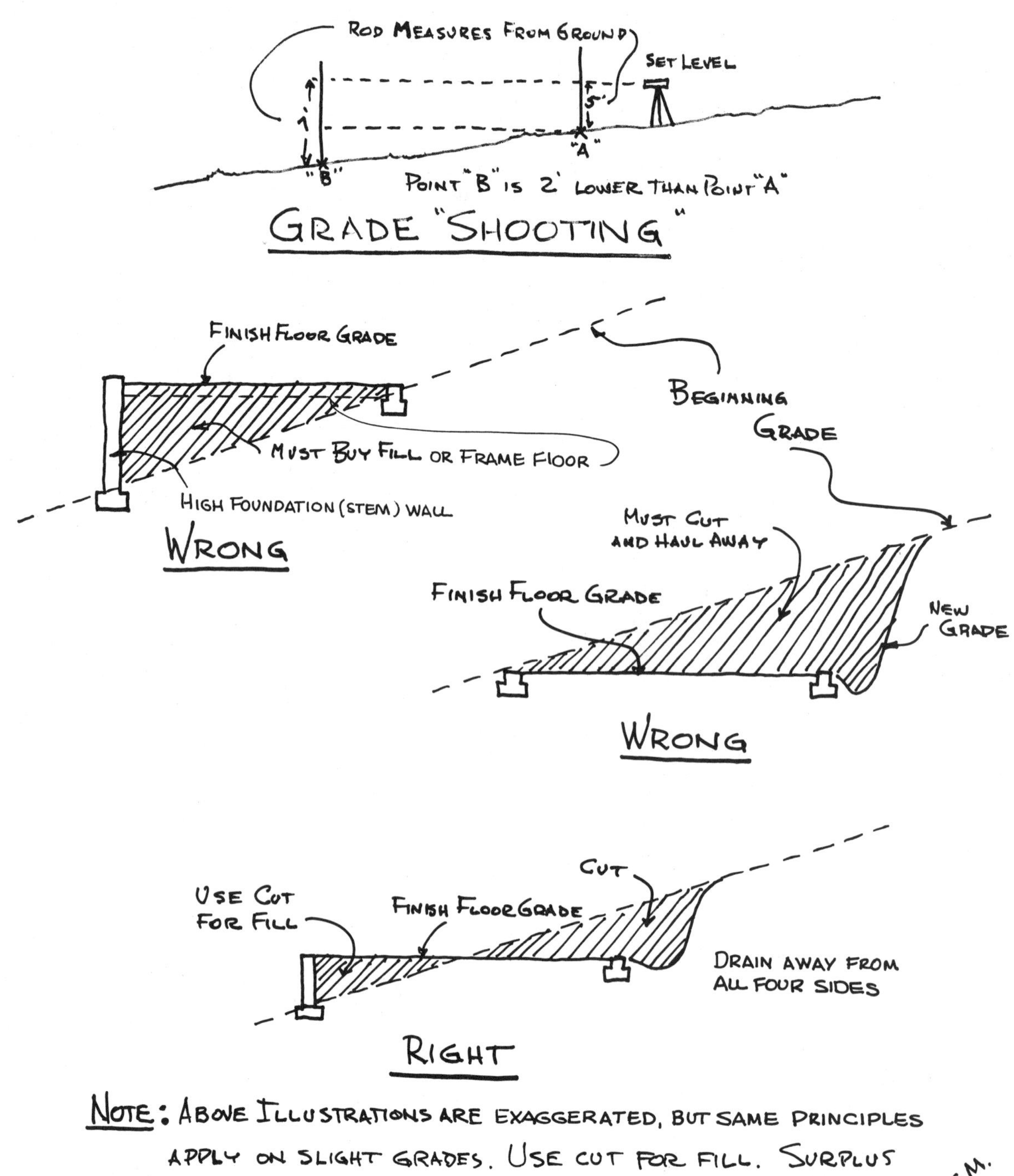

Fig. 5.3 Grade shooting and grade setting.

the foundations. The house consisted of 2,000 square feet, and two inches doesn't sound like much, but it represents 13 cubic yards (approximately 150 wheelbarrows). As my seven-year-old son asked while we shoveled away, "Why didn't you do that when the graders were here?" If you don't calculate the grades carefully, you may ask yourself the same question.

Figure 5.3 indicates two wrong ways to do the job, and the more sensible way. Please remember that you cannot always do it the ideal way exactly, and there may be unavoidable reasons why you can't. Check the beginning grades carefully against your plans before starting excavation. Don't create extra work through careless planning!

If you have a quantity of dirt to move, by all means use the most efficient piece of machinery for the job. A bulldozer or a grading tractor may be much cheaper than laborers with shovels for several weeks. In calculating the cost, be sure to check minimum charges for moving a large piece of equipment to the job.

SETTING THE STAKES

The next step after site preparation is to set the exact stakes at all corners, called "hubs." The corners should be checked carefully to make sure that they are exactly 90 degrees, or whatever angle you have planned. Remember that measurements must be taken on the level rather than along the slope of the ground, even if only a very slight slope. A plumb bob will help: hold the tape level, and let the plumb bob indicate the proper point on the ground. The squareness of a 90-degree corner can be checked very simply by using the Pythagorean Theorem whereby in a right triangle the sum of the squares of the two sides of a right triangle is equal to the square of the hypotenuse (see Fig. 5.4). Any multiple of a 3′ x 4′ x 5′ right triangle will work conveniently. Another simple method is to measure diagonally across the corners of the rectangle. If the corner angles are accurate, the measurements will be the same, or very close.

In most adobe homes, it will not be an error of great consequence if the corners don't come out exactly square. You will be working with rough, imprecise materials. But if you plan to use precise materials for floors and ceilings such as ceramic or acoustic tile, corners that aren't square will show.

After you have the corners staked, you will find it useful to set "batter boards." These are merely a pair of stakes, with a board nailed across them, that can be marked with a saw cut, and a string stretched between them, to show exactly where the building line occurs. Two batter boards are required for each line, one board being located at each end. The batter-boards should be set back far enough from the building site so that they will not interfere with construction machinery or work. Once the walls or at least the stems are up, the batter boards may be removed.

You may find it useful to set a permanent marker for the finish-floor grade in a location where it won't be disturbed, to use as a reference. The distance to the bottom of your footings that must next be excavated will be measured from the finish-floor grade. It is an important reference from which all heights are taken.

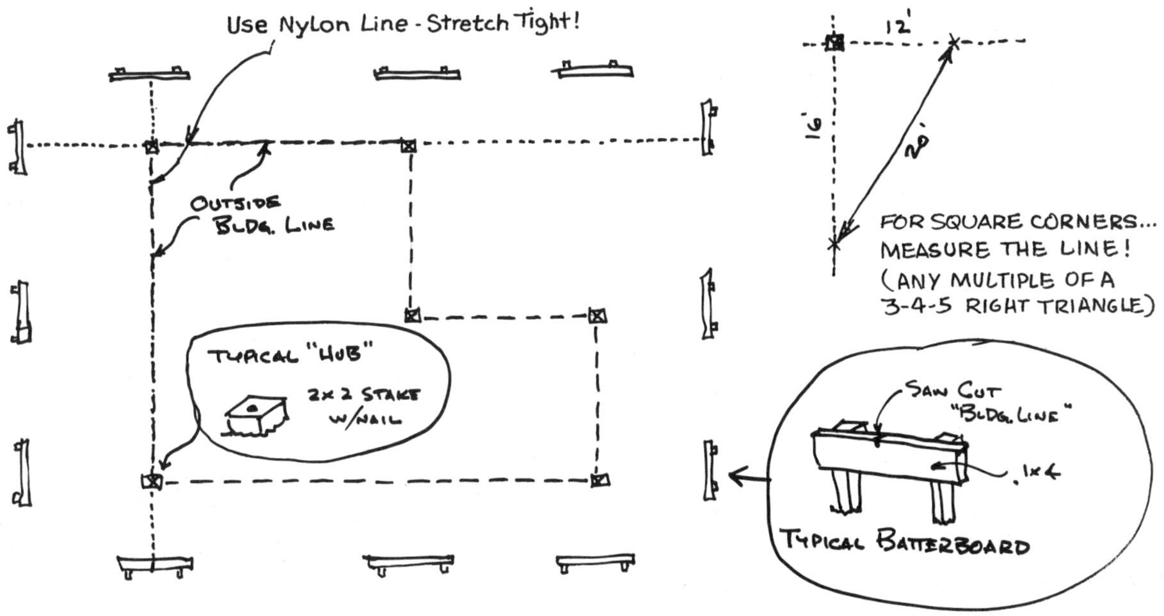

Fig. 5.4 Staking your home.

6

Foundations, Concrete, and Slabs

FOUNDATIONS AND SLABS built by nonprofessional builders frequently are either more substantial than necessary, or inadequate. We will deal with typical adequate foundations that are generally applicable. It costs very little more to construct an adequate rather than a skimpy foundation. One that is bigger than necessary is a waste.

FOUNDATIONS

Without going into a highly technical discussion of the engineering involved in a foundation, we might point out the basic purposes and principles that will apply. First of all, a particular square foot of undisturbed earth on your specific site will support a certain number of pounds without mashing down appreciably. There are specific tests to determine this, but we will not concern ourselves with them here. Most undisturbed soil in the arid Southwest will test out at approximately 3,000 pounds per square foot. The house, wall, roof, and all will weigh a total number of pounds. This must be distributed onto the soil with the required number of square feet so as not to exceed the soil-bearing capacity.

The bottom of this foundation, which is called the footing, must be deep enough into the ground so that it will be below the frost line. (The depth of the frost line depends on your climate.) If this is not done, water or moisture may get under it, freeze, and thereby lift the whole building. In a masonry structure, particularly with plastered walls, a ⅛″ shift will create large cracks in the wall. Concrete, while hard in itself, can be greatly strengthened (requiring less concrete) by the use of reinforcing steel bars, generally known as rebars. If there are filled or soft spots in your foundation line, these must be excavated to undisturbed earth, or bridged over by means of a grade beam (a stronger concrete beam poured at grade) which is supported at each end on undisturbed soil. Small excavations for pipes, and so forth, under the footing need not concern you.

Figure 6.1 illustrates an adobe wall foundation which will be adequate, in most cases, where a 10″ thick adobe wall is planned. If your adobe wall is to be thicker than 10″, a rule of thumb is to provide at least 3″ more width to the footing on each side than the thickness of the wall. Severe cold climatic conditions may require a deeper footing for frost protection, hot climates less. Consult your local codes.

Rock may be used for foundations where desirable or necessary. It is best laid up with cement mortar, but mud may be used for mortar if reasonably flat rocks are available so that the wetting of mud joints won't cause settling of the foundation. Most early structures were made this way, bringing the rock foundations above exterior grade to avoid groundwater and rain. In most cases they should be wider than a concrete foundation because they will not have as much cohesive strength. (See Figure 6.5)

The stem is the lower portion of the wall that extends from the footing up to the wall above the finished exterior ground grade. It can be made of poured concrete, or of hollow concrete block that can be filled solid with concrete or

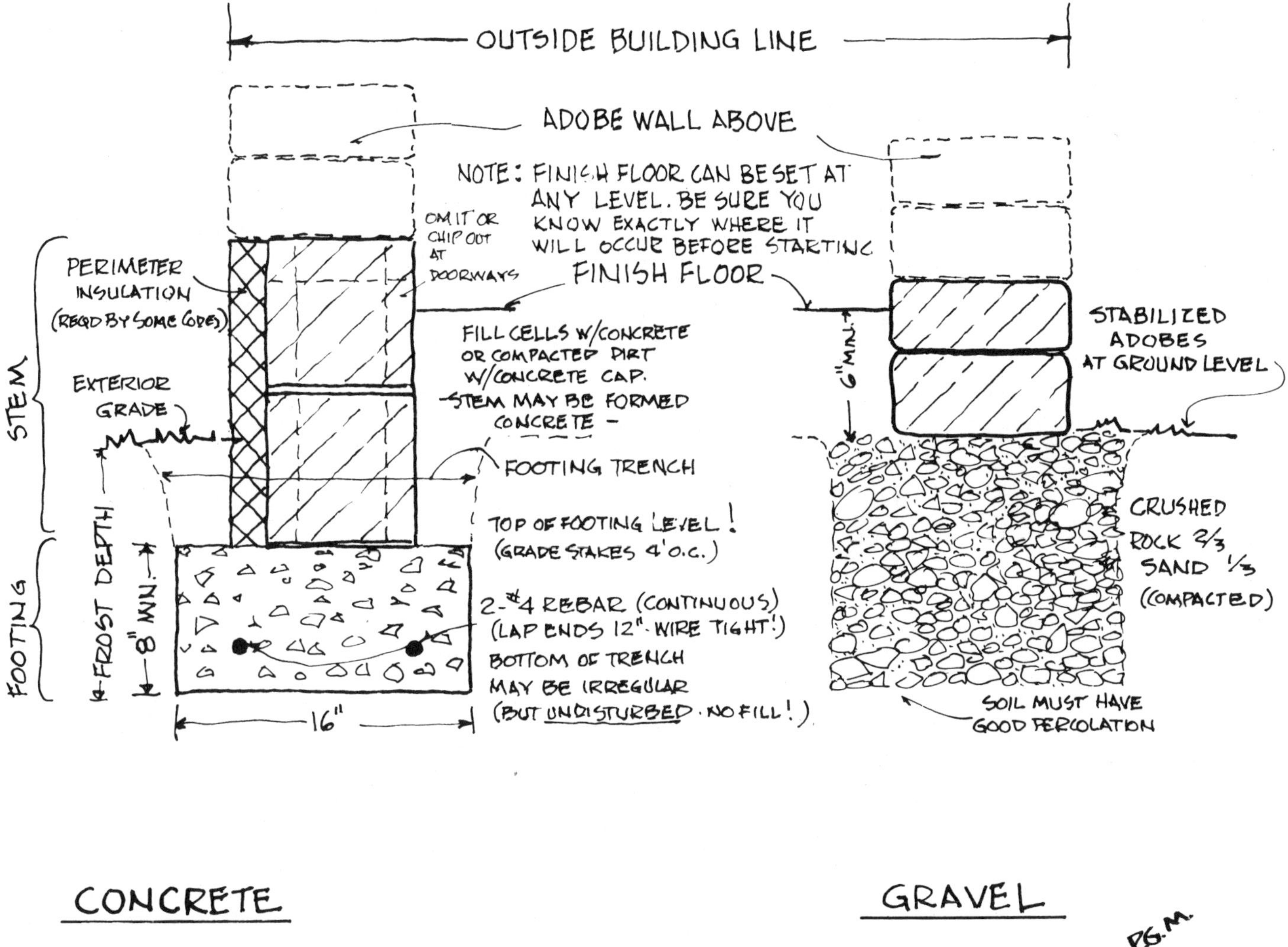

Fig. 6.1 Typical adobe wall foundations.

compacted adobe dirt capped with concrete. The latter is perhaps the most suitable way for the homeowner to build, since it doesn't require extensive (and expensive) forming. You will note from the dimensions given in Figure 6.1 that the stem should be at least two blocks high. (Hot desert climates may not need the frost protection.) This will also provide a waterproof material for a short distance above the finished floor inside the building. The waterproof feature is the most important aspect of the foundation construction. Adobe must be protected from water. Occasional rain will damage the surface slightly, but groundwater into the wall will destroy it. The top of the stem should be sealed with portland cement mortar so that capillary action can't occur and allow water to seep up into the adobe wall above. It has been suggested by some builders that an asphaltic material of some sort is more efficient.

Retaining walls are almost identical to stem walls, except they must be provided with vertical steel reinforcing, extending into the footing, in order to provide enough strength to hold back

Fig. 6.2 Concrete footings. In most instances where the building site is flat, footings are contained in a trench. Where an unlevel site is used, it may be necessary to step the foundations, using forms where needed, at levels which will accommodate the materials going on top of the foundation. Note vertical reinforcing rods imbedded in the footing.

Fig. 6.3 Block stem foundations. Block, the width of adobe wall which will go above, is placed on footing and filled with concrete, making a solid stem. Note simple forms and bulkheads which provide steps in this footing for an uneven site.

Fig. 6.4 Concrete forms. This form broke when it was filled with heavy wet concrete. The poor example above was cobbled together to contain it before it began to harden.

the earth they are to retain. This may be minimal with two big IF's — IF the top of the retaining wall is not too high (18″–24″), and IF a floor structure helps to give it lateral stability. If a retaining wall is to be free standing, it must have a footing width of approximately 60 percent of the height, elled into the bank, and with #4 rebar (½″) vertical reinforcing as close as 8″ on center if the wall is to be 6′ high. The ell into the bank works on the same principle as a bookend. A gravel well and drains must also be provided to release water that might be trapped behind the walls thus creating additional weight and pressure. Rubble rock may be economically employed on a sloping bank with some of the stones being keyed into the bank, when merely used to hold back earth, not used as a foundation. (See Figure 6.6)

If you plan to have a concrete slab floor in your home, it is possible to use what is called "monolithic slab" construction, which makes it possible to perform several steps at one time. This has certain drawbacks with adobe, shown as notes on Figure 6.7, and is usually more suitable where the entire floor of the building is to be concrete, and the walls of a non-water-vulnerable material.

In some cases, you may have to, or will find it more practical, to use a frame partition on some interior walls. Figure 6.7 shows the easiest way to do this.

Wood floors require a higher stem, to provide a crawl space below the joists. This may be obtained by raising the floor level, by excavating the area within the foundation, or a combination of the two. The crawl space is needed for access, prevents termites and rotting of wood, and in most cases is required by code. Some building codes and lenders may require that the ground be treated against termites before construction is started, where termites are a problem. (See Figure 6.8)

Excavation of this footing trench is the first thing you must do. It can be done by hand or by machinc. A number of subcontractors have trenching machines that will dig a trench of exact width and depth quite economically. If you have a reasonably flat site and room for the trencher to work, it will probably be more economical to use such a machine than to do it by hand. It will be necessary to do some handwork in any case, to clean out the trenches and straighten up the corners. A clean, accurate

Fig. 6.5 Rock foundations. Have been used traditionally with great success before the invention of ready-mix concrete plants. If using this method, it is best to make sure the rocks fit well without mud mortar, which may melt under severe rains.

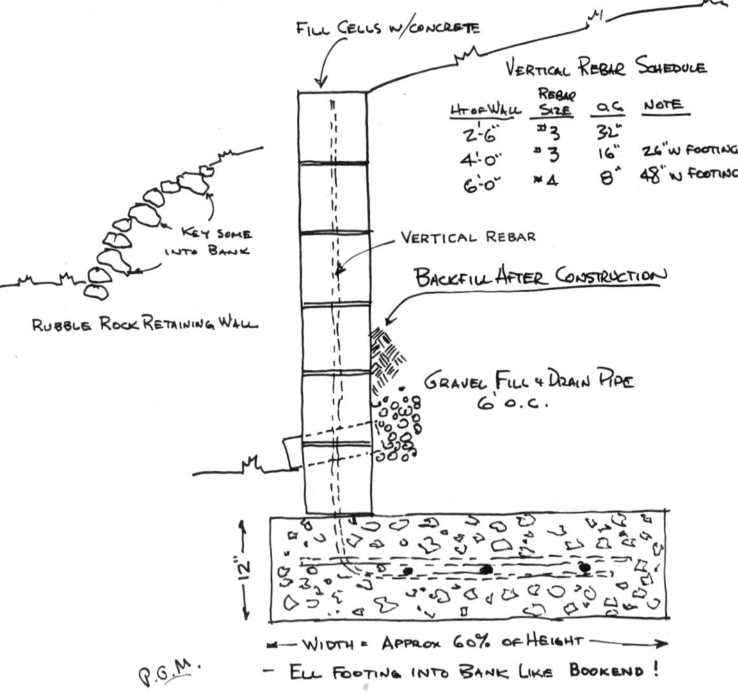

Fig. 6.6 Simple retaining walls.

trench is helpful in estimating the quantity of concrete that will be required. If the trench is irregular in depth and width, average dimensions may be used for estimating quantities of concrete.

Grade stakes should be placed in the bottom of the trench to indicate readily the top of the concrete level to be poured. These can be made of wood, placed along the edge, or of short pieces of rebar set in the center, and abandoned in the concrete. They may be most easily leveled by use of a transit, but a 4-foot level may also be used. If you use the latter method, make sure that there is not too much difference between the starting point and the final point, since small errors may creep into each measurement, creating a wide difference at the end. (Figure 6.9)

CONCRETE

Concrete mixes are generally specified as to hardness and aggregate size. Full curing (design hardness) is not achieved until the concrete has aged for 28 days. It might be mentioned that concrete is relatively easy to remove while still green (uncured), but gets harder daily. If some excess must be removed, do it now! The cost of concrete will increase (although only slightly) with the strength, and finer aggregate size. It is nearly always advisable to use ready-mixed concrete if available at reasonable cost, except in small quantities. Remote building sites, far from the plant, may make ready-mixed concrete prohibitive in price. Try to plan your "pours" so that small-load charges (usually less than 4 cubic yards) can be avoided.

The following is a rough guide for required concrete strengths:

Footings .... 2,000#, 1½" aggregate
Stems, beams,
  most floors .... 2,500#, ¾" aggregate
Polished floors, bond beams,
  heavy traffic,
  sidewalks .... 3,000#, ¾" aggregate

The quantity of concrete needed and the estimating thereof may seem a great mystery to many people, but is actually quite simple. Concrete is estimated in units of cubic yards. This means a cube that is 3′ x 3′ x 3′ will contain 27 cubic feet. Figure all quantities in cubic feet to start with, then convert to cubic yards. A standard heavy-duty contractor's wheelbarrow will hold approximately 2 to 3 cubic feet (larger ones are available if you're real strong). This means that it will require from 10 to 15 wheelbarrows of concrete to make one cubic yard, depending on how full you load them. If you plan to mix more than minor amounts of concrete by yourself, buy or rent a barrel-type mixer. It will save a great amount of hard work. If ready-mix concrete is to be used, it may be placed with a chute, which is a part of the truck equipment, up to perhaps 20 feet. If the site is inaccessible to the truck, you must figure on "wheeling" this in a wheelbarrow to its required location. If at all possible, try to make the chute placement usable. Uphill wheeling is rough!

If you must mix small quantities of concrete, the wheelbarrow makes an excellent measure. It is very difficult to accurately mix concrete to a specific hardness in the field. Better too strong than too weak. The following table should prove adequate:

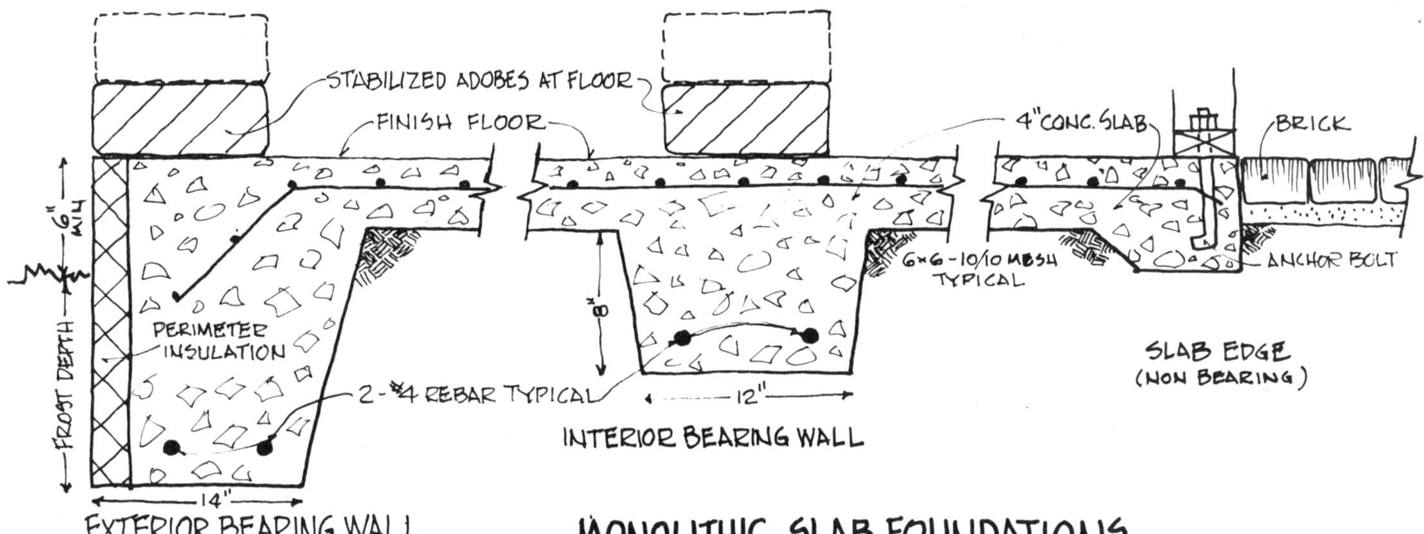

BRICK FLOORS ON SAND

ANCHOR WITH CUT NAILS

FROST DEPTH

8" MIN.

14"

EXTERIOR BEARING WALL

12"

INTERIOR BEARING WALL

SAND BED

MIN. SIZE

NON BEARING CURTAIN WALL

P.G.M.

MISC. CONCRETE FOUNDATIONS

Fig. 6.7 Foundation details.

Use	cement	Parts of sand	gravel	Gallons of water per sack of cement
Footings (2000#)	1	3	5	7½
Other (3000#)	1	2	3	6

One sack of cement (94 lbs.) is one cubic foot. Your shovel is a reasonably accurate measuring spoon. The quantity of water should be added slowly, until usable as you mix, since too much water will reduce the strength. Chances are that unless it looks real sandy, the mix will be twice as strong as you really need.

First estimate your quantities in cubic feet, then convert to cubic yards. It is very simple!

EXAMPLES:

FOOTING 8″ thick x 18″ wide x 100′ long:

8″ = .66 ft.
18″ = 1.5 ft.
.66 × 1.5 = .99 cu. ft. per lineal foot of footing (use 1.0).
100 lineal feet × 1.0 = 100 cu. ft.
100 cu. ft. ÷ 27 cu. ft. (1 cu.yd.) = 3.7 cu.yds.

SLAB 10′ x 10′ x 4″ thick:

4″ = .33 ft.
10′ x 10′ = 100 sq. ft.
100 sq. ft. × .33 = 33 cu. ft.
33 cu. ft. divided by 27 = 1.2 cu. yds.

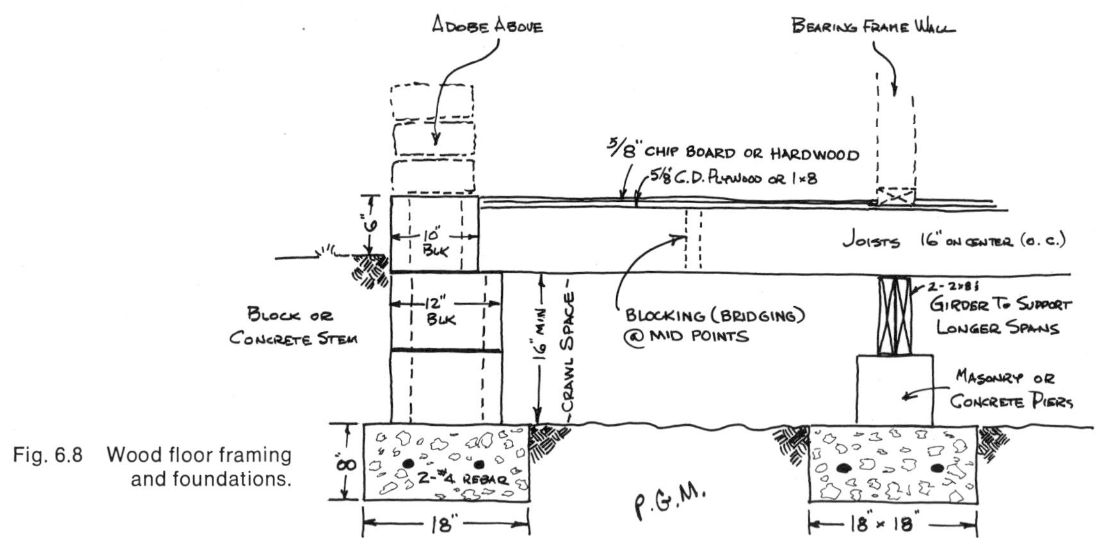

Fig. 6.8 Wood floor framing and foundations.

POURING CONCRETE SLABS

Concrete slabs must have forms placed at the edges before they are poured. The ground, or surface on which the concrete is to be poured, should be clear of grass and vegetation that may decay and allow the slab to settle, and should be reasonably uniform. If not, the slab may be more than 4″ in some places, requiring additional expensive concrete. Forms should be set so that the level surface of the slab may be determined by the top edge of the form when placing the concrete. Your eyeballs are not accurate enough — use a screed! The tops of the forms will serve as screed (leveling) points if smooth and unobstructed by stakes and the like, if the slab is not too wide. After the edge forms have been set (level if no drainage is required), the concrete is poured inside the form, starting at one end, placing more concrete than is necessary (slightly higher than the forms). Then the concrete should be tamped to insure that it has settled into all voids. Select a straight two-by-four, place it across the tops of the forms, and use it as a drag device (screed) to scrape away any excess concrete which is higher than the form. This is repeatedly done as the form is filled, until you reach the end of the slab. (See Figure 6.10)

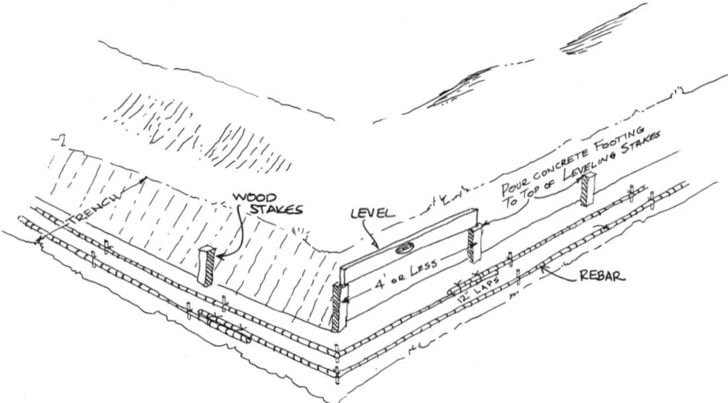

Fig. 6.9 Grade stakes for pouring level foundation.

If the slab is too wide to reach from form top to form top, temporary screed bars must be placed in the center (on stakes), level with the tops of the exterior forms, and used as screed points as you pour. The screed, or two-by-four used for dragging away the excess concrete, is used in the same manner. As large areas are poured and screeded level, the temporary screed bars are removed and the slight void filled with a shovel. If an edge of a slab is to be exposed, as in a patio or driveway slab, thicken the edge by digging deeper, to perhaps 6″, to provide additional support.

Once an adequate quantity of concrete has been placed to fill the form and screeded reasonably smooth, a "jitterbug," or screened tamping device should be used over the entire surface to push down any aggregate protruding from the surface. Then the concrete must be floated, the first troweling done with a trowel on a long handle, called a "bull" float. The concrete is then allowed to set up (dry) until the surface becomes somewhat firm. Do not walk on it at this point.

After it has dried to the point where a board will not sink into the surface, the concrete can be troweled by hand. For a smooth slab, this should be done at least twice, waiting for additional drying in between. This is quite hard work, and most large slabs are troweled by means of a gasoline-powered mechanical

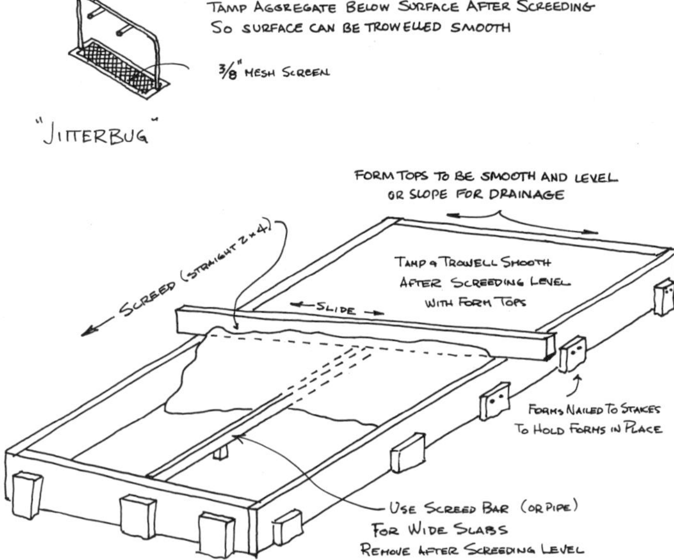

Fig. 6.10 Concrete slab forms and screeding.

trowel. These may be rented. However, for any large areas, such as garage or driveway slabs, for example, it would be wise to hire an experienced concrete finisher. It is skilled work to get a smooth, good surface. Experiment with a small area before tackling a large one.

You may want a nonslip finish for walks. To get such a finish, you use a broom to rough up the surface, just before the concrete takes a final set.

Use an edging tool to round off edges that will be exposed. This cannot be done later; it must be done as the concrete sets.

The concrete slab will set up in a matter of hours, but it is usually an all-day job to finish a slab of any size. The time required for drying depends on many factors, such as temperature, humidity, and wetness of the mix. The trench or surface on which the slab is to be poured should be wet down prior to pouring to prevent too rapid drying. Once the slab has been poured, and finished, it must be protected — in the winter from frost (frozen concrete turns to mush), and in the summer from rapid drying. If a strong wind is blowing, "monkey blood" should be used, which is merely a light coating of paraffin, suspended in a liquid. This will seal the surface so that the moisture cannot escape too rapidly. A large plastic sheet will also serve to prevent rapid drying. The slab should be sprinkled with a hose repeatedly for several days to help insure a good hard surface.

Summary of steps in pouring concrete:

1. Primary grading; excavation if required.
2. Set forms (and screed bars).
3. Final grade leveling and soaking.
4. Set reinforcing, if any.
5. Place concrete, tamp to fill voids.
6. Screed level, "jitterbug."
7. Float fairly smooth (stop here for footings and rough slabs).
8. Trowel (1st), edging.
9. Trowel (2nd, 3rd, etc.), broom finish if desired.

REINFORCING STEEL AND MESH

Reinforcing steel comes in a number of sizes. The most common are:

#3 — 3/8″ diameter for bond beams
#4 — 1/2″ diameter for general use
#5 — 5/8″ diameter for long concrete lintels, extra strength

Please note that the number designation indicates eighths of an inch of diameter.

It is sometimes worthwhile to use reinforcing mesh in concrete slabs. It is more important in exterior slabs that may be subject to frost heaving or tree roots than on interior slabs. The common mesh used is 6″ x 6″ (squares) of 10/10 (10 ga.) wire.

Expect your concrete slabs to show cracks. Very few will not, no matter how careful you are. If a slab is to be more than 20 feet long or wide, expansion joints (1/2″ expansion-joint material) should be inserted flush with the surface of the slab, in some sort of pattern. Slabs to support ceramic tile need not be carefully finished, but must be level, and at least 2″ thick. Footings, naturally, do not need and should not have smooth finishes, since the roughness helps the stem bond securely.

Pouring concrete is hard work. The amateur need not fear the rougher concrete work such as foundations and footings. Larger slabs that will be exposed to view require skilled finishing, sometimes special tools, and I feel you would be well advised to employ skilled help to do this phase of the work. Skilled concrete contractors can do this for a surprisingly reasonable cost. At least hire a good cement finisher for large areas.

7

Adobe Walls

ADOBE BUILDING BRICKS are a very simple material. They are simple to make, and by following a few rules can be laid by anyone with a strong back, using a reasonable amount of care. A great deal of misinformation, myth, and old wives tales has been circulated about this great building material, to the point that many individuals, even builders—who are a fearless breed—are hesitant to tackle adobe construction.

The raw material can be found under your feet almost anywhere. Some soils have too much clay, or too much sand, or too much organic matter to be ideal, but in most cases with a minor amount of tempering they can be used. Not too many years ago in Albuquerque, it was the practice to hire a crew that would dig your basement, and make adobes out of the resulting dirt. It is still a good idea, if you want a basement. Otherwise, I suggest that you either buy dirt and make the adobes yourself, or buy them ready made. Walls, although the most prominent part of any structure, are not the biggest item in your budget. In many cases the cost of adobe walls will constitute less than 10 percent of the total cost of construction. Don't be fooled by the relatively small cost for the walls, but examine everything else as well, and then the total when preparing your budget. This perhaps will help you decide whether to buy the adobes or make them yourself.

The price that you'll pay for the bricks can vary, depending on many factors, such as how many are needed, how many are available, how badly the adobe maker thinks you need them, delivery charges, and so forth. Many adobe makers prefer to make and install the bricks in the wall for a set price per thousand. This is a good idea, provided you are able to keep an accurate count (usually he will expect to count all the broken pieces too), or you may be able to estimate the approximate number required as accurately as the adobe man, and settle on a lump sum price for so much wall to a certain height. This is more satisfactory, to me at least, since it doesn't leave much argument as to the number of adobes that were put in the wall. Bear in mind, also, that the lower courses of adobe bricks are easier to install than the higher ones that must be laid from a scaffold or the roof. Make sure that any "deal" you make includes all the adobes, not just the ones that are easily reached at the lower levels. And expect to be cheated, at least a little. This is part of the game.

MAKING SUN-CURED ADOBE BRICKS

Making adobe bricks is quite simple, but very hard work. First you must have a level, dry area where they can be left to dry as you make them. You can buy adobe dirt by the truckload, usually five to eight cubic yards at a time (one dumptruck full will make 400 to 500 adobe bricks). The soil ideally should be a mix of clay, sand, and fines (very fine silt); it will probably have a reasonable amount of tin cans, bottle caps, broken glass, small rocks, and almost anything. These won't hurt a thing.

The proportion of sand, clay, and fines may vary widely. If the soil has too much clay, the bricks will shrink too much on drying and have a tendency to show shrinkage cracks. If the sand is too high in proportion, the bricks will erode very easily from water. The proportions can be checked to some degree by putting a handful of earth you plan to use into a jar of water, then cap and shake vigorously. The sand and silt settle rather rapidly, while the clay tends to remain in suspension for a while (cloudy) and settle last. The resulting stratification will give a sort of preliminary check.

The best way to determine the suitability of the soil is to make some test bricks. The most frequent problem is too much clay. This will result in shrinkage cracks on drying that will appear rapidly (24 hours or less) as the brick dries. This can be corrected by adding sand or straw to mix. Experiment to find the best proportions, note the quantities. Remember, highest clay without cracks is the best. Make a form of the size brick you intend to use. It can be of virtually any size you can handle, but the usual size, in the Albuquerque area at least, is 10″ x 4″ x 14″. This will give you a dry brick that should weigh between thirty-five and forty pounds. Any bricks bigger than this will result in extreme fatigue to you by noon or before. This "standard" size seems to be optimum in terms of weight, insulation, and wall strength.

Mix the dirt into a doughy mass with enough water to make the mix handleable with a shovel, and place into the form which should be resting on a dry flat area of ground, with a thin layer of sand placed in the bottom. The form should have been wetted thoroughly before filling. After an initial set, depending on how much water has been added, the form should be lifted off, and the resulting mass should be dry enough to stand by itself without slumping (much). The test brick should be left in place for at least three days, or until dry enough to pick up and stand on edge without too much crumbling. After it has stood on edge for three or more days, it should be dry enough to stack, or at least handle with minimum breakage and crumbling. Let it dry for perhaps two weeks. If the soil is right, and the weather hot and dry, the adobes can be used within seven or eight days of manufacture, wet weather taking longer. After thorough drying, the resulting brick should be quite hard, and resist the scratching action of a knife, and a drop of two feet or so without too much damage.

Assuming that you have suitable soil, and your test bricks are reasonably usable, you will now try to make these in quantity. Remember that adobe is a very unbusiness-like material. The quality of the soil for the bricks will vary from one shovelful to the next. Don't worry about it! "Reasonable" is the key word. Make a gang form, that will mold perhaps eight adobes at a time. If you make the form larger, you'll need help to get it off. (See Fig. 7.2)

Mix your mud thoroughly. The clay content tends to get lumpy, like flour in gravy, and will resist efforts to make a smooth mix. The best way to overcome this is by soaking. If possible, soak overnight, in a pit—with dams, or any way

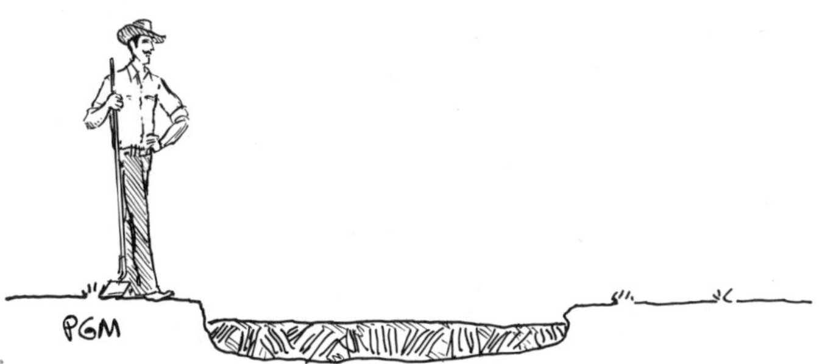

Fig. 7.1a Mixing and soaking pit.

you can—the amount of dirt you hope to use the next day. You'll be surprised at how much dirt can be used, so try to keep a backlog (See Fig. 7.1a). If you are really in earnest, a tractor can be used to push and mix, and mash with the wheels. I think this will increase the cost of your adobes beyond the bought range. Forms may be soaked in oil, which helps separation. Use cheap oil. Used motor oil is great.

Straw is sometimes suggested as a necessary ingredient. It is not! Most adobes made with reasonable adobe soil don't need it. Straw provides a ready home for insects, so sand is the preferred additive, if readily available. Once the bricks are plastered, it probably won't make much difference, but it must be better to make them without straw if possible.

Stacking of the finished bricks must be done to get them out of the way and make room for more manufacturing. Strangely enough, there is a special way that seems superior to any other (See Fig. 7.1b). If the bricks are laid flat, they will be broken by their own weight. Placing them on edge, against a center pillar, and stacking them not more than three or four rows high seems to be ideal. You will lose one or two of the bricks on the bottom of the pillar, but the rest will remain in fairly good condition. If you plan to leave the stack for any period of time, protect it on top with a layer of asphalt paper, plastic, or some weatherproof covering to prevent undue rain erosion. (See Fig. 7.3)

Fig. 7.1b Correct stacking of adobes.

Handling of finished adobe bricks should now be discussed. It costs almost as much to move a stack of adobe bricks 100 feet as it does to move it across town on a truck. Plan your stacking very carefully! I estimate that it costs me about $50 per thousand (5¢ each) for each move. If the bricks can be made and stacked exactly where they will be used, it will save surprising amounts of time (and money). Any advance planning at this point will pay big divi-

Fig. 7.2 Adobe gang mold. Foreground: Empty molds ready for filling. Center: Damp bricks with mold removed. Background: Bricks turned on edges for drying.

Fig. 7.3 Adobes stacked. Note that to minimize breakage, adobes are stacked on edge, not flat. Tarpaper on top protects bricks until used. Chipped corners and ragged edges won't hurt a thing.

dends in future labor. Adobe does not travel well, and should be manufactured as close to the site as possible.

SPECIAL KINDS OF BRICKS

TERRONES are sometimes available in certain limited areas. Basically these are "bricks" of cut sod, cut from a boggy area, and dried in the sun. The size presumably could be whatever you might desire. Most I've seen, and I never did measure one, would appear to be 6″ x 6″ x 10″. The high proportion of organic material (roots) seems to harbor bugs and has a poor compressive strength. I've been told that walls of *terrone* blocks have a tendency to compress downwards, probably from the drying of the vegetation in the bricks. Many old homes built of *terrones* are still standing, however. Terrones, like mud adobes, are laid up with mud mortar.

STABILIZED ADOBE is made with additives that make it resistant to moisture. It will cost more to manufacture (or buy) bricks with the water-resistant feature. In most cases, I don't feel the extra expense is justified, unless you intend to leave the bricks exposed to maintain a masonry texture. This texture can be beautiful, and may be more to your taste than a plastered surface. It can sometimes be used effectively in combination with the main plaster areas as a change in texture, or for special effect. More care must be exercised in installation to maintain an even brick appearance.

Asphalt emulsion makes a good stabilizer and is simply added to the mud and water as it is mixed. The resulting brick will be slightly darker upon drying than regular mud adobes, and may be soaked for days in a pail of water without appreciable damage. The percentage will vary from 5 percent to 15 percent of the total mix depending on the exact soil conditions. Make several test bricks with varying portions of asphalt to find the lowest level at which the brick will be satisfactorily waterproof. Percentages can be measured by comparing the volume of asphalt with the volume of water (buckets). Mortar for layup is mixed with asphalt, just like the bricks.

Portland cement may be added to achieve the same effect, but it will be more expensive, and the same soil variations will require experiment as in the bitudobe above.

Other additives may also be used, such as chemical compounds, which must be mixed with the raw material to be effective. These may prove costly. Certain plant juices are used traditionally by some native cultures, but little is known of the effectiveness.

Coatings, sprayed or brushed on, seem to be ineffective as they change the physical properties of the material and may do more harm than good.

Mortar for stabilized adobes should be stabilized too, for full protection, or use regular cement-lime mortar.

BURNT ADOBE (kiln-dried) is a suitable, durable, attractive material where severe cold is not often experienced. If moisture gets into these burned adobes (they are very absorbent), and the nighttime temperatures fall below freezing, severe spalling (flaking off of the surface) will usually result. Burnt adobe construction is popular and logical in the desert areas where frost is not a problem.

The quality of kiln-fired adobe bricks may vary tremendously, depending on the care with which they are manufactured. Inquire locally as to which supplier is best or most consistent in quality. It is a common practice in many areas to coat the surfaces (after the wall is finished) with a clear liquid preservative such as silicone or some other waterproofing product. This may need to be done at regular intervals (2–4 years) depending on the quality of brick and climate.

Burned adobes are usually laid up with cement-lime mortar, as are regular bricks. This is made by using 2 parts cement, one part lime, to 12 parts sand. "Masonry Cement" may be used (with the lime already added) at a ratio of 5 parts sand to one part masonry cement.

LAYING UP BRICKS

Mortar, with which the adobes are laid up in the wall, seems to be best made from the same material as the wall itself. From time to time, I have encountered those builders who recommend a cement-lime mortar be used, but I never could justify this. The walls are of mud—what advantage can possibly accrue from waterproof joints? The raw material for the mud mortar must differ in only one respect from the mud used in making the adobes. A certain amount of extraneous matter can be tolerated in the mud for adobes, but the mud used as mortar must be free of most of this, particularly rocks and stones of more than ¼″ diameter. The mud joint will vary from ¼″ to ¾″, perhaps even more or less, and the presence of ball-bearing type stones in the mix as you lay the next course of bricks will prevent a smooth and even lay. The occasional stray stone will occur in the best of mixes, and this can be dealt with by checking the mud bed by passing a trowel over the surface lightly after it has been put in place with a shovel. If any stones are present, they will be felt, and can be flicked out with the point of the trowel.

The procedure for mixing the mud mortar is the same as in mixing mud for the adobes. Namely, you must let it soak long enough to become wet all the way through. It will most likely be mixed at a central point near the work; perhaps more than one "pile" may be used effectively. Frequently the surplus dirt that results from excavation may be used for this purpose. It can be stockpiled as it is dug. The mud should be mixed with a hoe, and transported in a large wheelbarrow.

Fig. 7.4 Adobe bricks being laid up in the wall. Ends and corners of wall (leads) are measured and leveled carefully, with bricks in between laid to the string stretched between leads.

It might be mentioned at this point that a helper is quite useful. The change in pace of having to mix mud, load and wheel a wheelbarrow to the location needed, and perhaps carry the adobes to where they may be used, breaks the rhythm and thus slows down the progress considerably. It will also be of value to use your helper to shovel the mud onto the top of the wall, where you plan to put the next course. If too long an area is spread too soon, the mud has a tendency to dry out before the next course of adobes can be placed upon it. A short-handled shovel (perhaps one that has been broken) works admirably for this purpose. A little practice will smooth out the operation. Do not lay more than 6 or 7 courses at any one point in the wall on any one day, or the wet mud joints may compress before drying. The end (head) joints of the brick should be staggered at least 4 inches so that no vertical joint occurs.

"Leads" (pronounced *leeds*) is a masonry term for the corners and interruptions of a straight wall, such as window and door openings. Hopefully you will be starting with a reasonably level stem, and you must strive to keep the top of the wall the same way. You know at what height you wish to terminate your wall, from the plans and wall sections that you have already drawn, and from the thickness of the adobe bricks. A little simple arithmetic will tell you the number of courses of adobe bricks that will be required to reach the desired height. Allow for ¾ ″ as the ideal joint. It may be more or less, since the thickness of the bricks will vary, and your mortar may not always be of consistent texture. (See Fig. 7.4)

You may best use a "story pole" (see Fig. 7.5) at the leads that will predict where the joints should occur. The leads should be laid up plumb (true vertical), using a long level (4′ is

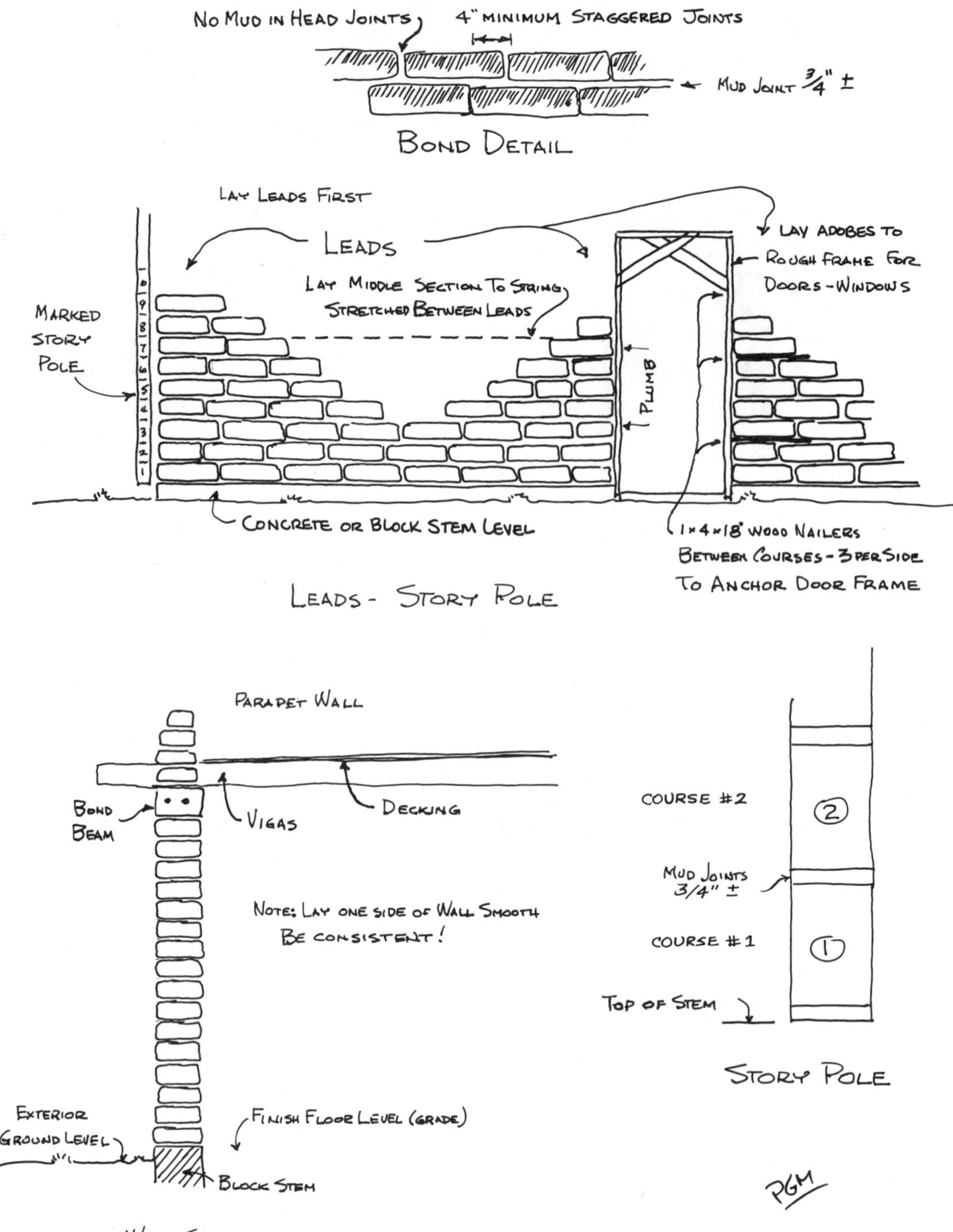

best) and as accurately to the story pole as you can. If this is done, and the leads are accurate, it is a simple matter to stretch a string between corresponding courses of two leads, and lay adobes to the string in between. This is one reason that additional corners in a house are expensive. More leads must be laid, each with a considerable amount of care, requiring more time than a straight wall. The wall itself must be constantly checked with a long (4′) level to make sure that it is plumb, although careful leads and a taut string will eliminate most of the problem. If the wall is not plumb (straight up and down) it will have a tendency to tip over with time. Slender columns of adobe bricks must be avoided.

Provision for doors and windows should be planned in detail before starting up with the walls. Opening locations, widths, and anchoring devices must, in most cases, be determined and installed as the wall is built. The details of this are covered in Chapter 8. Plan your details before starting up with the walls. (Fig. 7.6)

Adobe is a great building material. It is quite economical (in itself at least), found nearly everywhere, and tremendously plastic and versatile. It must be protected from moisture, however, since its vulnerability to water is its greatest drawback. This fact must be kept constantly in mind. An hour's work with a hose can destroy an unplastered adobe wall completely. It must be protected from rain, from groundwater that may seep into the wall from flooding or heavy downpours, and also from the runoff from the roof during rains. If a wall becomes wet all the way through, the great weight above it will squeeze the lower wet courses out like toothpaste from a tube.

It is wise to extend the block or concrete stem a few inches higher than the finished floor inside. Adobe's compressive strength is limited. If you put a concentrated weight, such as a *viga* (a reasonably straight tree with the branches and bark removed, used to support the roof) at one point in a wall, it may compress the adobe down, leading to all sorts of complications. Any weights that will be concentrated (such as a roof beam) should be spread over a larger area through the use of plates (pieces of flat lumber), bond beams, or pads of concrete that will spread the load over a wider surface. One other drawback to adobe is its refusal to hold most anchoring devices for cabinets and the like. You must try to provide for this in advance, by the use of nailer blocks or inserts of wood that are installed with the bricks in the wall. A piece of wood, 1″ x 4″ x 18″ long, may be inserted between courses of adobe to provide a secure nailing point for doors, windows, or kitchen cabinets, or you may use "gringo" blocks (see fig. 7.7), which are merely adobe-sized blocks of wood laid up with the adobe bricks in necessary locations. In the event these are overlooked at the outset, nailing strips or wood plugs can be inserted later.

The quantity of adobe bricks required may

Fig. 7.6 Rough bucks. These rough lumber frames provide an accurate square opening to receive a door or window. The rough portion is normally covered with plaster. The top of the buck also acts as the bottom of the form for a poured concrete lintel beam.

be determined by the wall area: height times length. Adobes laid with 4″ x 14″ dimensions exposed will require approximately 2.25 adobes per square foot. Ignore window and door openings unless very large. These "outs," as they are called, will provide for breakage loss.

Earthquake-prone areas require some additional treatment in the construction of masonry walls. Any masonry wall is extremely vulnerable to earthquakes where sharp lateral movements of the earth will tend to bring down the whole structure. The most successful earthquake-proof structures have proven to be of steel-reinforced concrete. You may incorporate this principle in your wall construction by the use of reinforced concrete pilasters at the corners, and at window and doorjambs. The construction of forms to contain this concrete can be tedious, although a superior method.

The University of California publication, *Adobe Construction Methods,* suggests that vertical and horizontal reinforcing will suffice. The vertical reinforcing must be embedded in the

Fig. 7.7 Adobe wall with "gringo" blocks, block stem. Wooden "gringo" blocks have been set in place of adobes to provide anchorage for doors, windows, or as in this case, a gate. This wall has been exposed to the weather for approximately five years with little damage. Note concrete blocks extending above ground level, preventing ground water from damaging bottom of wall.

concrete footing at the bottom, and extend to the concrete bond beam at the top of the wall. You need not have this all in one piece, however, since the height of this limber rod makes the placement of adobes quite awkward. You may make this of two or more sections of reinforcing bar, lapping the ends at least 12″ and wiring the joints tightly as you extend them up (see Fig. 7.8). These verticals should be placed on 2- to 4-foot centers. The adobes may be drilled and put down over the rod, or split and laid to each side. Horizontal reinforcement may take the form of several types of patented devices, such as "Durowall," or possibly #3 reinforcing rod, laid in the joint, each third course. In earthquake prone areas, consult a structural engineer.

BOND BEAMS

Bond beams are used to tie the tops of masonry walls together. Contrary to the popular phrase "solid as a brick wall," masonry walls are really quite fragile unless they are tied together at the top. This is less true of adobe than most masonry walls, because of its mass and weight, but any masonry wall—brick, block or adobe—should make use of the bond or collar beam. This is usually of concrete, and is reinforced with one or more steel reinforcing rods.

Perhaps you have seen old adobes with large cracks at the corners, where one wall has separated, from inadequate foundations, erosion at the bottom, or the wall being out of plumb, so that one or both sides of the intersection tends to tip in an outward direction from its original vertical position. The cure for this in older structures has been to "batter" the walls, by building buttresses at the corners to support the walls and prevent further movement. These buttresses are large masses of masonry (adobe) that are stacked against the corner for support (see Figs. 7.9 and 7.10).

Installing a bond beam with block construction is quite simple. It is merely a matter of using a bond-beam-type block in the course in

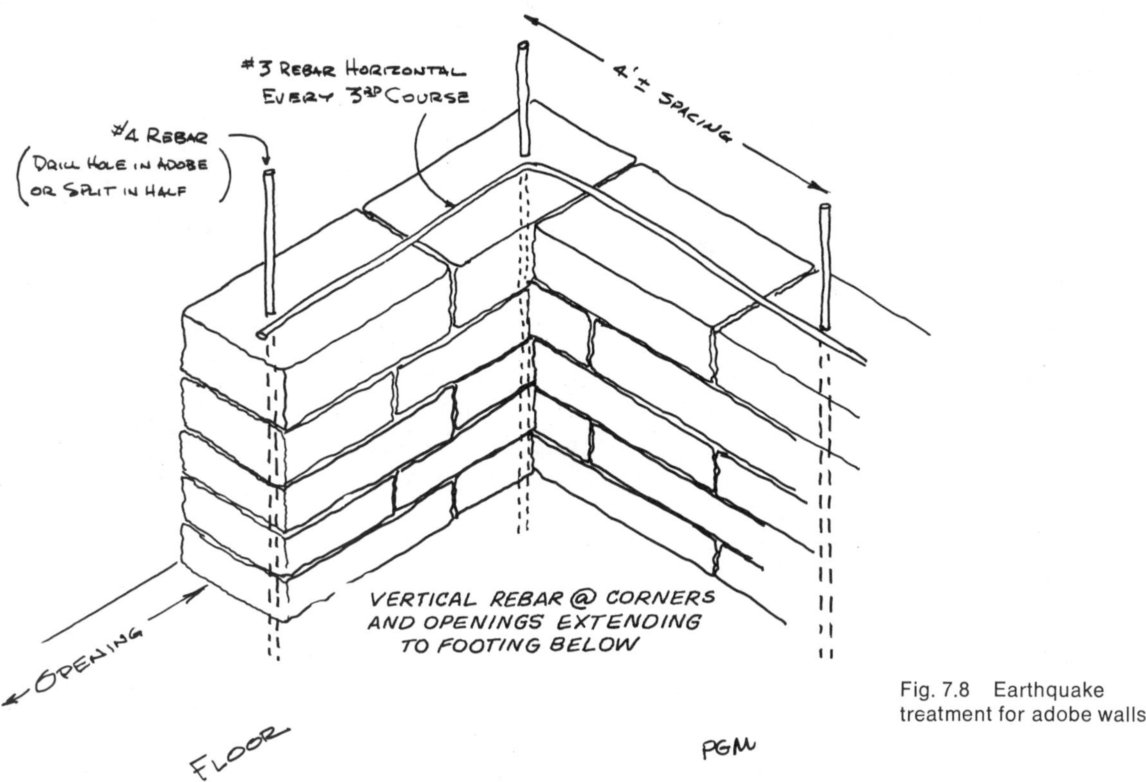

Fig. 7.8 Earthquake treatment for adobe walls.

which you want the bond beam, laying in reinforcing rods, and filling with concrete. This is most commonly done so that the roof structure will rest upon the top of the bond beam.

Bond beams for adobe construction are somewhat more troublesome. Since a bond-beam-type block is not presently available in the necessary 10″ width (or other width you may select) for the adobe wall, you must set a small form and fill it with concrete. A wood bond beam may also be used. It should be a minimum of 4″ thick and the ends and corners must be securely fastened together. Figures 7.11 and 7.12 illustrate two types of bond beams. (See Fig. 7.14)

The wood bond beam may not be acceptable under certain codes. There is one style of construction where it should be employed, however. If you plan to use stabilized adobes, or intend to preserve the masonry texture of the wall for its decorative effect, the wood bond beam will be more attractive. A concrete bond beam with this style may well be unsightly, since it will not have the same texture as the balance of the wall. An additional drawback of the wooden bond beam, where the wall is to be plastered, is that the wood will shrink, causing cracks in the plaster surface unless properly covered with tar paper and metal lath.

LINTELS

Lintels are bridges over openings in the walls where windows, doors, and passages through walls occur. These may be made of concrete, where long spans are required, or they can be of wood timbers for a decorative effect. If a lintel is to be made of concrete, this is most easily accomplished by thickening the bond beam at this point. If of timber, sufficient bearing must be provided on each end, and the lintel should be anchored in some manner to the bond beam. Careful attention must be given to the dimensions that will be involved. Frequently the wood lintel will be in a bearing wall and will be required to carry the main roof structure, so it will be necessary to have the top of the wall level to carry the *vigas* or roof timbers. Additional steel reinforcing is usually desirable in the concrete

Fig. 7.9 Ranchos de Taos Church, Ranchos de Taos, New Mexico. Masses of heavy masonry help support a corner which has started to tip, from either a lack of a bond beam or weakened foundations.

Fig. 7.10 Ranchos de Taos Church, Ranchos de Taos, New Mexico. High walls may also need some support.

Fig. 7.11 Bond beam form. Form may be held in place with simple metal brackets. A patching piece is used at windows and doors to cover the thicker lintel. Note 1 x 4 nailer strips laid up with the adobe wall, in place of "gringo" blocks.

Fig. 7.12 Bond beam. Form has been stripped off, *vigas* placed, and adobes continued above bond beam.

Fig. 7.13 Grand junction. Concrete bond beam, heavy timber lintel, and frame wall all come together at one corner. Note support for timber lintel (concrete pad atop adobe wall).

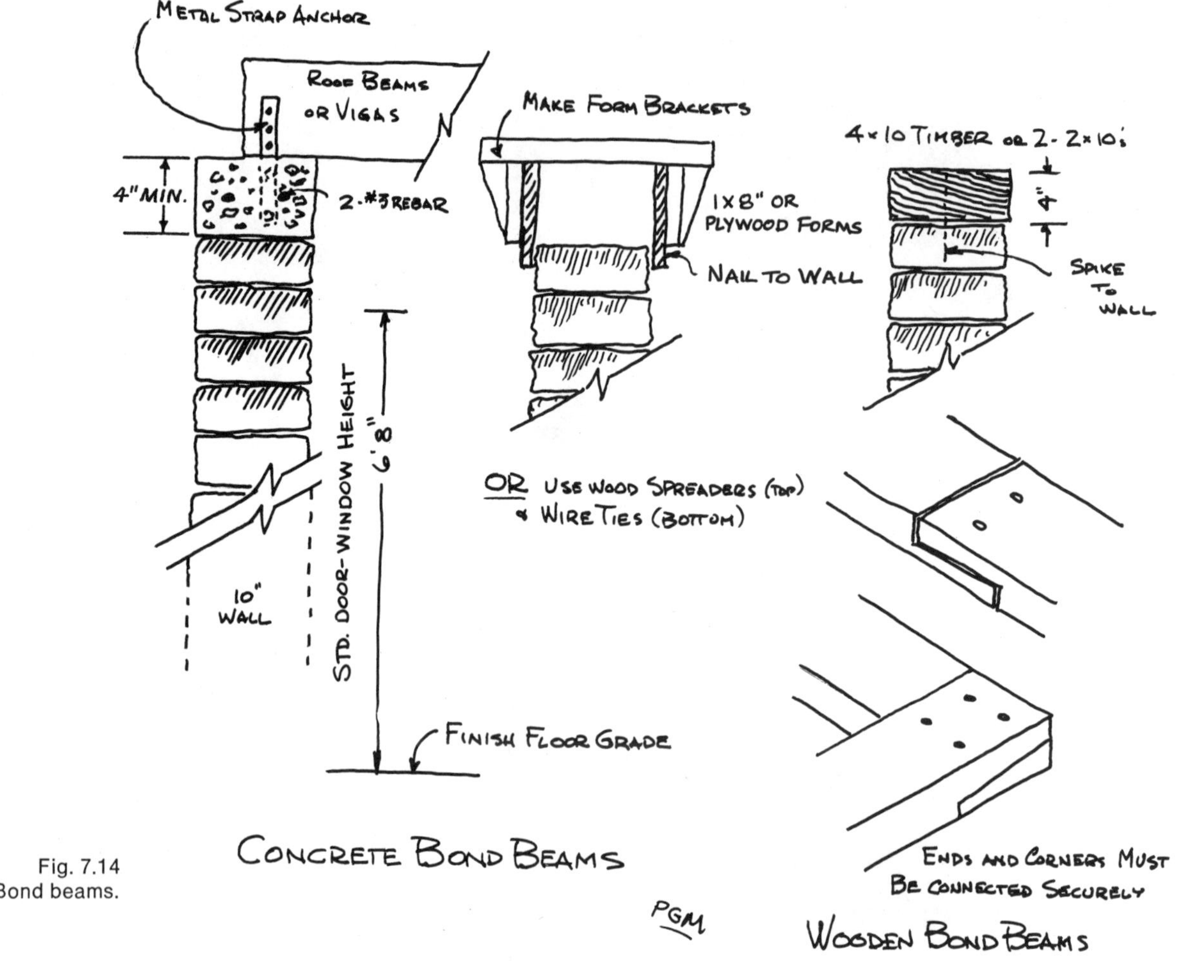

Fig. 7.14
Bond beams.

lintel. One additional #4 rebar is required in most cases; however, if a span in excess of 8 feet is required, the concrete lintel depth should be increased to 18″, with four #4 bars. This may increase the ceiling height, or lower the opening height. Check measurements carefully on paper to make sure in advance. (See Fig. 7.15)

Make sure the additional reinforcing bars extend into the bond beam at least 24″. This additional thickness should be sufficient for spans to 16 feet. Handsome, unusual effects may be obtained by carving lintels for decoration. This carving can best be done on the ground before the lintel beam is erected, but may be done later when you may have more time, or as rainy-day work.

Careful attention to detail must be given in planning how the door or window frame will fit to the lintel. Special trim may have to be provided for, or a special treatment given to the lintel before it is installed.

FRAME WALLS

Frame walls are frequently used in an adobe home for a variety of reasons. They may be used either as bearing walls or merely curtain walls. A curtain wall is one that carries no weight other than its own, and is generally installed after the structural walls and roof are in place. Its sole purpose is that of a divider. Frame walls may be used — bearing or nonbearing — where sound transmission, and massive appearance are of no great importance. They are particularly useful for short walls that must carry a quantity of plumbing or heating pipes. It is more difficult to build a masonry wall around pipes than it is frame walls. A typical frame wall is shown in Figure 7.18.

The sketch indicates that standard two-by-fours will be used for the frame-wall construction. It may be desirable to make this wall from two-by-sixes or two-by-eights, in order to accommodate plumbing, or for other reasons.

A cast-iron drain line hub (joint) will measure more than 3⅝″, and may be slightly out of plumb, making an intrusion into the room. This wall may be furred out with lathing strips later, or may be made thicker by the use of wider lumber. If furring is required, it may cause complications with the size of the room. Therefore, it may be better to plan on the thicker wall to begin with, thus avoiding unpleasant surprises later on.

Building a frame wall can best be accomplished by the following method. The wall should be laid out on a flat surface — the floor will do admirably — close to where it will be used. The studs can be precut to a uniform size, in accordance with ceiling height and plate thickness. Lay out stud and trimmer locations in pencil on the plates, which go at the top and bottom. Start from one end and lay out on 16″ centers. This way it will carry either 32″ lath or 48″–96″ sheets. It may be some advantage to arrange door and window openings to take advantage of stud locations on one side at least, but not greatly so. If you don't hold to the 16″ centers consistently from the starting end, considerable cutting and waste of sheet material will occur. Make sure that nailing blocks are provided at each corner or wall intersection to provide support for sheet material.

Determine your window and door sizes exactly, and allow for frames. If you have made an error, it can be corrected, but it will save time to do this accurately the first time. Nailing this wall frame together in the flat position is the easiest. Make sure that the surfaces of all framing are flush. After nailing together, the entire section can be tilted up into place and attached. If a long section will be too heavy to lift, build it in more than one section. After it is fastened in place, you may then put on the second top plate, if this is to be a bearing wall. This plate may also be incorporated while it is flat. Stagger the plate joints to make the wall stronger. (See Figure 7.19)

DIMENSION LUMBER is generally used for framing because of its uniformity. It might be well to explain at this point the definition of "dimension lumber." When logs are cut at a sawmill, they are cut approximately to the correct size such as a two-by-four or two-by-six. The actual dimensions are subject to the skill of the sawyer. These boards are now known as

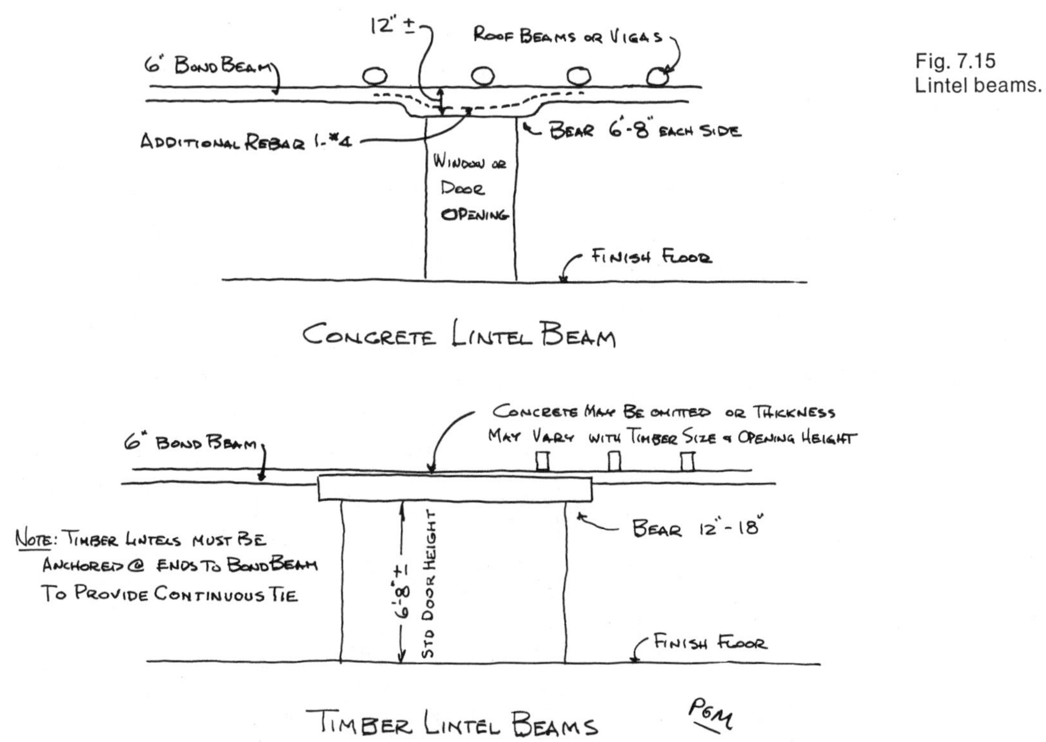

Fig. 7.15
Lintel beams.

Fig. 7.16 Residence, Albuquerque, New Mexico. Various combinations of lintels may be required to accomplish roof timber framing.

Fig. 7.17 Residence, Albuquerque, New Mexico, P. G. McHenry, Jr., architect-builder. Heavy timber lintels resting on adjacent walls support roof beams.

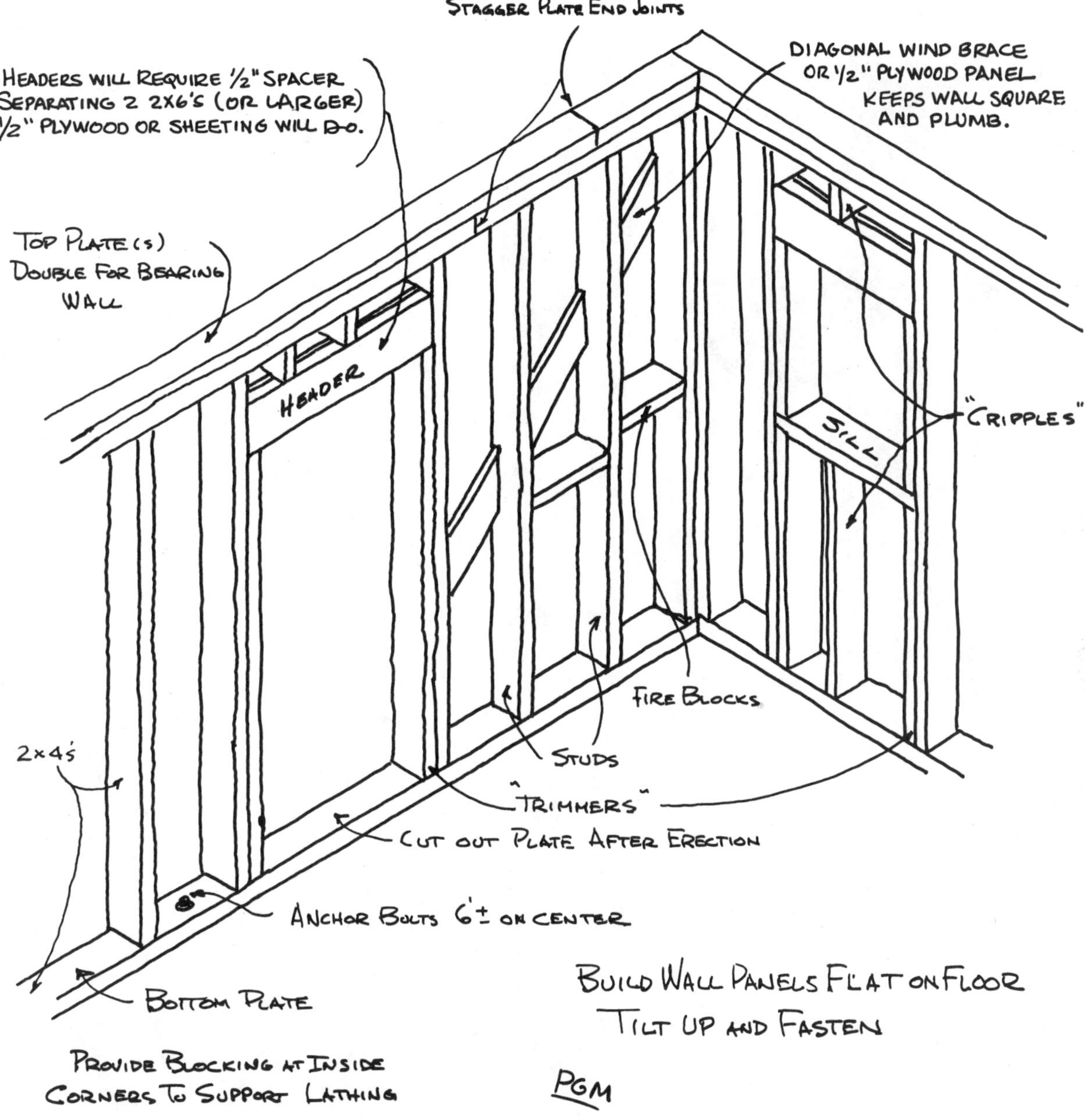

Fig. 7.18 Typical frame wall.

rough sawn, will not be too uniform, and will not have been dried or graded for quality. They are further processed at a planing mill, where the rough blanks are fed into a machine that surfaces them on all four sides, creating "dimension lumber" of a precise size. The S4S (surfaced 4 sides) lumber is then dried in a kiln, and shipped to the lumber yards for sale.

A lack of uniformity will create problems. For many years the industry standard for a two-by-four has been not 2″ x 4″, but 1⅝″ x 3⅝″. But now the standard is 1½″ thickness. Lumber must be assembled much more exactly than adobe.

The new sizes are as follows:

Kiln-Dried Lumber

Nominal	Actual	Nominal	Actual
1″	= ¾″	6″	= 5½″
2″	= 1½″	8″	= 7¼″
3″	= 2½″	10″	= 9¼″
4″	= 3½″	12″	= 11¼″

Fig. 7.19 Frame walls. Note diagonal bracing to keep walls square. Door header, cripples, trimmers, and additional blocking provide nailing surfaces at corners. Top plate is doubled to carry framing for roof above.

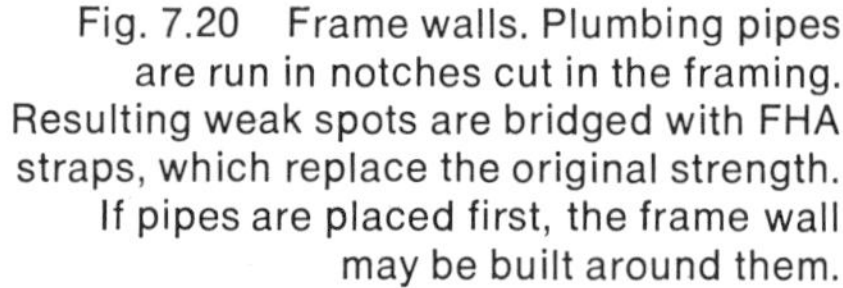

Fig. 7.20 Frame walls. Plumbing pipes are run in notches cut in the framing. Resulting weak spots are bridged with FHA straps, which replace the original strength. If pipes are placed first, the frame wall may be built around them.

If rough lumber is used, it may be full dimension and may not be kiln dried. Shrinkage will occur on drying.

It is also desirable to protect any lumber stored on the building site from the elements, and it should be left in strapped bundles until used. If this precaution is not taken, lumber stored on the site will be warped and twisted to the point where it may become unusable.

Lumber grading is a rather inexact science, but various species of wood may be used, which are available in several different grades. Consult your lumber dealer for the correct, cheapest grade that will suit your purpose. There is no need to buy lumber of a higher grade than is required. Purchases are made by specification (e.g. #2 or better, Pine). It will be to your advantage to sort the shipment for clear (without knots) straight lumber, separating the particularly bad ones for use as short pieces.

NAILS are best chosen from a display chart shown by a manufacturer or supplier. The chart will show length and special features. If a quantity of a single-size nail will be required, by all means buy a 50 lb. box (half keg). The largest quantity of a single size that you'll need will probably be 16d, which is the size most commonly used for wood framing. A small quantity of 20d (larger) nails will be required for heavier duty, and where you need to "straighten" a board by nailing. A small quantity of 10d for miscellaneous framing will also be needed. "Cut" nails for nailing to masonry will be used in small quantity. If the nail head will be exposed to the weather, the nail should be galvanized. If it will be used in conjunction with plaster, it should be "blued" to retard rusting. Where decking is to be nailed, "cement coated" nails should be used. Ask the advice of your supplier.

8

Doors and Frames, Hardware, and Windows

DOORS AND WINDOWS are used by all of us, all our lives, with very little thought given to their size, construction, style, or detailing. In order to be satisfactory, they must have certain features and quality (dry lumber, straight, etc.). We will examine these in more detail later in the chapter.

SWING-TYPE PASSAGE DOORS

The types of these doors available fall into three general categories: flush, panel, and special. They range in price from a very few dollars for economy flush doors, to several hundred dollars each for special hand-carved doors. Doors will be a big item in your construction budget, and they should be chosen carefully. I will not attempt to go into all the types available, since you may do this more readily and satisfactorily at your supplier's. General considerations for the three types follow:

FLUSH DOORS are usually the most economical, unless you specify a particularly unusual grade of plywood for the face. Interior doors of this type are generally made hollow core, to reduce the cost and the weight. Exterior doors, to be satisfactory, should always be solid core. They will have a smooth, plywood surface on both sides which can be stained or painted. The most economical grade is rotary-cut mahogany. This type has very little grain, since the plywood surface is peeled off the log in the manner of a pencil sharpener, making a continuous sheet of plywood from one log. The hollow-core doors frequently have a cardboard core of honeycomb construction. This is not bad necessarily, because it reduces the weight and cost, and makes them more stable and free from future warpage. The solid-core types usually have a core of flakeboard, or inexpensive plywood. Very attractive finishes can be achieved with stains and varnish on birch, gum, walnut, and other plywood varieties.

PANELED DOORS come in an almost endless variety of panel arrangements. The more economical have thin plywood panels. The more panels, the more expensive the door. They are also available in raised panels, one of the more popular being designated a "6 RP" which stands for a six-panel, colonial-style door, with raised panels, made of special millwork. These are obviously more expensive. (See Figure 8.1) There is also a choice of wood available. They may be made of fir, which is the more economical, or of clear pine, which is more expensive. The clear pine has higher raised panels, and will accept stain more readily and uniformly. Some paneled, and flush, types are available with glass panes of various sizes as well. There is probably no "typical" door that would be historically correct in an adobe house, except that the territorial style made use of a great amount of very detailed millwork. This could perhaps be reflected in your doors.

SPECIAL DOORS must be ordered as a rule. Very ornate doors can be imported from Mexico, although my experience would indicate that there is not much saving to be made in cost, and the quality (stability of the wood) is not as dependable as in domestic doors. It is fun to make your own doors, but a word of warning. It is quite difficult, and the result is sometimes disappointing. In order to fit properly, the door must be straight and true, and it is difficult even for the average contractor to purchase material from which good doors may be made. If the door is not accurate, it will be extremely difficult to hang, and it may not be possible to plumb it properly — so that it will have a tendency to swing open or shut. It also may be difficult to weatherstrip. Frequently, standard doors can be modified by the application of moldings or panels to create unusual and original effects more economically than a special order.

OTHER KINDS OF DOORS

SLIDING GLASS DOORS, although they may not seem consistent with the adobe style, have many advantages that cannot be ignored. They serve double duty by admitting light and air as well as functioning as doors. These units are extremely economical, and where large glass areas are desirable, can be installed with insulated glass. Their standard height is the same as the others (6′8″), and they come in many width combinations. Be sure to specify tempered glass to reduce the possibility of serious accidents.

BIFOLD OR BYPASS DOORS, commonly used for closets and as dividers, frequently have the same pattern used on swing-type doors, but utilize different hardware. Bifold doors are available in many widths and patterns, and are perhaps more satisfactory for wardrobe-type closets, which are very practical and economical. Bypass doors also serve this purpose.

OVERHEAD GARAGE DOORS come in several sizes, but two are common. These are 9′ x 7′ and 16′ x 7′. I personally prefer the 16-foot width since it is easier to negotiate, and usually cheaper than two 8-foot doors. These can be solid panel or sectional, and made of wood, steel, or fiberglass. Make sure that you have sufficient headroom between the top of the door and the ceiling for the door to operate properly. It frequently makes sense to have a glass or fiberglass panel incorporated in the garage door, since this eliminates the necessity of putting an additional window in the garage to provide daylight. You should have natural daylight in any garage or storeroom when the doors are closed.

INTERIOR DOORS

Panels are ¾″ raised solid White Pine.

	Sizes	Stiles	Top Rail	Lock Rail	Cross Rail	Bottom Rail	Mullions
ND 103	2-0x6-8x1⅜	4⅝″	4⅝″		4⅝″	9⅝″	
	2-6x6-8x1⅜						
	2-8x6-8x1⅜						
ND 108	1-4x6-8x1⅜	3¾″	4⅝″	8″	4⅝″	9⅝″	
3-PANEL	1-6x6-8x1⅜	4⅝″					
	1-8x6-8x1⅜						
ND 108	2-0x6-8x1⅜	4⅝″	4⅝″	8″	4⅝″	9⅝″	4⅝″
6-PANEL	2-4x6-8x1⅜						
	2-6x6-8x1⅜						
	2-8x6-8x1⅜						
	3-0x6-8x1⅜						
	2-6x6-8x1¾						
	2-8x6-8x1¾						
	3-0x6-8x1¾						
	3-0x7-0x1¾						

16

Courtesy Ideal Company, Waco, Texas.

Fig. 8.1 Page from door manufacturer's catalog.

SIZES OF DOORS

Standard-size doors throughout the house are certainly the most desirable from a cost standpoint unless architectural considerations make this inadvisable. You can order doors of any size and pattern you want, but be prepared to pay a premium for them.

The normal height for doors is 6′-8″ (finishing height of the door itself), except garage doors which are 7′-0″. The standard widths, and most common uses are listed on the next page.

STANDARD DOORS

Width	*Common Use*
1′-8″	
2′-0″	most bathrooms
2′-4″	
2′-6″	most bedrooms
2′-8″	most back doors (wide enough for a refrigerator)
3′-0″	most front entries
3′-6″	special-effect entries

The difference in cost between most sizes is quite small. Make sure that the door width is adequate for anything you may conceivably want to move through it.

Thickness of doors may seem unimportant but the standards call for 1¾″ for exteriors, and 1⅜″ for interior swing doors. Many bifold louver and panel-type doors, as well as screen doors, may have a thickness of only 1⅛″, which is satisfactory.

DOORS — GENERAL INFORMATION

For a door to be satisfactory, it must swing, close, and latch easily and securely. It must be hung plumb, which means that the door and frame must be in an exact vertical position. If it is not, the door will tend to swing open or shut of its own weight. The material it is made of must be almost completely dry, or it will warp or twist, throwing the latch or stops out of alignment. Extreme care must be used in the protection of exterior doors to protect them from the elements and warping. They should be laid flat in a stack — clear of any possible floor moisture — until they are hung. *Do not* lean a door against a wall for any period of time.

Any exterior door that is hung must be protected at once with a coat of paint, varnish, or some sort of sealer to prevent the pickup of moisture that will cause warping. If a door is to be coated with some such substance, it is important that both sides, and the top and bottom, be coated. If not, the shrinkage from surface tension on the coating when drying will bow the door. Exterior doors should be further permanently protected by some sort of canopy or overhang, to prevent direct exposure to the sun and rain. If an overhang is impossible, at least coat the door with a marine polyurethane material. The Southwestern sun will eat Spar varnish or paint off of a surface within a few months if not protected. Weatherstripping and a sealing threshold should be incorporated in all exterior doors.

PREFABRICATED DOOR UNITS may sometimes be worked into a plan. These are factory-assembled units, where the door is hung, fitted, and locked in a frame. It is more economical to have this done in a shop with production methods than in the field. Where plaster, as opposed to drywall, is to be used, prehung units may cause trouble because the wet plaster will cause the frames to swell, making a refitting of the door necessary after setting.

THE HAND of a door swing is frequently misunderstood. It must sometimes be specified for hardware and door units particularly. The way to determine the hand is to face the door on the side where it swings toward you. The knob will be on the right or left side in this position. The side the knob is on, as you face it, will be the door's "hand."

SWING. Plan the door swing on your particular floorplan to make sure that the swing will not interfere with furniture, light switches, or other doors, if possible. Number each door on your plan and make a "door schedule" with necessary notes and dimensions, perhaps even frame sizes and rough opening dimensions as these may differ between masonry and frame wall openings that will receive them. It is useful to note hardware requirements on the schedule.

DOOR FRAMES

The frames for your doors are finished woodwork that will be exposed to view. You must plan them carefully. They must be of sufficient width, and in the correct position to enable your door to swing completely open, flat to the wall. With adobe construction and its thick walls, this requires some careful planning and setting of the frames. These must be set to one side or the other of the wall, to permit the doors to swing flat to the wall, and nailing devices,

Fig. 8.2 Hand-carved door, Tucson, Arizona. Imports can create magnificent effects.

Fig. 8.3 Modern production doors. The handmade effect may be approached by careful selection of premium products by reputable manufacturers.

Fig. 8.4 Hand-carved doors, Hermosillo, Sonora, Mexico.

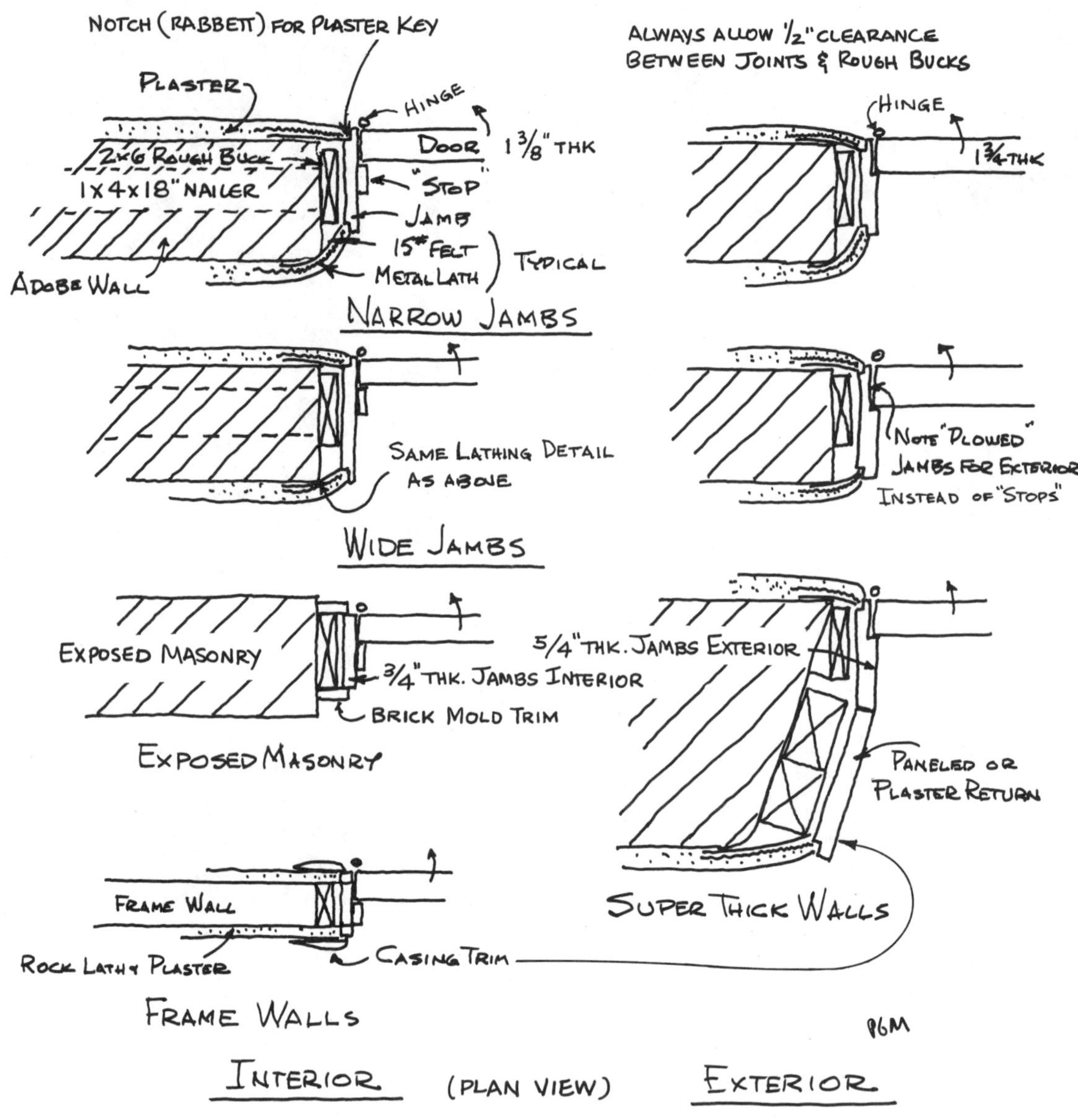

Fig. 8.5 Typical door jamb details.

or rough bucks (rough wood frames to receive finished doors and frames) must be provided in the proper location.

The frames must be of almost the same rigid specifications for dryness and so forth as your doors. They can be built on the job or it may be more convenient to order the frames only from a door-unit manufacturer. Frequently frame manufacturers can provide "finger joint" jambs, which are made of short pieces joined with glue. If the frames are to be stained, specify "solid," since the different colors of wood in "finger joint" may show through. If they are to be painted it won't matter.

This is finished carpentry work and all care must be exercised to avoid hammer marks and abuse that are permissible with "rough" carpentry work. The frame must be provided with some sort of "stop" to stop the door in its closed position. This may be accomplished by the use of nailed-on stops, for interior doors, and preferably with rabbetted or milled stops for exterior doors. A "rabbetted" or "milled" frame is made of a solid piece of wood, run through a router or milling machine to remove a notch as thick as the door. The exterior door frame may be milled or rabbetted on both sides for the installation of screen doors, and as a result, should be made of heavier material than the interior frame. Interior frames are usually made of ¾″ thick stock and the exteriors of 5/4″ (1¼″) stock. (See Figure 8.5)

DOOR SCHEDULE (FOR FIG 5.1)					
NO.	SIZE	TYPE	FRAME	HARDWARE	NOTE
①	$3^{0} \times 6^{8} \times 1\frac{3}{4}$	SPECIAL PANEL	$\frac{5}{4} \times 6\frac{1}{2}$ - SOLID PINE DBLE. RAB. FOR SCRN	$1\frac{1}{2}$ PR. 4×4 BUTTS LOCKSET *	ALUM. THRESH. & WEATHERSTRIP -FUTURE SCREEN-
②	$2^{8} \times 6^{8} \times 1\frac{3}{4}$	KC-½ GLASS	$\frac{5}{4} \times 6\frac{1}{2}$ · SOLID PINE DBL. RAB. FOR SCRN	$1\frac{1}{2}$ PR. 4×4 BUTTS LOCKSET *	ALUM. THRESH. & WEATHERSTRIP -FUTURE SCREEN-
③	$9^{0} \times 7^{0}$	O/H GAR. SECTIONAL	ROUGH ONLY	INTEGRAL	
④	$2^{6} \times 6^{8} \times 1\frac{3}{8}$	6 PANEL COLONIAL	$\frac{3}{4} \times 3\frac{1}{2}$ W/STOPS SOLID PINE	PRIVACY	
	-ETC-				

* KEY ALIKE

Fig. 8.6 Typical door schedule.

If you have particularly thick walls or want an unusual effect, you may wish to "case" the door opening. The casing is a wood face on the interior of the opening. It must be carefully provided for, and details of exactly how you plan to install this should be made prior to ordering doors and material, or laying up the wall.

Hanging your doors is a skilled job. If you do not feel up to the task, it is advisable to hire a "trim" carpenter who will do as much of the finish carpentry work as you may want him to. Such carpenters are hired by the hour, by the unit, or on a lump-sum basis for a specific list of items on the job.

A typical door schedule is shown in Figure 8.6 above.

THRESHOLDS AND WEATHER STRIPPING

Thresholds are extremely important to obtain a tight fit on an exterior door. Most have a rubber or vinyl strip which is flexible, and to which the door must be fitted. The threshold can be of metal or wood, and comes in several heights to accommodate carpet or floor covering of different thicknesses. Nothing is more aggravating than a door that drags on the carpet. A correct-height threshold with the door fitted to it will solve the problem.

Weather stripping is vital on most exterior doors, unless they fit very tightly without it. Several types are available. The most common, and most economical, is a spring bronze strip, which is nailed to the frame. The door, on closing, compresses the strip to a tight fit. If a door becomes badly warped, it may be impossible to use this type, in which case a felt sweep, or flexible stop can be attached to the frame.

HARDWARE

Hardware for your project can be selected from a bewildering array that should suit any taste, and the choice is limited only by your pocketbook and imagination. The quality will vary from the most economical to specially ordered items. If you have lived in some of the older tract homes that made use of bargain hardware, you may have discovered that the doorknobs needed replacing after perhaps ten years. Recently I had occasion to remove a number of items from a house built almost one hundred years ago, and was pleased to discover that all the original hardware was intact and completely workable. I'm sure that it was quality hardware! The only adjustment that had been made was to shim up the hinge pins about ½″ on the swing side of the front door. The bearing part of the hinge had actually worn down that much over the years and was held up with a series of small washers. Every twenty years, put in another washer!

Let us cover the main hardware items and their nomenclature now:

HINGES. These are known in the trade as "butts" and are ordered in pairs (1½ pairs equal 3 hinges). They come in a bewildering variety. Even the contractors may have difficulty in describing exactly what they want to order. The material may be brass, steel, or plated, and in several finishes, such as polished brass, chrome, satin, antique brass, bronze, and so forth. A few of the common types of hinges are as follows:

Full mortise: These are set flush with the surface of the door *and* the frame. The wood must be chiseled out to receive them.

Full surface: These are mounted on the surface of both the frame and the door.

Half surface: These are a combination of the two types described above.

Offset: They may have an offset hinge in one side to accommodate a rabbetted door (cabinet doors most commonly).

Piano: These are continuous hinges such as are found on pianos, and are usually used for special cabinet doors and lids.

Many other hinges are available for special uses.

KNOBSETS. As with hinges, these come in several types, and in a variety of styles and finishes.

Locksets usually have keys, and most locksets fall into two quality ranges: Pin-tumbler (the best and most expensive) and wafer-tumbler types. The exterior appearance may not indicate the difference in quality, but the price will. The cost difference between the cheapest available, and the commercial types for school and industrial use may be as much as twenty or thirty times. A good pin-tumbler lockset will last for many years, while the wafer type will wear out in a few years, but will cost only half as much, or less. Make your own decision!

A current good practice is to "key alike" all exterior doors. The hardware supplier will do this at no extra cost and you only need one key for all exterior doors.

Passage sets are merely operating knobs, without the key feature.

Privacy sets have a locking latch on one side and are commonly used on bath and bedroom doors. The bathroom-door set may have a chrome finish on one side to match the chrome fittings in the bath. Blind or dummy sets are sometimes used on closets, but the cost is frequently as high as for passage sets.

Most modern knobsets come assembled to the point that you need only drill a relatively small hole in the thick portions of the door, and a smaller one for the latch. However, you may encounter what is known as a full-mortise lockset, which necessitates the hollowing out of a sizeable portion of the door in order to insert the mechanism. Follow directions and templates carefully! They are usually included in the box.

BOLTS. Bolts are nothing more than sliding latches and come in several types, from simple, surface-mounted, barrel bolts, to full-mortise flush bolts for which the door must be hollowed out. One of these must be placed at both the top and bottom for satisfactory operation and installation of "French"-type doors.

Every hardware supplier has many patented locking devices that you may want to use. Start with only the basic requirements and then buy whatever else you need.

WINDOWS

Windows serve several functions. They provide light, air, and a view, can be decorative, and maybe even serve as exits and entries. The amount of light required in a home is largely a matter of personal preference. Some people prefer a snug, rather dark atmosphere in the tradition of the older frontier homes, while others like a light, wide-open feeling. Strange as it may seem, you can have too much window area in your home. Large glass areas in a hilltop home, for instance, feel exhilarating at first look, but can create a feeling of uneasiness and exposure, to the point where some people actually feel uncomfortable. Certain government-loan regulations require that you have a minimum percentage area of glass in relationship to the floor area. Some codes require that at least one window in each bedroom be of a sufficient size and height to be used as an escape route in case of fire. I believe that if you provide windows in a quantity that seems to feel good, and look attractive, you will be well within the required limits.

TYPES OF WINDOWS fall into six general categories. Most windows can be purchased as a unit that incorporates sash, frame, glass, hardware, and perhaps even the trim. This last is usually an optional item that may be changed to meet your particular construction or architectural requirements. The price will vary tremendously depending on quality. You may purchase any style, in a wide range of quality and price. You must also consider the cost of installation in evaluating a particular choice. Windows cost more than walls, so it behooves you to keep the glass area to a minimum, consistent with the considerations mentioned above.

The main types are listed below:

Double hung: Two vertical sections, both of which slide up and down.

Single hung: Similar in appearance to the double hung except that the upper section is fixed.

Casement: Hinged on the side to swing out, and operated by a crank or lever. These are generally hard to weatherstrip and seal tightly. Screens may be a problem.

Slider: Units that slide horizontally in a track. In recent years these have been made of aluminum, are pre-glazed, sealed tightly to the weather, and are quite economical. Unfortunately, they are perhaps not architecturally suited to adobe homes.

Projected: Hopper type that is hinged on the top or bottom to swing out like a basement window. This type is more frequently found in school or industrial use, usually in combination with fixed panes. One fringe benefit of this type is that the window may be left open in the rain.

Fixed: These are for light and view, and effect, only. Special care must be taken in detailing the frames for these, since they have a tendency to leak if not properly designed. The window manufacturers go to great lengths to prevent leakage, so we take manufactured units for granted. In many cases, the fixed-pane frames must be specially built on the job or by a millwork shop, so particular care must be taken in the design. Rabbetted or milled stops should be incorporated in the frame.

FRAMES usually come as a part of the window unit. Each manufacturer has slightly different sizes, dimensions, and details. You should have made a choice of window design and manufacture prior to actual construction so that the rough openings will be built to the correct size. The manufacturer's detail sheet will show exact dimensions of the unit to be supplied, and suggested details for installation in several types of wall construction. Familiarize yourself with these details and plan accordingly. The location of the frame in relation to the wall line is extremely important in adobe construction. Most window units are designed for thinner walls than adobe, so a window casing, or return, must be made either in the inside or the outside.

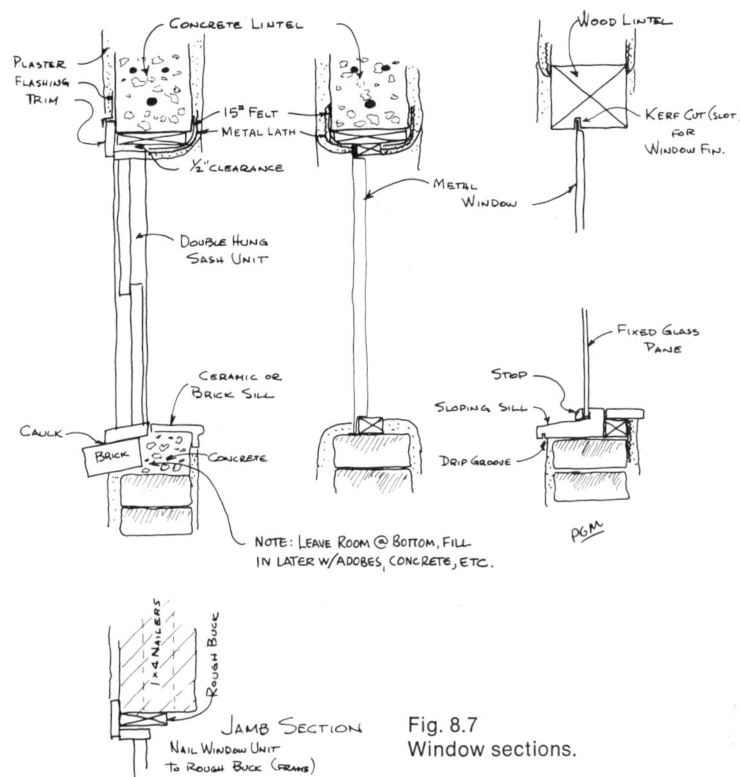

Fig. 8.7
Window sections.

Determine this by detailing on paper the jamb, head, and sill sections of this window.

SILLS are an integral part of your window, and will be subject to the elements, inside and out. You must provide a way for the water to run off with minimum effort (both for the water and for you), and with minimum damage to the structure. This is usually accomplished by the use on the exterior of a sloping sill, of a waterproof material, that will carry the water away from the wall, and allow it to drip to the ground. The interior sill is not subject to as much attack as the outside, but condensation will cause the flaking of paint or deterioration of plaster at the window sill. It is desirable to provide some material at this point that will resist the water and require as little maintenance as possible. Terra cotta, ceramic tile, or marble make excellent interior sills. (See Fig. 8.7) The tops of windows are normally located at the same height as the tops of doors (6′ 8″ above finished floors), but can be elsewhere. The span of the opening will dictate what strength glass will be required:

UNIVERSAL CHECK RAIL WINDOWS
(Available Factory-Primed on Special Order)

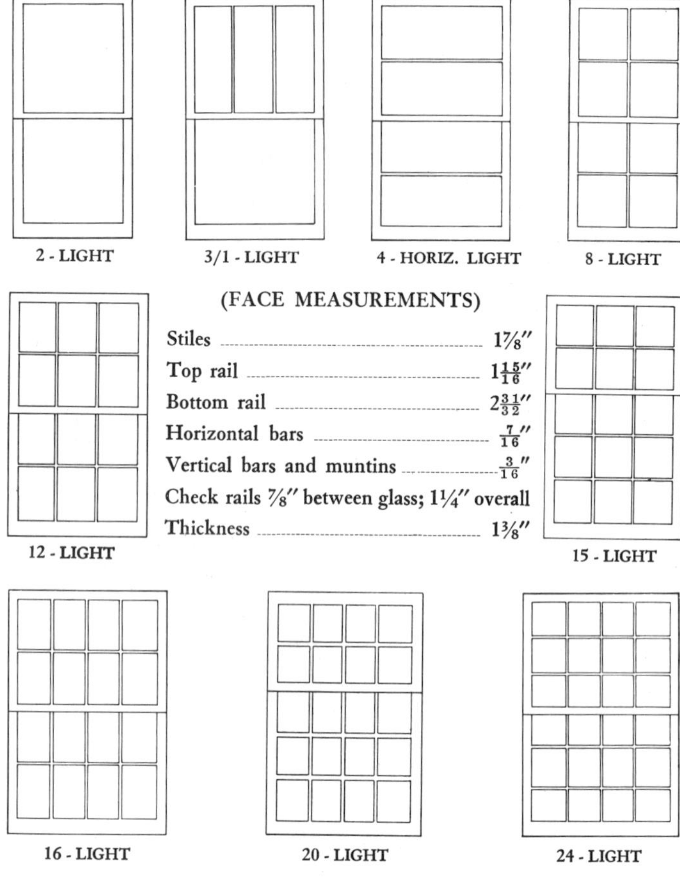

PLAIN RAIL WINDOWS

EIGHT LIGHT

Size of Opening	Glass Size	Wt. Lbs.
1-8½x3-10	8x10	10
2-0½x4- 6	10x12	15
5- 2	14	18
2-4½x5- 2	12x14	19
5-10	16	22

(FACE MEASUREMENTS)

Thickness, 1⅛″; Stiles, 1¾″; Top and Bottom Rails, 2¼″; Meeting Rail, 1″ face; Munts, $\frac{3}{16}$″; Bar, 8-light, $\frac{13}{16}$″; Bars, 12-light, $\frac{3}{16}$″.

TWELVE LIGHT

Size of Opening	Glass Size	Wt. Lbs.
2- 4x3- 2	8x 8	14
3-10	8x10	16
4- 6	12	18
2-10x4- 6	10x12	21
5- 2	14	23
5-10	16	26

56

Courtesy Ideal Company, Waco, Texas

Fig. 8.8 Page from window catalog.

Thickness	*Maximum one dimension*
3/32″ SS Single Strength	24″
1/8″ DSB Double Strength	48″
3/16″ Crystal	60″
7/32″ Crystal	60″
1/4″ Polished Plate	120″

TEMPERED GLASS is necessary in locations where breakage is a real threat. (i.e., doors, windows close to a floor). Building codes have specific requirements. This is glass that has been heat-treated so it will break into small squares rather than spears. It cannot be cut after tempering so must be ordered to a specific size, or the frame sized to receive standard tempered sizes. Special orders are costly and may delay construction. Laminated glass is also effective for such locations.

INSULATED GLASS was once a costly extra, but is now almost standard in many production doors and windows. It can include tempering if required. Two pieces of glass are separated by a spacer and the edges sealed. Any leakage will allow moisture fogging, dust, etc. in the cavity. *NOT ACCEPTABLE!* The "guarantee" may vary, and will be priced accordingly. Insulated glass reduces heat transmission and will repay its higher original cost in energy savings. Check to see what sizes are standard, and design accordingly. Job-built double glazing is usually unsatisfactory.

SOLAR GLASS made without certain minerals, allows more light/energy to pass through it and is better for solar features.

Make a window schedule! (Fig. 8.9)

Fig. 8.9 Typical window schedule.

WINDOW SCHEDULE (FROM FIG. 5.1)

MARK	SIZE (ROUGH OPNG)	TYPE	SILL*	NOTE	NO. REQD.
Ⓐ	3¹⁰ × 5³	16 LIGHT DBLE HUNG 8/8	BRICK	W/HARDWARE, SCRN, SPL. TRIM*	5
Ⓑ	2⁸ × 3⁰	12 LIGHT DBLE HUNG 6/6	BRICK	- SAME -	3
Ⓒ	6⁰ × 4⁰	FIXED*	BRICK	—	1
-	- ETC -				
				* SEE DETAIL THIS SHEET	

9

Roof Beams, Decking, and Insulation

A TYPICAL ADOBE HOME has a flat roof. The beams that span between the walls can serve two purposes, structural and decorative. The ideal, of course, is to combine both functions for economy.

ROOF BEAMS

The first consideration in beams, *vigas,* or whatever roof or floor structure to be used is the necessary strength to carry itself and whatever loads will be imposed on it from above. Different varieties of wood have different strengths, and each is further classified as to grade (e.g., select structural, construction, economy, and so on). Ponderosa pine, for example, one of the more economical varieties, is not as strong as fir and hemlock, which are further classified as to coast or inland grade. The whole system is so complicated that we will make no attempt to go into it here, other than to make you aware that such classifications do exist, and advise that savings can be made by using the most economical grade for your purpose. Your local lumber supplier will have facts and figures with which he will be pleased to supply you.

The variety, size, and spacing must be of adequate strength to carry the total "load" of roofing, decking, insulation, gravel, snow, and people that will be imposed upon it. It is not our purpose here to go into a technical discussion of the engineering, except to say that the general tendency for the amateur is to make the structure stronger than it need be. If you barely meet the structural requirements, it will probably look skimpy, or at least it does to me. The best practical approach is to design for appearance first, and then have your lumber dealer, or local building inspector check your planned sizes for strength to make sure they are adequate.

VIGAS, the traditional round, peeled-log-type beams, serve very well as the main roof structure. They are decorative and economical. They may sometimes be purchased locally from the stock of a specialty lumber dealer, but frequently must be ordered from loggers who deal in posts and native materials. Sometimes you can buy used telephone or power poles from your telephone or utility company. It is possible to obtain a permit to cut these yourself from a national forest, but in my opinion, it is better to purchase them delivered, because the cutting, handling, and transportation of these heavy materials require special equipment, and can be prohibitively expensive in small quantities.

The primary problem in using *vigas* is the frequent lack of uniformity. These logs may taper from 10 inches or more on one end to 6 inches or less on the other. If the taper is too great, and the span too long, or the sizes irregular, you may have problems in installing the flat lumber (deck) which goes on top of them. It must be remembered that, like a chain, the *viga's* strength is only as strong as its smallest diameter. Each *viga* or joist will have a "crown." This is the high part of any bend or irregularity that the *viga* has. It is normally placed in the top position, the bend up. After initial placement, a string should be used to determine the relative

Courtesy Larry Roybal, designer-photographer.

Fig. 9.1 Residence, Corrales, New Mexico. Traditional round *vigas* contrast with exposed tongue-and-groove decking. Note herringbone effect which can also be achieved through the use of *latillas* or *cedros*.

flatness across the tops of the *vigas*. This will immediately indicate any irregularities that may interfere with the placement of the decking. Irregularities can be trimmed off with an axe, hatchet, or perhaps an adz (if you can find one). If you plan to use short lengths of deck, the problem will be relatively minor, since the deck material may run up and down slightly without too much effect. If the deck material is to be long, there may be *vigas* in the way, or you may have voids where a particular part of the *viga* is too low. The natural taper of the *viga* may be used to provide a built-in runoff slope for rainwater. Assuming the top of the bond beams is level, and the butt ends are all placed on the same side, you will have built-in drainage.

RECTANGULAR ROOF BEAMS are probably easier to deal with. They will not (or should not) have the irregularities inherent in *vigas*. You can predict accurately where the upper and lower sides will occur. All *vigas,* beams, or joists should be securely anchored to the bond beams. If a concrete bond beam is used, it is necessary to install a nailer in, or at the top, of the bond beam. This may most simply be accomplished by the use of "FHA" straps, or plumbers tape (perforated metal strips). These metal anchors are inserted into the concrete as you pour the bond beam. (See Figure 9.2)

JOISTS are members that span a roof or floor area, just as the beams or *vigas* do. So far, in our considerations of beams and *vigas,* we have assumed that these members will be exposed, in which case appearance is a factor. The same can also be true of joists, but these are usually constructed of dimension lumber and covered with plaster, wallboard, or some additional material to conceal them. You may have some particular reason for this, such as in the kitchen, which has a tendency to get more dirty than other rooms from cooking. Rougher surfaces that are desirable in most other areas may be objectionable to some.

Standard dimension lumber is usually placed on 16″ centers. The required depth of the board, which is placed on edge, will vary depending on the span it must cross, and the load it must carry. The span table given below will be of some use in determining the correct size. In some cases, particularly for floors, it may be desirable to double (fasten two boards together side by side) the joists, and perhaps place them on closer than 16″ centers. The reason that 16″ centers have been developed as a standard is that they will exactly accommodate increments of 32″, 48″, and 96″, the usual widths and lengths for paneling, boards, and sheet material.

Bridging (spacer blocks or ties) should be used between the joists on any span of more than 6 feet; otherwise the joists will tend to bow out of alignment. These bridging blocks may be either mechanical patented devices made of metal, or may be cut from scrap lumber on the job. When precutting these bridging blocks,

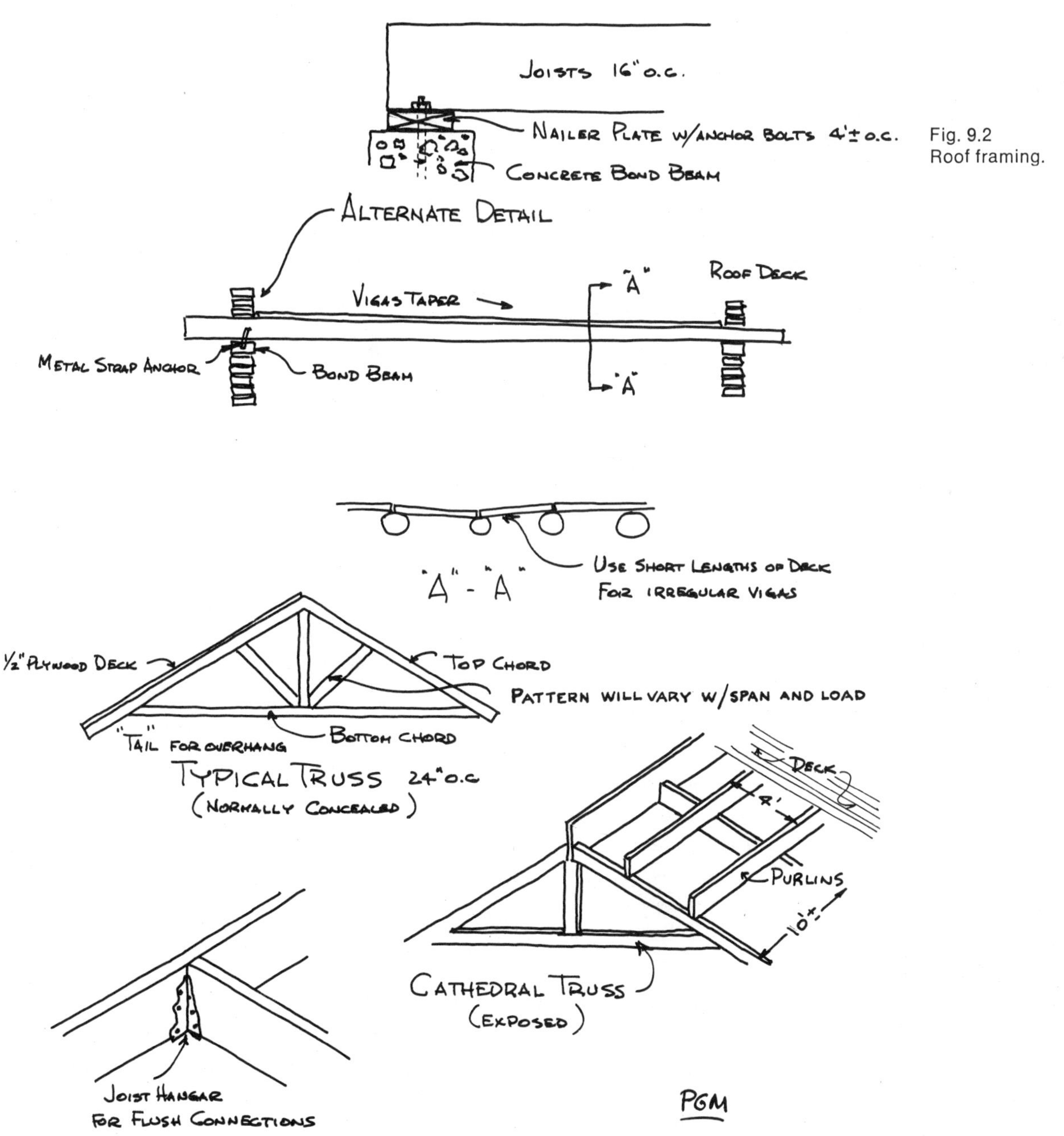

Fig. 9.2 Roof framing.

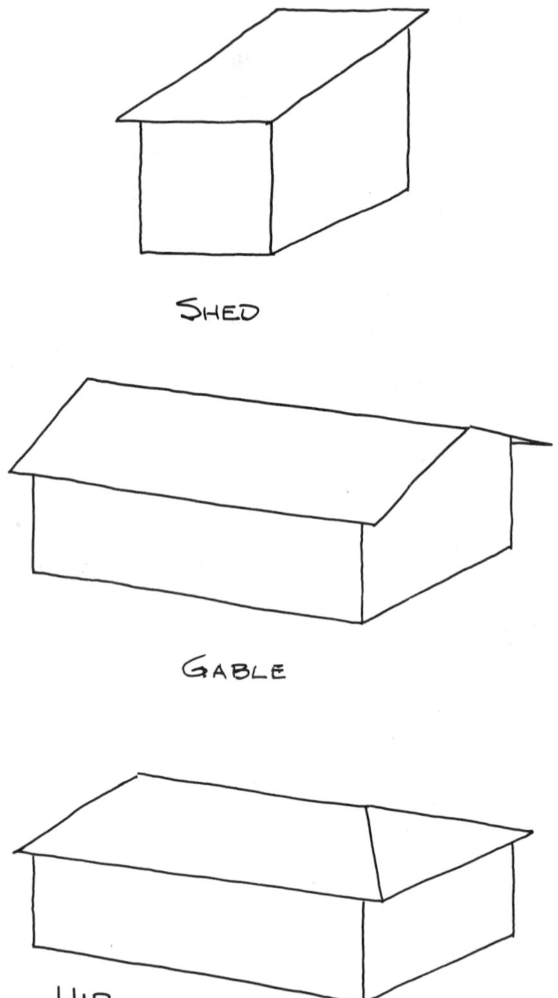

Fig. 9.3 Roof framing types.

remember to allow for the thickness of the joists. For example, if the joists are on 16″ centers, the net length for the block will be 16″ less 1½″ which equals 14½″. The same is true for fire blocks in vertical walls. Joists may be required to be attached to other joists or nailing headers, maintaining a flat face. There is a sheet metal device not frequently seen by the amateur called a joist hanger. This will help achieve a flush attachment of joists to a wood nailer piece to provide a flush bottom surface for ceiling board.

RAFTERS are merely joists that are placed at an angle to the horizontal. They serve the same purpose, to hold up the roof deck. Your roof may be framed with rafters to provide several types of construction, the nomenclature of which is sometimes misunderstood. The types are shed, gable, and hip. Figure 9.3 illustrates the differences between them.

TRUSSES are a fabricated assembly of rafters, chords, and braces that may prove useful, economical, or decorative. They can be made on the jobsite, or may be purchased from a specialty manufacturer, usually local. If you plan to use trusses, inquire as to cost and design from the local manufacturer, to make sure of adequate design for code and load requirements. Most commonly these are made from dimension lumber, two-by-fours or larger, and are spaced 24″ on center. You may wish to include a "tail" on the top chord (rafter) to provide an overhang. In most cases, these trusses will be concealed from view inside the home with ceiling board or plaster. If they are to be exposed, some consideration should be given to their appearance. By using heavy timbers for the truss, spacing them farther apart, and adding purlins or high-strength decking, a cathedral or vault ceiling may be obtained. (See Figure 9.4)

SPANS: The following span table may be used as a general guide. Bear in mind that this is not a precisely engineered and calculated table, since there are so many variables and loads that it would take a volume in itself to do this with complete accuracy. The sizes listed are adequate in most cases.

VIGAS (Not advisable for floor framing.)

Diam.	Max. span
6″	10′
8″	16′
10″	20′

BEAMS (4″ to 6″ wide)

Depth	Max. roof span
6″	10′
8″	16′
10″ to 12″	20′

spacing: 3′ to 4′ on center (O.C.) for roofs; 2′ to 3′ O.C. for floors.

Floors should be rigid and feel solid. A springy floor is most unpleasant. It is advisable to reduce spans for floors by the use of girders, decorative beams or bearing walls. Maximum span, 16 feet.

Fig. 9.4 Residence, Albuquerque, New Mexico. P. G. McHenry, Jr., architect-builder. Cathedral truss roof framing.

JOISTS 16″ O.C.; 2″ wide fir or hemlock.

Depth of Joist	Joist Span
6″	8′
8″	10′
10″	14′
12″	20′

DECKING

DECKING material may be selected from an almost endless variety. The first consideration, as always, is the strength of the material that is to span the distance between beams, *vigas,* or joists. The second is appearance, if this material is to be exposed. A third consideration should also be kept in mind — the insulating value of the material used. You must insulate the roof, and the total thickness and combination of material used will provide a certain insulation value. It may be advisable to use a thicker material than the structure requires, because of its insulation value. Every combination of steps you take will require a certain amount (dollar value) of material and labor, whether it is your own or you hire it done. The only way to make a cost comparison is to figure carefully what each combination of material and labor will cost, and then compare them.

For most purposes, traditional adobe construction (which is our primary consideration) will be one-story, relatively flat-roof construction, with the beams, or *vigas,* and deck exposed. You may use flat boards, surfaced or rough sawn. You may or may not want to use material with a tongue-and-groove edge. This edge supplies additional strength, and you may span a larger distance with thinner material if you use this feature. Tongue-and-groove material can be obtained in thicknesses up to 5″ which will adequately span 15′ to 20′. The following guide may be used:

Thickness	Max. Span (Roofs)
1″	3′
1″T&G	4′
2″	4′
2″T&G	6′

If decking is to be used for flooring for a second story, special considerations must be looked into. Maximum span should probably be 3′ with 2″ tongue-and-groove material used, and perhaps a further plywood treatment above to provide additional strength and rigidity. Noise transmission from the second floor can also be extremely objectionable. This may be minimized simply by using ½″ wood fiber wallboard beneath the rug pad, assuming the floor will be carpeted. Otherwise, the noise of footsteps and the moving of furniture is unbelievably loud.

All wood shrinks with age and drying. The boards used as decking will shrink—the amount depending on its dryness when fastened down—possibly leaving unsightly gaps between the boards. If the tongue-and-groove material is used, it will help conceal this, since the shrinkage will seldom exceed the tongue.

LATILLAS AND CEDROS are traditional material to use for roof decking. The *latilla* is a peeled pole of about 1½″ to 2″ diameter (aspen is best because of its uniformity). It is usually laid in diagonally between the beams, creating a herringbone pattern. The use of shorter decking lengths will help compensate for uneven *vigas. Cedros* are split cedar poles, used in the same manner; they can impart an unusual texture to your ceiling. This type of treatment requires a great amount of hand labor. In early times when sawn materials was almost unobtainable, labor was also of smaller concern.

INSULATION

INSULATION is sometimes the most ignored part of a building. Its cost is not insignificant, but the cost will be recovered repeatedly over the years, not only in comfort, but in actual cash on fuel savings. It is possible (although not likely) to overinsulate. A reasonable amount is an absolute necessity.

Adobe walls have a reputation for good insulation. Actually, the heat transmission factor (R-4 for 10″) is poor when compared to rock wool (R-11 for 4″). However, the thermal mass (weight) of the walls slows down the temperature swings outside. Super-thick walls will create a "thermal lag" effect which may not be desirable. Adobe walls should be insulated to reduce energy costs. Insulation should be placed on the *outside* to preserve the thermal mass effect. Where cost is vital, it is most important to insulate the North side and *maybe* the East and West. The South can be omitted.

A typical example: I had a home under construction during the dead of winter, and it was necessary to shut the main gas line off for four days. The heat had been on in the house for several weeks, in spite of the fact that the window and door openings were not completely sealed. I was striving to dry out the walls, so that we would be able to plaster. In spite of the many openings around the doors and windows, the temperature of the interior of the house never fell below 65 degrees while the gas was off.

The old adobes had extremely thick walls, and a thick dirt roof. Builders did this because that's all they had, but we have better, lighter, more modern materials for roof insulation and roofing. The old way requires additional foundations, bond beams, window and door treatment, and tremendously strong ceiling supports, or narrower rooms. The labor for placing this much dirt on the roof is staggering. The old roofs were so thick that only a repeated series of heavy rains could penetrate the clay. They also required continuing maintenance. Most of us want to build a home that will require as little maintenance as possible.

An adobe home of the more modern variety will be hot if it has been closed up for a period of time. It will remain hot until cooled off by nighttime temperatures, with airing, or by air conditioning. The same situation holds true in the winter. When you get the house warm, it tends to stay warm, in spite of low temperatures

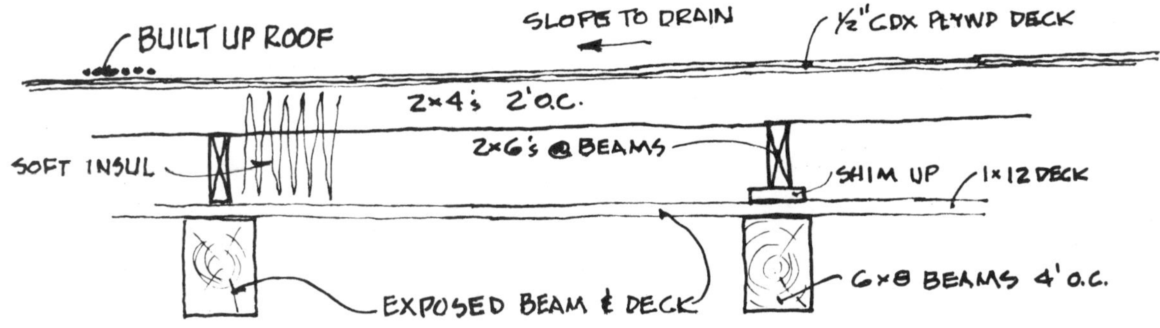

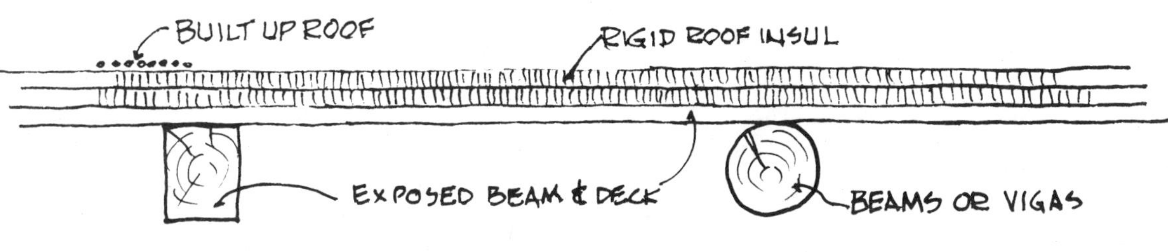

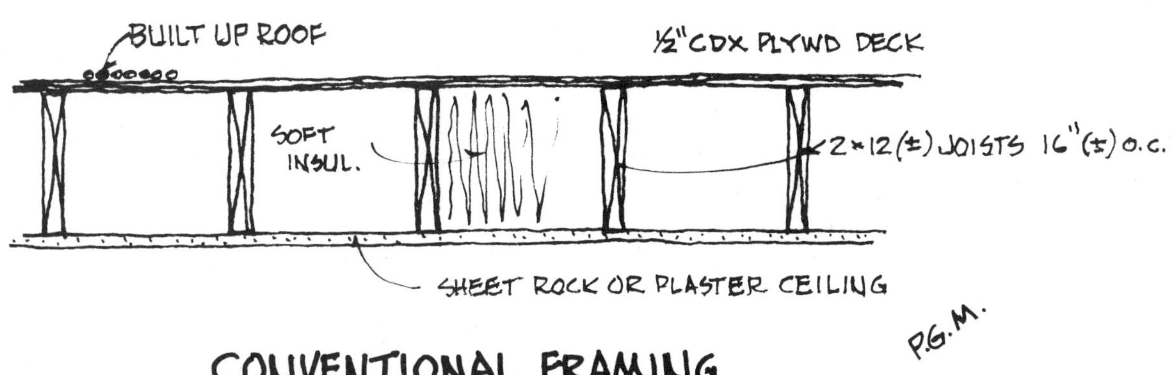

Fig. 9.5 Roof insulation.

outside, with a minimum of added heat. You must take advantage of and enjoy the thermal effect that adobe has.

Assuming that you will have all exterior walls of adobe, let us consider the roof insulation. You will have a finished deck of some sort, on top of the beams or *vigas*. The thickness of this deck material will account for some insulation value. From this point upwards, you have two choices — a rigid insulation, on top of which the built-up roof may be placed, or a soft insulation, which in itself will be more economical but will require protection in the form of another frame and deck. Make your own choice; the cost will come out surprisingly close. The double deck is the better construction, and will also provide more usable room for electrical wiring. Figure 9.5 indicates several possibilities.

10

Floors

ORIGINALLY, the logical choice for floors in our early Southwestern societies, both Pueblo and Spanish, was hard-packed clay. This was sometimes mixed with animal blood, to darken and give an additional hardness and shine to the surface. This would seem less than satisfactory today with all the new materials at our disposal. We will deal with many of these choices, not necessarily in order of their importance, or even their desirability. People feel strongly about floors, and I don't intend to enter into the argument as to which is best, but merely point out the way to accomplish the kind you may prefer.

CONCRETE FLOORS

Concrete is the logical successor to the original mud floor. The most common thickness for concrete floors is 4″. Less thickness can be used, but the floor will have a greater tendency to crack or heave. If an additional material such as flagstone or tile is to be applied to the surface, the thickness can safely be lessened. If you intend to impose extra loads on this, it may be wise to increase the thickness to 6″. A thickness of 4″ is adequate for a garage floor which must bear the weight of a car.

Reinforcing mesh should be used (6″ x 6″ — 10/10 wire) if the slab is not to be contained on all sides. A porch slab, for example, should be reinforced. Interior slabs seldom need this reinforcing, if the subsurface is reasonably firm and undisturbed. If you have old slabs, foundations, and filled spots, it is wise to spend the little extra to help keep a satisfactory floor.

Slabs will crack! No matter how carefully you prepare, pour, and finish them, cracks will appear. Now that you have accepted this premise, you must try to keep them to a minimum. Where large areas of concrete will be required (20′ x 20′ or more) you must use an expansion joint. This formidable sounding term is merely a strip of resilient material, about ½″ in thickness and as wide as the slab is thick. The most common material used is asphalt-impregnated wood fiberboard.

You may chose to use a "cold" joint, without the expansion material, where the slab is poured in two sections. It may further be merely scored at logical places, and hopefully the cracks will follow the scored joints. They will not in every case.

Caution: When pouring a new slab over an old slab, it is difficult if not impossible to get the new slab to adhere to the old one. The only solution other than removal of the old slab, which can be expensive, is to make the new slab at least 2″ thick, and isolate the original, underlying slab with a thin layer of sand (½″ minimum). There are bonding agents on the market that purport to bond new concrete to old, but they are not always satisfactory. Use the other method if at all possible.

TILE FLOORS

Tile floors (of the ceramic variety) are probably the ultimate in beauty, durability, and graciousness, and unfortunately the ultimate in cost as well. Do, however, compare costs carefully before selecting some of the exotic pure vinyls, which may equal or exceed tile in cost. Many

Fig. 10.1 Residence, Albuquerque, New Mexico, P. G. McHenry, Jr., architect-builder. Patterned concrete tile floors.

materials are available that can provide great beauty and durability. Quarry tile is perhaps the most readily available.

Pre-cast colored and patterned concrete tile is available in Mexico in an almost unlimited choice of colors and patterns, if you have the patience to order it and are willing to wait for it to be manufactured. Precast, polished terrazo tiles are available from stock in many places.

Any flat hard material will serve as a flooring material. It has always been my preference to use a material that added color, texture, or interest to the general decor. Many manufactured colored materials must be used with caution lest they clash with the softer hand-crafted finishes.

The main consideration in this type of hard flooring is a solid base. The top of the slab must be low enough to accommodate the thickness of the tile and the setting bed that will attach it to the slab, and still be level with adjoining floors. You have two choices in this case — a reasonably smooth concrete floor, and application of the tile with a "thin set" bedding mortar

Fig. 10.2 Residence, Albuquerque, New Mexico, P. G. McHenry, Jr., architect-builder. Patterned concrete tile floors.

of only about 1/8″ thickness, or you can use the older, and more difficult "mud bed" which will allow you to absorb variations in the thickness of the tile. They will occur. Many imported materials are not as uniform as the products we are used to that are manufactured in the United States. An allowance in the thickness of the setting bed must be made for this. The tile to be used must be soaked overnight in water so that it is completely wet, all the way through.

A damp mix of sand, rich in portland cement, should be spread on a dampened slab. This mix, when rich enough with portland cement (one shovel portland to four sand), will assume a greenish color. It will not set for several hours, giving you time to set the tile. The "dry pack" bed (which is actually damp) should be smoothed in the same manner you use for screeding a concrete slab that was discussed earlier — taking care to not prepare too large an area — the tile placed on top of it, and gently tapped in with a rubber hammer. This must be done in small areas, a little at a time. More of the same mix is put into the joints between the

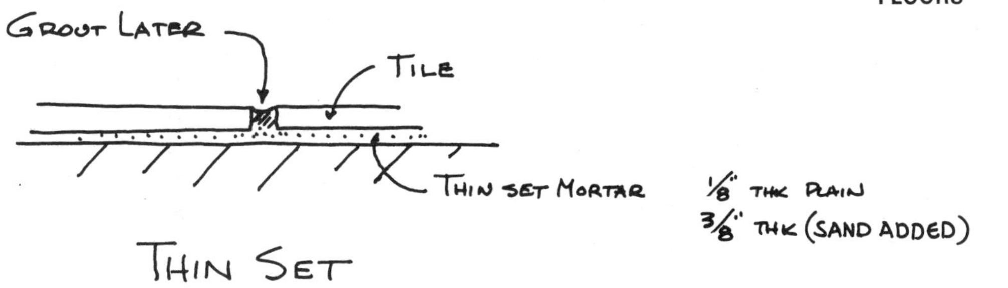

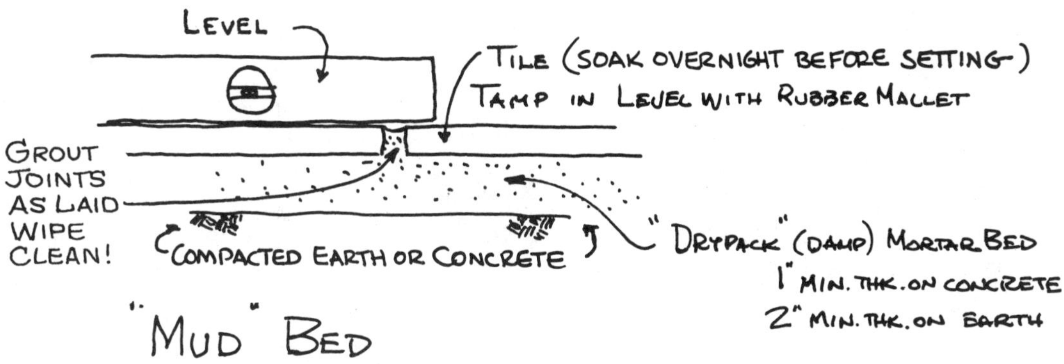

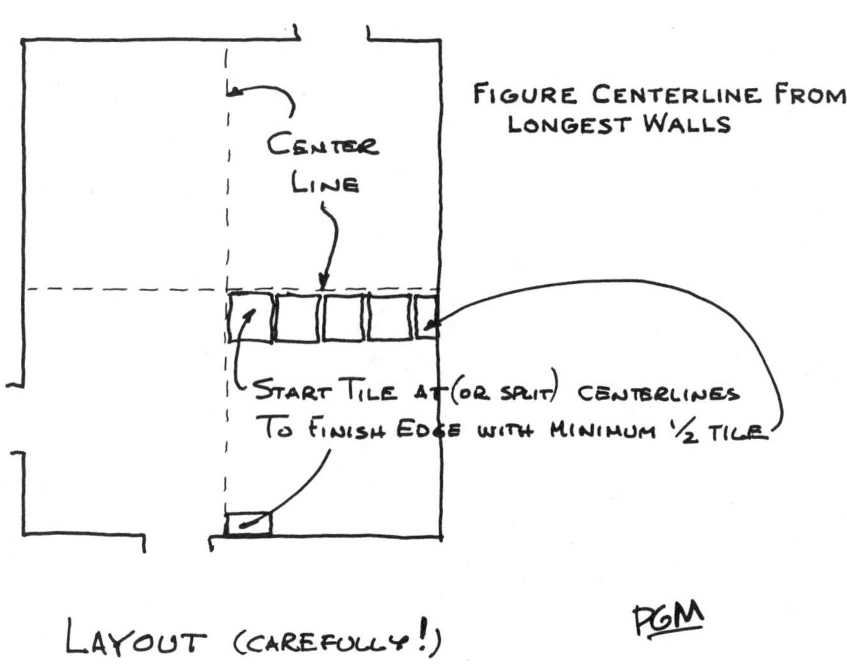

Fig. 10.3 Floor tile setting.

tiles as it is laid (this may actually be done later, at the risk of loosening tiles as you walk on them). (See Figure 10.3)

The joints should be repeatedly dampened in order to prevent the concrete from curing too fast and weakening its grip on the tile or the slab below. The amount of water used should not be enough to disturb the grout between the tiles, but only in sufficient quantity to keep the surface damp. This dampening should be repeated daily for several days to insure a good hard set. After curing has been accomplished, the cement stains must be cleaned from the tile. These can be lessened by the periodic wiping of the tile surfaces with rags during the curing. If serious stains remain, they may be removed with a solution of muriatic acid, one part muriatic to 10 parts water. This acid solution is used for removing cement and plaster stains from brick and glass. If cement tile is used, acid will attack and etch the tile surface. It is much better to keep the work clean as you go with a damp rag.

If you plan to do this work yourself, start with a small area where appearance is not too important. The layout or starting point for a given room is most important. You should have a reasonably even border on all sides of the room, avoiding small slivers at the edges. Plan the layout of tile squares, including joints, so that it will end on the edges as you plan it to. The best device for cutting heavy tiles is diamond-blue tub saw for a wet cut. It may be rented.

BRICK FLOORS

Brick floors are probably the most satisfactory for your purpose. Bricks make an attractive, traditional floor that can be laid accurately by a careful amateur.

The subsurface needs only minor preparation. There will be a quantity of surplus dirt left over from your foundation, plumbing, and heating excavation that should normally be left on the inside of the stem wall if you plan brick floors, to help raise the finished floor level above the ground outside. The subsurface should be raked, leveled, and wet down so that it will compact to a reasonably smooth, hard surface to a distance below the finished floor grade that will equal the thickness of the brick and the sand bed (approx. 3½″). The determination should have been done in the original planning, and the finish-floor grade marked on the stem wall—done best with cut nails in each corner of each room. You may need this reference point later. Some cutting and some filling of the earth will be required to level the floor below the brick. This need not be done too carefully, but you will want a sand bed of at least ½″ and not more than 1″.

Assuming that you have the dirt floor reasonably level, you should sprinkle the entire area liberally with insecticide, to hold back the ant and varmint population. Over this, spread a plastic sheet (4 mil thickness is O.K.). This material may be bought in rolls, in widths up to 36 feet or more. Buy a roll width that is slightly larger than the narrowest width of most of your rooms. Lap the edges where necessary, 2″ to 4″. On top of this, spread approximately 1″ of dry sand. I say dry because this seems to work best. Damp sand can, of course, be used, but it seems to have a tendency to bridge over soft spots that may sink later. This sand should be leveled by the use of screeds, like the ones discussed in pouring concrete slabs. The sand should be screeded level, using screed bars (pipes will do) and a straight 2x4, the pipes removed, and the resulting hollow filled up with sand. (See Fig. 10.4)

It is then a simple matter to place the brick firmly on the smooth sand bed. If you plan to use tight joints, without mortar between, the bricks should be butted tightly. I suggest that this is the ideal method for the amateur. If you plan a mortar joint between the bricks, the setting bed must be done a little at a time, checked with a level, set on dry pack, and grouted (cement in joints) as you go along. The same principles apply as in tile floors.

The next step is cutting in the edges, after the "field" brick have been laid over the main area of the floor. The edges must be cut in as required. This can be done with a masonry saw, wet or dry, or with a wide brick chisel and a sandbox; hit it as you might in chipping ice, and not with one mighty blow. Very hard bricks can be cut close to measurements this way if you are slow and careful.

THE PATTERN you choose should be determined before you start. Many patterns will be satisfactory, as long as you take into account the dimensions of the particular brick you want to use. Try out several patterns, with brick, before you start floor work. Incidentally, you must use "solids" or "patio"-type common brick. Regular common brick has holes in it to help hold the mortar. The bricks are not exactly twice as long as they are wide. Therefore, the "basketweave" pattern will cause problems. A "masonry bond" or "herringbone" pat-

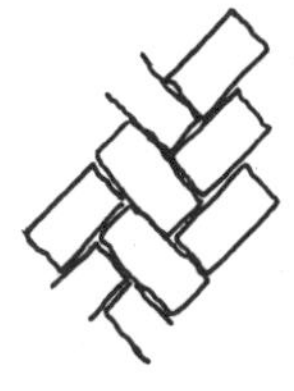

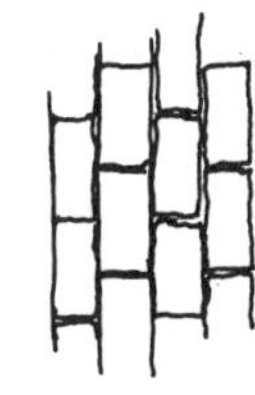

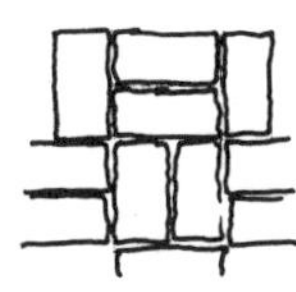

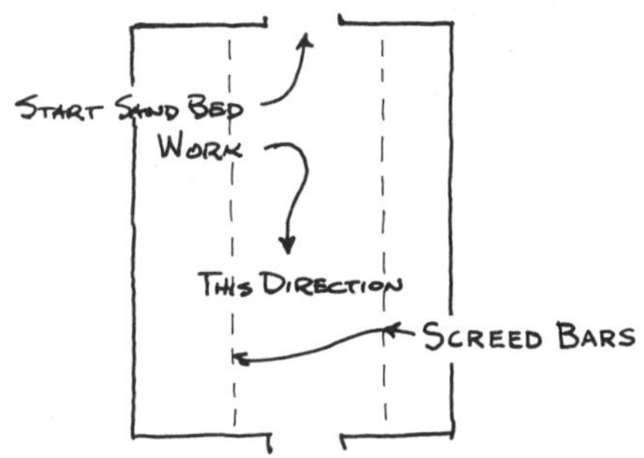

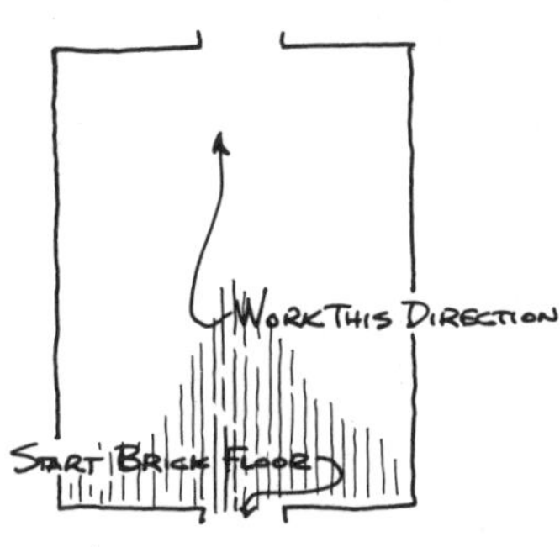

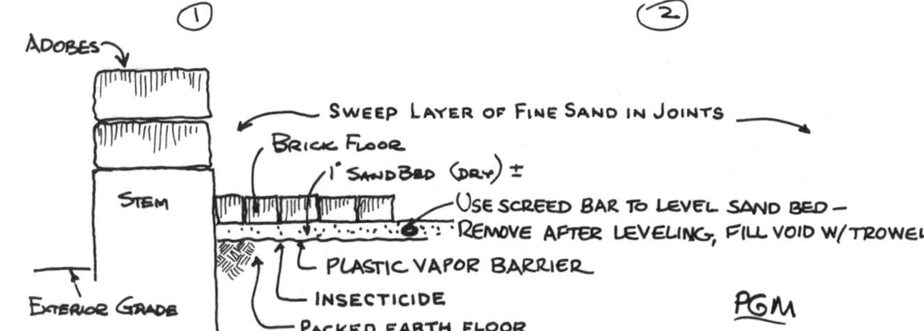

Fig. 10.4
Brick floors.

tern may be easiest. A few experiments will demonstrate the advantages of these patterns.

Paving-type bricks are best for exterior walks and patios. They are harder, more dense, and will resist weather much better than "commons," cost considerably more, and are more difficult to cut.

A helper is quite useful in laying brick floors. Your wife will do if she has a strong back—and doesn't object! Start at one end of the room, a doorway usually, and lay the brick down on your prepared sand bed, building outward in the pattern you have selected. If you must get off your knees (invest in crawler pads) to get more brick, it really slows things down. One bricksetter can keep two or three helpers busy carrying brick, and the job goes surprisingly fast. You will discover that the laying of bricks is extremely hard on your hands. The first impulse is to use gloves, but you will find that they are in the way and will prevent the bricks from fitting tightly against each other. The best solution I have discovered is to pick up a brick, note where it touches your fingers, and tape these areas completely with surgical tape before starting. Do this before you start the brick laying, because without the tape, you will discover that the skin will wear off right down to the flesh in a very short time. *Don't forget the tape!*

Caution: Once a floor is started in each room, it should be finished, or traffic kept off of it. You must sweep fine sand into the cracks of the finished product, to lock the bricks tightly, particularly at the edges, and at doorways. If the brick

Fig. 10.5 Residence, Placitas, New Mexico, P. G. McHenry, Jr., architect-builder. Brick floors can provide a hand-crafted feeling economically when done by the owner-builder.

is not contained securely, it will tend to creep outward toward the uncontained edge, making wider gaps between the bricks. A simple wood form will contain these at the doorways temporarily until the adjoining floor can be finished.

Once this is done, the floor is complete, except for sealing. From time to time, you may have some reason to grind the finished brick floor. Any serious leveling or grinding must be done with a concrete grinding machine, or with a terrazo grinder. This will change the texture of the brick surface every place where it is ground, and make a terrible mess. Careful laying is the best answer. Then if a few sharp edges still remain, and they will, use a regular rotary floor sander with #2 grit discs and a sprinkle of sand. Hand rubbing with another brick will soften sharp edges. A once-over lightly will smooth out the irregularities.

SEALERS have been suggested that I've never had the courage to use, such as used motor oil. I've tried almost everything else suggested, from kerosene and boiling water to expensive urethane coatings. You are free to try anything that sounds logical. The best method I have found is the following:

Use an economical grade of oil base varnish. It can be purchased in 5-gallon cans, and you will be surprised at how much it takes. The first coat can be diluted ⅓ with mineral spirits to get good penetration and cut cost. Subsequent coats will go on up to 400 or 500 square feet. Apply with a paint roller. After the floor has been sealed (one to two coats), additional coats may be applied for color effect. Each coat will deepen the color slightly. Additional coats may be desirable, depending on the finish you want.

The floor may then be maintained by additional applications of plastic sealer or wax. I personally prefer the sealer instead of wax, since the wax seems to turn white in the small pores of the brick. Colored wax seems to impart a false color to the brick. The first few days of use the newly finished floor will show dusty footprints which may cause some concern; however, the floor will take on an even patina in a few days and will require minimum care.

WOOD FLOORS

Wood floors are warmer and softer than solid floors of concrete or brick. They are also generally more expensive unless the topography of your lot will require a great quantity of fill. Two possibilities should be considered when planning a wood floor. First, will it have a decorative purpose? A well-finished wood floor is a thing of beauty. It can impart a texture and warmth unachievable with any other material. Second, is the floor to be strictly utilitarian, and to be covered with a carpet? If you plan to carpet, it seems foolish to go to the expense of a hardwood floor which will be covered.

Framing for a floor has been discussed earlier, so we will deal here only with the surface. The wood floor will have two parts — the subfloor, which decks the area, supported by the joists to provide strength and solidity to support that which goes on top of it. The subfloor can be made of either ⅝″ plywood (CD grade) or of 1″ boards, laid (diagonally for boards) across the joists. The contractor usually chooses plywood, because the savings in labor costs to place it more than offset the higher price. For your purposes, make a comparison with flat boards; (1″ x 8″) is optimum. The subfloor should be nailed in place with 8d cement-coated nails, approximately 6″ to 8″ on center. The cement coating helps them hold tightly.

If you plan to carpet the wood floor, or to use a resilient floor covering, such as vinyl asbestos tile or linoleum, you will now nail down a second layer of ½″ plywood. The best to use for this purpose is called "particle" or "flakeboard." It is stable, economical, and provides the most inexpensive smooth surface.

Hardwood floors are normally nailed directly to the subfloor, without the second layer of plywood. Obviously it is best to lay this at right angles to the floor framing. A wide variety of hardwood floors is available, and different grades within the species. Make sure you plan for correct thickness where floor finishes will be different. Most hardwood flooring comes tongue and groove, and is toenailed through the groove. This is not too difficult, as long as the joints are held tight; these are further tightened by the toenailing. This hardwood flooring can be purchased in a prefinished state, or unfinished. If you plan to use an unfinished flooring, it may be necessary to hire a specialty contractor to finish it for you, because it requires special tools and know-how. Before making firm plans, compare prices on a complete job from flooring contractors. The combination the contractor can offer may be more economical.

RESILIENT FLOOR COVERINGS

The varieties of resilient flooring (tile, linoleum, and vinyl) are endless, and the price range unbelievable. These materials are particularly suitable and desirable for bathrooms and kitchens. Laying floor tile is an excellent job for the amateur. The installation of sheet goods is not. If you plan to install linoleum or sheet vinyl, by all means have an expert do it. You may want to purchase the materials and contract the labor, but don't attempt it yourself.

The procedure for laying floor tile is quite simple. The floor, even though it may look quite smooth to your unpracticed eye, will need some preparation. Make sure that all your nails are flush, or even indented a little, and all holes filled. All joints in the plywood should be sanded flush and smooth. Further, use a powder preparation, mixed with water, called "floor stone." This should be troweled on with a flat plastering trowel; it will fill up any voids or cracks when troweled smoothly over them. It also serves to fill and cover any nail holes, hammer marks, or indentations in the wood. After applying it, sand the fills again, by hand.

Any imperfections, ridges, bumps, and the like will "telegraph" through the finished floor material, and become even more visible from the polished surface. The same considerations for smoothness apply to concrete floors that will be covered with resilient tile or sheet goods.

11

Plumbing

A GOOD PLUMBING SYSTEM is perhaps the least romantic, but most necessary, part of your home. Camping is fun, with primitive facilities, but one of its best purposes is to point out to us how dependent we are on the modern conveniences. Your plumbing system must include provisions for an adequate supply of drinkable (unpolluted) water, a means for easily and conveniently heating it, and a sewage-disposal system to get rid of the sewage. There are two different situations, one in the city, where full city utilities are available, and another where you must provide your own disposal system.

We cannot here make master plumbers of you by any means, since most plumbing work requires a great deal of skill, experience, and expensive tools. But it is possible for a determined, resolute individual to take out a "homeowner's" permit under certain conditions and do his own work. The advent of many new types of plastic pipe and fittings has made the homeowner-type installation much more feasible than in past years. Building codes have prevented the use of many of these new materials, but it would seem that changes are currently taking place to make possible their use. A minimum of tools is required, beyond a knife, hacksaw, and glue brush. An excellent source of more detailed information than we will go into here is available from the Home Building Plan Service, 2454 NE Sandy Boulevard, Portland, Oregon. They have a detail plumbing sheet, showing typical installations with the older-type materials, which is available at a nominal cost. If you choose this route, you'll have my unqualified admiration.

THE WATER SUPPLY

Water supply from city mains may require tapping by city crews. This may involve several hundred dollars, depending on the tie-in charges and any cutting or patching of a paved street that may be required. When you purchase a building site, the water and sewer may be roughed in to the lot. If so, it may be marked on the curb with a "W" and an "S," or some other designation, at the location of the line. Whether either one is roughed in or not may affect your budget, or the price you pay for the lot. In some cases, a meter is even set, or at least paid for. Incidentally, there should be in every case a shutoff valve at the meter or connection, which often requires a meter key to operate the valve. This is not a key in the usual sense, but merely a long-handled wrench that must be used to exert enough torque to turn the valve. The valve operates by means of a rectangular metal bar at the top of the valve. It is frequently covered with dirt in the meter box. Meters come in different sizes, the larger sizes costing more. The standard size for most residences is ¾″, although if you plan to have a quantity of sprinklers or irrigation, it may be advisable to install a larger size initially.

THE WATER SUPPLY LINE to your home should be at least ¾″. Many codes require that a "stop-and-waste" fitting be installed outside the building line. This fitting acts as a shutoff for the entire water supply to your home, and in most cases is operated with that square metal rod you trip over in flower beds close to the house. This fitting has a further function, in that when it is in the closed position, it opens the bottom of the valve, to drain the entire house system. The whole water system in the house should be graded so that it will drain to this point. Frequently, however, this valve becomes frozen (jammed) after several years, so that it is wise to include a "meter key" in your tools in the event the "stop-and-waste" valve will not close.

The stop-and-waste provision is designed more for climatic zones that experience hard freezing conditions. The valve is normally located below the frost line. It further helps to prevent freezing of the pipes in the house when it is unoccupied. Warm-desert dwellers, of course, have no need for these considerations.

MATERIAL that you use for the water system may be either *copper* or *galvanized pipe* (some codes now permit plastic). The copper tubing will be somewhat more expensive, but probably worth the additional cost. If you plan to do this work yourself, all you need is a tubing cutter and a soldering torch to solder the fittings. It is quite simple. The copper pipe will resist rust and corrosion, and should last virtually forever. Galvanized pipe, and you will have to use some because of its rigidity, will eventually require replacement (it may take 30 years). It requires more tools and skill to work with galvanized pipe, although most of the tools may be rented.

HOT WATER ARRANGEMENTS should be carefully considered. You must have an adequate supply that can be heated economically. The difference between the cost of a smaller hot-water heater and a larger one is minimal. The heater should be located close to the point of most frequent (and quantity) use. In many homes the most frequent use is in the kitchen, but the biggest volume is the bathtub, shower, or perhaps the washer. The bathrooms require hot water only a few times daily. It would seem advisable therefore to locate the hot-water heater near the kitchen and washer. If the bathrooms are a far distance from the water heater, it may take a minute or more to get hot water to these fixtures. In most cases, this is acceptable. However, should you have widely separated plumbing fixtures, it may be advisable to set up a return line from the farthest fixture and install a pump on this line so that it will circulate the hot water constantly, providing instant hot water at each outlet. The cost for such an arrangement is surprisingly low. The pump should have either a manual or thermostatically controlled switch.

CAUTION: If the hot-water circulating line is used, make sure that the hot-water line and cold-water line are separated adequately to prevent heat transfer, or you may have hot water from both lines, for several minutes at least. Nothing is more aggravating than trying to get a drink of cold water in the middle of the night and have hot water come out of both taps.

The specifications and warranty for water heaters should be carefully examined. The best guide to quality is the warranty period stated (5 years, 10 years, or more). Frequently the water heater wears out shortly after the warranty period expires. This may involve rupture of the tank, causing flooding of the adjacent floor area. It is advisable, therefore, to locate the heater in an area where this will do the least damage. If you must locate it in the house proper, install a floor drain close to it. This floor-drain feature is most desirable for washer locations as well. Perhaps you can manage to locate both the water heater and washer in the same utility room or closet.

Water softeners are a desirable feature for most homeowners. Water is surprisingly corrosive. The minerals in most water will attack surfaces of pipes and tanks; the harder the water, the more corrosive it is. Water softeners eliminate or minimize the problem. They can easily be installed after the home is completed, so that it may be wise to hold this item from your budget until you have the more important items that will be much more expensive to install later. The softener can be tied into the entire system or the hot water only, as you prefer. Two types are usually available, a permanent type which is recharged with chemicals at regular intervals, or tank units that are changed at the same intervals. These systems can be purchased, or rented on a month-to-month basis.

FIXTURES AND TRIM for your plumbing system can vary tremendously in price. Nearly all manufacturers make comparable quality

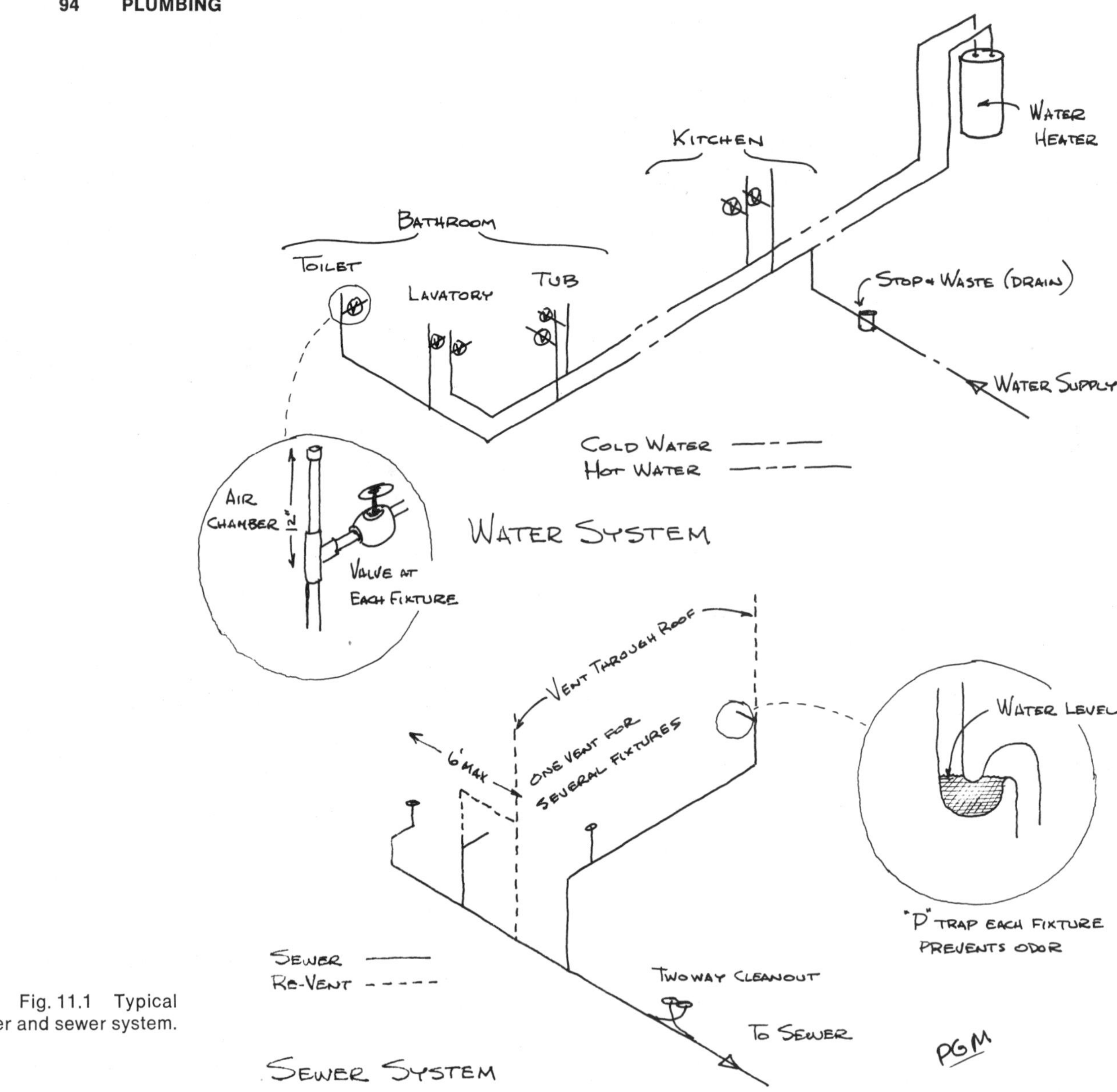

Fig. 11.1 Typical water and sewer system.

lines. You may spend $25 for the "trim" (valves and spigot) at a shower over tub, or you may spend six or seven times that much depending on quality. It is possible to spend more than $50 on a shower head alone. Water closets (toilets) can be economical, standard, or special wall-hung units costing several times the minimum price. A plumbing bid may only be accurately evaluated by specific fixture models. Choose what you want from a plumbing-supply house, and then specify this particular brand and model, with the phrase "or equal." If your plumber suggests something other than what is specified, check it out. You may want to solicit his suggestions on what to specify. It may save a great deal of money. Each fixture should have a valve to shut off the water supply so you may change or service the fixture without shutting off the whole system.

Sunken tubs, if you fancy the idea, provide an elegance that can't be achieved any other way. The cost of owner-built construction is surpris ingly small. It is only necessary to determine the grade for the bottom of the tub, install the nec- essary plumbing, and build a reverse form (for the inside of the tub). The forming can be a very sketchy affair, and after pouring the concrete you knock the form out, and line the surface with ceramic tile. (See Fig. 11.2) Calculate the number of gallons of hot water it will require to fill your tub... Is the water heater big enough?

Prefab systems are becoming more and more

Fig. 11.2 Sunken tub details.

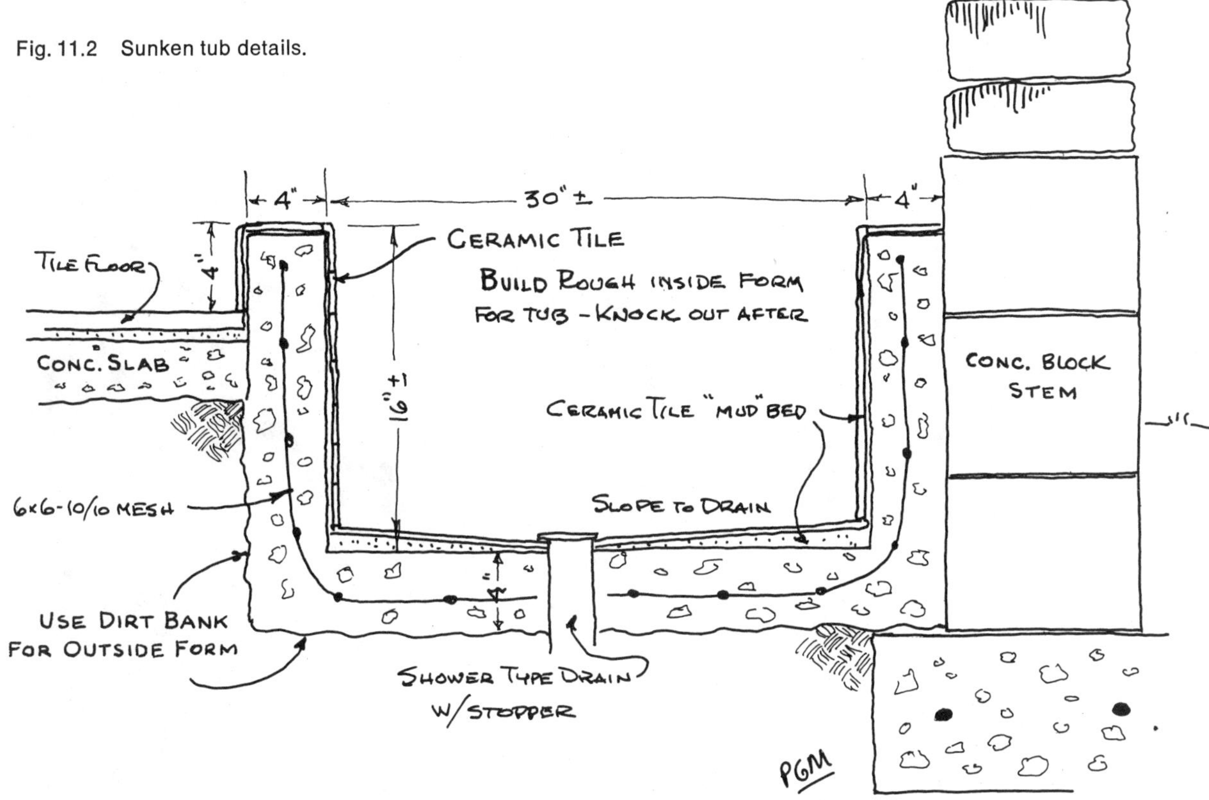

available from local supply houses. They range from prefabricated "trees" of drain and re-vent piping, which need only to be connected, to one-piece fiberglass tub or shower-tub enclosures. If you plan to do much of your own plumbing work, take your plans to a plumber who may be willing to prefab some of the more difficult parts, or to a supply house who will help you analyze your requirements for specific fittings and supplies. Why not use all the professional help you can get?

WATER WELLS can be drilled almost anywhere and I want to emphasize the word *almost*. Some places there *is* no water, some other locations are not likely to produce good water, and still others are to be avoided because of the proximity to sewage systems. You'll find that you will be somewhat at the mercy of the well-drilling contractor. You may want to drill your own well, but it seems more advisable to have it done by a person who is highly regarded by past customers. The ideal well man will have had experience in your particular area and should be more aware of the problems he will encounter. The well contractor will not guarantee that he will find water for you for a specific price. He will quote a per-foot price for which he will drill and install a casing of particular size. Usually, a deeper well will require a larger casing, and a larger pump, costing more. Different depths of the well may require different specifications for the pump, or even a larger size. Water may be found at several depths, some strata of which may be better than others. A "good" well should give a virtually endless supply of good water for domestic use. Ask your neighbors who drilled their wells how they like theirs, what they know about good water depths and locations, and who they recommend. Then, follow the recommendations of the well contractor. The total cost of a well must include the pump, pressure tank and other accessories desired or required by code.

SEWAGE DISPOSAL

Sewage is a smelly problem that must be dealt with adequately and as economically as possible. We must emphasize the first word — *adequately!* The cheapest price in the world is no good if the system is inadequate. In the city, you hook into the sewer in the street and then the

Fig. 11.3 Residence, Albuquerque, New Mexico. P. G. McHenry, Jr., architect-builder. Sunken tub lined with decorative tile gives a super luxury touch with little added expense.

sewage is a city problem. In the country, it still belongs to you, and you must dispose of it. Incidentally, most plumbing bids are based on "stubbing out" from the house (usually 5 feet), and the water and sewer yard lines that connect to the street will be an extra item, quoted at a per-foot unit price. This is not an unreasonable way to prepare the bid, because if the plumber does not know exactly where the connection to the street will occur, he must protect himself by figuring an additional amount to cover his costs.

THE HOUSE SEWER SYSTEM is a fairly simple matter, consisting of drain lines which used to be of cast iron and required special tools for cutting and joining. Now they are more commonly of hard plastic which can be cut with a hacksaw and glued together. The whole system must be vented through the roof (re-vents) at specified intervals in the house to prevent air locks in the system. Another feature that should be included and is sometimes overlooked is an adequate number of "cleanouts." These are access fittings to the drain system where "snakes" or routing tools may be inserted to clean clogged drains. The re-vent system may cause complications in your framing and wall construction, but is necessary, and must be dealt with. It is customary to have the waste and re-vent system installed after the stem is in and prior to construction of the walls (see Fig. 11.1).

SEPTIC TANKS are almost as good as city sewers, and they usually don't cost a whole lot more if you must cut streets and the like. The system consists of a waterproof concrete (or block) tank that will hold liquids and solids. Bacteria break down the solids into a liquid which then flows into a seepage pit or drainage field. The seepage pit is simplest and least costly, *if* you have adequate subsoil conditions. It is merely a rock-filled pit that has been dug to a gravel bed below the surface, or to some strata where the liquid will leach into the soil. The drainage field accomplishes the same purpose, but by utilizing a quantity of perforated pipe to distribute the liquid over a larger area. Each state has its own regulations as to size and technical construction requirements, and will probably require a permit. Failure to secure one may cause difficulty with financing, or unnecessary delay and expense. From time to time, the septic tank may need to be pumped out when the seepage system becomes overloaded. Additives can be put into the septic tank to help insure good bacterial action. (See Fig. 11.4)

Fig. 11.4 Typical septic tank requirements. New Mexico Health and Social Services Department.

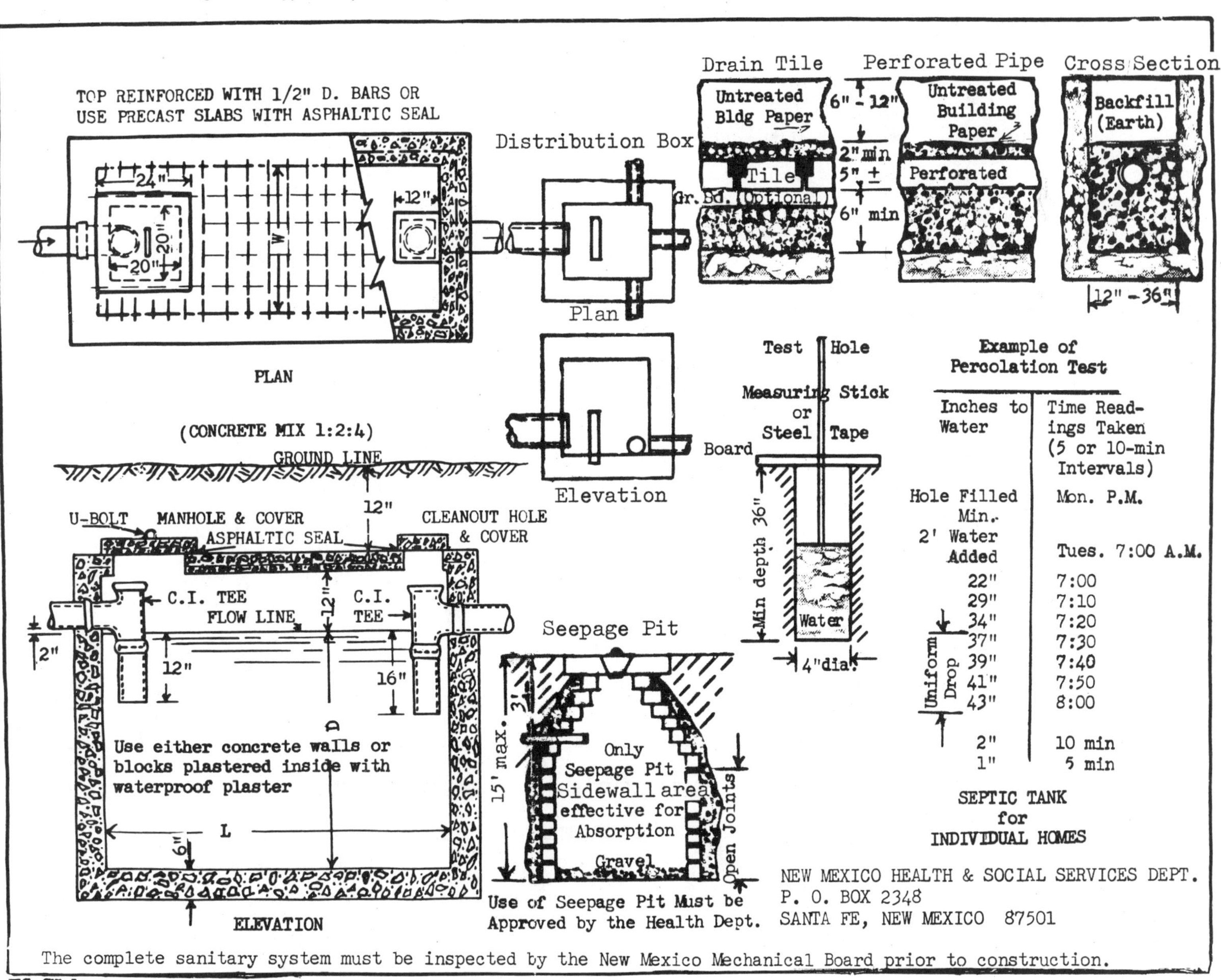

The function of a septic tank is to remove the suspended solids from sewage. Bacteria feed upon the solids and reduce most of them to gas or liquid. The remainer stays in the tank as sludge. Under ordinary conditions, sludge should be removed from the septic tank every two years, and either buried or discharged into a municipal sewer. It is not necessary to seed a septic tank. No surface disposal of septic tank effluent is acceptable. Walls of a septic tank may by of either concrete or blocks. If blocks are used the inside walls are required to be plastered with a waterproof plaster. A septic tank is required to be water-tight.

Minimum lot sizes are recognized as necessary for private sewage disposal. New Mexico Department of Public Health Policy requires the following lot sizes for each individual house: One-half acre (21,780 Sq. Ft.), or larger, where both private water supply and a private sewage disposal system are to be located on the same lot. One-fourth acre (10,890 Sq. Ft.), or larger, where a public water supply is available, but a private sewage disposal is located on a lot.

The minimum grade on the 4" sewer line between the house and septic tank should be 1/8" per foot, and preferably 1/4" per foot, with the 10' section of sewer immediately ahead of the septic tank being 1/8" per foot. The seepage field must be installed carefully with the tile or perforated pipe laid on a grade of 2" to 3" per 100' of length, and never greater than 6" per 100' of length. The minimum clear distance between seepage trenches should be not less than 3 times the trench width. Only the trench bottom is used in determining absorption area for trenches, while only the sidewall area below the inlet is effective on seepage pits.

A percolation test is made by digging a 4" diameter or '2" square hole to a depth equal to the proposed depth of the seepage trenches. The test holes should be a minimum of 36" deep, and be representative of the seepage area. At least 2 test holes should ordinarily be made. Test holes should be filled with water and allowed to stand overnight before tests are made. At the time of the tests are made, the holes should again be filled with water to a depth of at least 2 feet. At 5 or 10-minute intervals record the time and depth to water. When the rate of fall is uniform note the time required for water to drop one inch and then use Table No. 2 to determine the square feet of absorption area required.

Steps to follow in planning a septic tank and seepage facility: (1) Determine number of bedrooms and septic tank size. (2) Locate septic tank site. (3) Make percolation tests and determine amount of seepage area required. (4) Determine depth and grade of sewer line from house to septic tank inlet. (5) Determine location of seepage facility. (6) Determine depth of septic tank inlet below ground level. (7) Determine depth and grade of seepage lines. (8) Check Table No. 3 for compliance. (9) Obtain approval of the New Mexico Mechanical Board prior to construction. (10) Construct septic tank, sewer lines, and seepage facility.

Table No. 1 REQUIRED SEPTIC TANK CAPACITIES

No. Bedrooms	Septic Tank Capacity	Septic Tank Dimensions: Length	Width	Liquid Depth	Total Depth
2 or less	750	7' - 6"	3' - 6"	4' - 0"	5' - 0"
3	900	8' - 0"	3' - 6"	4' - 4"	5' - 4"
4*	1,000	8' - 0"	4' - 0"	4' - 6"	5' - 6"

*For each additional Bedroom add 250 gallons

Table No. 2 ABSORPTION AREA REQUIREMENTS FOR PRIVATE RESIDENCES

(Provides for garbage grinder and automatic-sequence washing machines)

Percolation Rate (Time required for water to fall 1-inch in minutes)	Required Absorbtion Area In Sq. Ft. per Bedroom, Standard Trench and Seepage Pits	Total Sq. Ft. Absorbtion Area Required — Number of Bedrooms: 2	3	4
1 or less	70	140	210	280
2	85	170	255	340
3	100	200	300	400
4	115	230	345	460
5	125	250	375	500
10	165	330	495	660
15	190	380	570	760
30	250	500	750	1,000

Table No. 3 LOCATION OF SEWAGE DISPOSAL SYSTEM

Minimum Distance in Clear Required From

Septic Tank	Disposal Field	Seepage Pit	To
5 feet	5 feet	20 feet	Buildings and structures
10 feet	5 feet	10 feet	Property line adjoining Private property
10 feet	10 feet	10 feet	Water lines
50 feet	100 feet	100 feet	Water supply wells*
10 feet	25 feet	100 feet	Streams*
10 feet	10 feet	10 feet	Large trees
6 feet	6 feet	3 diameters	Seepage pits

*Where special health hazards are involved the distance required shall be increased as may be directed by the New Mexico Health and Social Services Department and the New Mexico Mechanical Board.

Some subsurface soil conditions have little if any percolation, and it may be necessary to build an especially designed drainage field which allows moisture to go up (evaporation) instead of down (percolation). Write Los Alamos County Health Department, Los Alamos, NM, for details.

THE DRAINAGE GRADE of your sewer system will be less than you might suppose. The grade is generally estimated at ⅛″ to ¼″ per foot. This helps insure that solids and paper will float out to the disposal system. If the pitch is too steep, the line may have a tendency to clog. In most cases the grade of the system between house and sewer is no great problem. If the sewer depth is shallow, and the house set low, the grade should be verified before setting your finished floor grades. (See Fig. 11.5) If natural grade is impossible, you may install a "sewage ejector" (pump) to do the job. This may involve an expense of several hundred dollars, and it is better to avoid if possible.

Fig. 11.5 Typical septic tank requirements, continued. New Mexico Health and Social Services Department.

12

Heating and Cooling

WHATEVER THE METHOD of heating or cooling you select for your home, it will be determined by several factors, such as the type of fuel available, climatic conditions, initial installation cost, operating cost, and your personal preferences. You can range from a simple fireplace or stove to a sophisticated system that completely conditions the air temperature and humidity on a year-round basis, without opening a window or moving the controls. We will deal with heating and air-conditioning systems separately. Each system must have the capacity to heat or cool adequately for local climatic conditions.

HVAC

HVAC is the abbreviation of Heating—Ventilating—Air Conditioning, and systems should be selected that deal with all three. Our standards for comfortable living (or what we regard as standard) are constantly being upgraded. Adobe homes, contrary to some beliefs, do need heating and air conditioning. Ventilation in an adobe home is even more important than in conventional construction, to take advantage of the thermal mass storage and lag.

DIRECT HEATING of the air is perhaps the system most familiar to us all. This is usually accomplished by means of a furnace which has an air chamber in which the air is heated and then circulated through the home. Warm air rises so a basement "warm air" furnace sends warm air up, and cold air returns naturally. A refinement of this system adds a fan which circulates the air more efficiently. In either case, the circulated air must be returned to the furnace where it can be re-heated and circulated again. This circulation may be accomplished by return air ducts or sometimes by the hallways and rooms of your home. In most cases a thermostat, placed in the path of the returning air, controls the heat in the heat exchanger and the fan which moves the air. These furnaces are fueled by natural gas, liquified petroleum gas (LPG), fuel oil, coal, or even electric heating elements, over which the air passes to be heated. Efficient heating and air conditioning units are now available for roof mounting, attics, crawl spaces, and in areas which would not have adequate space for older style equipment. (See Fig. 12.1)

The action of the heat exchanger and thermostat perhaps needs some explanation. People wonder why the furnace does not come on immediately when the thermostat is activated. Within the heat exchanger are two thermostats. These override the wall thermostat, and measure the air temperature in the heat-exchanger box. It would be undesirable to have the fan push air through the ducts before it has been heated, and it would be equally bad to have the heat exchanger get too hot from having the heat on with the fan not operating. These additional controls are set at the factory, should be adjusted only by a competent heating mechanic, and not by the homeowner.

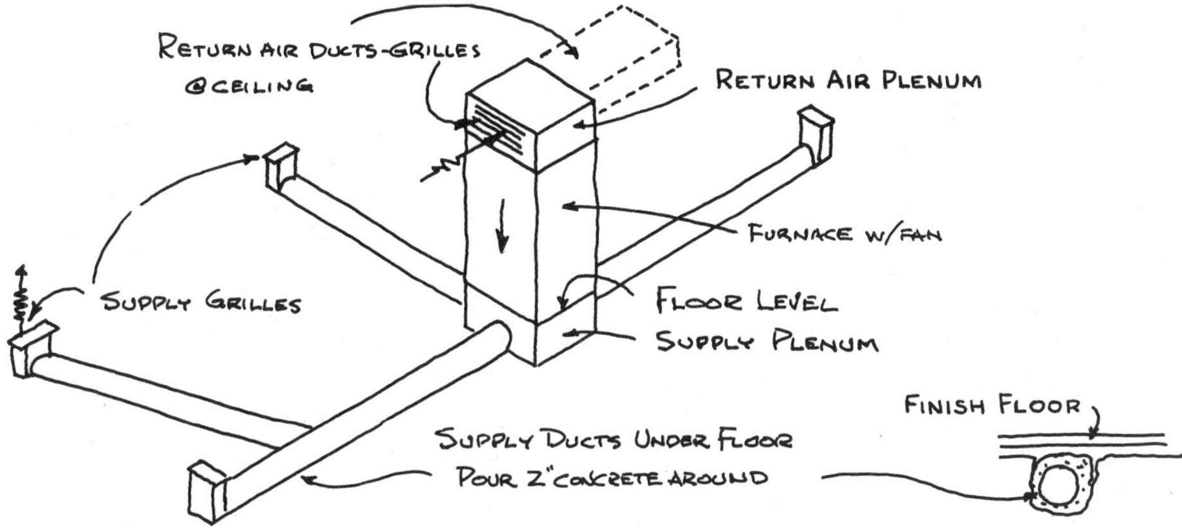

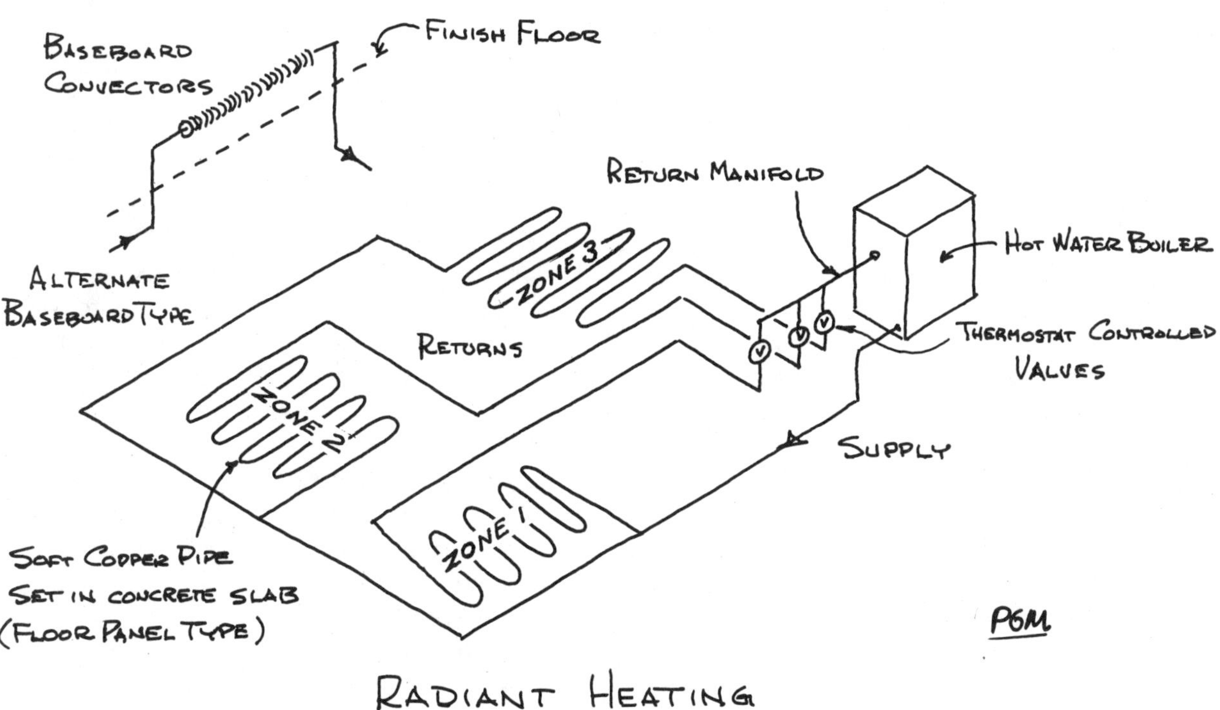

Fig. 12.1 Typical heating systems.

The updraft furnace is perhaps the more common type in use, but not the most desirable in homes without a basement. It heats the air, which rises in a duct and is distributed throughout the home by means of additional ducts at the ceiling level. This system provides hot air at the ceiling level where it tends to collect. A newer and more desirable type in homes without a basement is the "counter-flow" furnace which heats the air and forces it downward for distribution. In my opinion, this is the optimum heating system for most adobe homes. The air ducts can be located in the earth fill on which the brick floor is placed, or can be easily run in a crawl space, with supply registers located around the exterior walls. In this system, the warm air is introduced at the floor level, into the room that is to be heated, so it will rise and heat more pleasantly and efficiently. The ducts under the floors also provide a certain amount of radiant effect to warm the floors as well. If the ducts are to be buried directly in the earth fill, you have several choices of material, some of which must be protected from the corrosive effects of the earth fill. If you use sheet-metal ducts, or "Sonotube," which is a round cardboard duct, you must encase either kind in concrete (at least 2″ thick). One major drawback to this type of heating system is the difficulty of zoning the heat for different areas of your home. Additional furnaces or heating systems are required to heat different zones. Forced air systems have the advantage of providing air circulation, important in adobe homes.

Collection of the returning air to the furnace can be a problem in typical flat-roofed adobe-style homes, particularly with exposed-beam ceiling construction. A logical answer to this is to furr down (enclosing at a lower level) the ceiling area in a hallway, or closets where appearance is not too important. This will provide a quiet collection system for the return air, and by reversing the flow, may be used as a more efficient distribution duct for cooled air. In the event that it is not possible to enclose such a return-duct system within the house, it may have to be roof mounted. The resulting ducts exposed on the roof must be carefully insulated and protected from the weather for full efficiency. It is far better to enclose the ductwork within the house if possible.

In locations where heating needs are minimal, very simple, economical systems may be used, such as a wall-type direct radiant heater. If gas or combustible fuels are used, make sure that local code requirements are met to provide adequate combustion air and venting. We read daily in colder months of the tragedy of deaths by carbon-monoxide poisoning from improperly vented heaters. These unfortunately seem to be more common in the areas where little need for heat is the rule.

RADIANT-TYPE HEATING may assume several forms, either a radiant-panel arrangement in the floor or ceiling, or a baseboard type which provides heated strips at the perimeter walls that in turn heat the air. In general, the radiant-type system costs more to install, but is more efficient, resulting in lower operating costs. The major drawbacks for radiant-type heating are its lack of air circulation and incompatibility with cost-effective air conditioning systems, which must be provided separately. Radiant heating seems best for colder climates. We will look at the systems separately.

Panel-type radiant heating involves the use of a small water boiler and hot-water heating coils, placed directly in a concrete floor, through which hot water is circulated. The system is easily zoned by means of thermostats which operate valves, allowing the hot water to circulate, or restrict the flow to reduce the heat. In some areas, the electric power companies offer lower rates to users who install electric heating systems and will provide free design engineering. Investigate this carefully before making your decision.

The primary drawback of floor radiant panels is the lag. In most parts of the Southwest, there is a wide daily temperature fluctuation. It will be extremely cold at night, and quite warm in the daytime. Several hours will be required for the radiant panel to become heated and do its job. By the time this has been accomplished, the heat may not be needed because the outside temperatures have risen. This may be overcome by anticipatory controls, which anticipate the changing temperatures and cause the heat to come on in time for it to be at peak efficiency when it is needed (see Fig. 12.1).

Baseboard radiant heating, either hot water or electric, may be slightly more economical in many cases, and will operate more quickly than the panel type. This system involves a boiler to heat water that is circulated through finned, convector-type pipes that are run around the base of the exterior walls. These, although ugly in themselves, are usually hidden with an attractive metal cover. This type of system is reasonably low in initial cost (although not quite as economical as a forced-air system), is quite efficient in operating cost, and may be zoned easily by the use of return lines and thermostatically controlled valves.

Liquid propane gas (LPG) fuels can provide a source of fuel for outlying locations. The homeowner can either buy the storage tank or rent it. Most state plumbing codes require a licensed LPG installer to do this type of work. Careless work can be extremely dangerous.

COOLING

Some method of cooling is very desirable in the warmer Southwestern climates even though you have an adobe house. In the days before modern air conditioning systems, natural methods were used for cooling homes in the hot desert areas. In earlier times, the best remedy for hot climates was a high ceiling, with provision to vent off the overheated air, introducing cooler air from outside through a window. In the hot deserts of the Middle East, ingenious schemes using prevailing winds and below-ground temperatures for natural airflow were developed thousands of years ago, and are in use today. We can learn from their examples. The reverse was true in colder areas of the Southwest, where heating was of prime importance. In these areas, low ceilings were used so that the amount of air to be heated was lessened.

The capacity of the cooling equipment need not be as great with adobe as in other types of construction because of the stabilizing effect of the massive adobe wall. You will need some, however, to maintain the "softy" standards to which we have become accustomed. Two types may be considered, the older evaporative "swamp coolers," and the more modern refrigerated type.

EVAPORATIVE COOLING works well in areas with low humidity. It requires only a relatively simple unit that may be roof- or wall-mounted, containing a pump and fan. Water is supplied in small quantities, and electricity operates the fan and pump. The pump drips water over absorptive pads, and fresh air is drawn through the pads on the sides of the unit, the evaporation reducing the air's temperature. The additional air pumped into the home creates an added air pressure within the house which may be released by the opening of windows, thus directing the flow of cooled air. The fan unit should have a two-speed control switch for varying conditions. The pump should have a separate switch. In my experience, adobe homes in the colder desert areas need be cooled only a few hours each day, late in the afternoon, to keep the temperatures of the adobe walls low. Without air conditioning, this can be accomplished by a thorough airing during the evening when outside temperatures are naturally lower.

Hot desert areas make cooling of some sort an absolute must. The evaporative-type system works well here, too, where the humidity is low. Increased farming activities have significantly changed the humidity patterns in some places making refrigerated air conditioning the only logical system. In lower desert areas where high day and night temperatures are experienced in the summer, it is common to have air conditioning systems run continuously for several months at a time. The operating cost under these circumstances is most important. Costs for cooling may be comparable to costs of heating in cold areas.

REFRIGERATED AIR CONDITIONING can be either gas or electric and works on the same principle as your refrigerator. Again there is a "heat exchanger" cooling coil over which the circulating air is passed. You must, in most instances, for economy's sake use the same ducts you use for heating for the air conditioning. However, it may take a different air change to cool than it does to heat. Since you have the same volume of air to deal with for heating or cooling, you must circulate it more rapidly for cooling. Heating ducts ideally sized for heating are smaller than the ideal sized ducts for air conditioning. Frequently it is logical to compromise between the two sizes and have one duct that is not quite efficient for either. This is common practice. The main drawback usually is the noise made by the cooled air passing over or through ducts that are slightly too small.

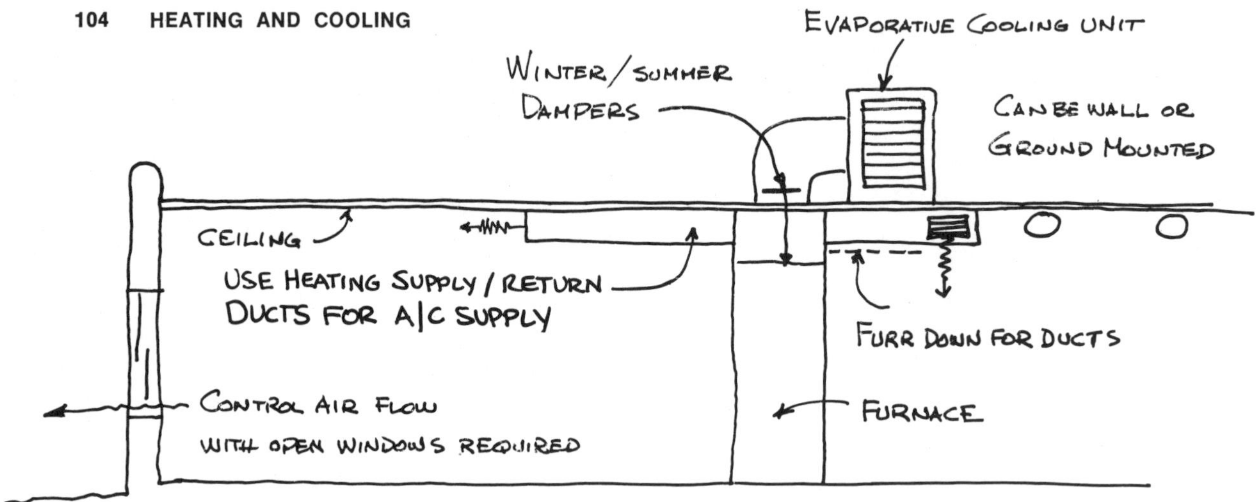

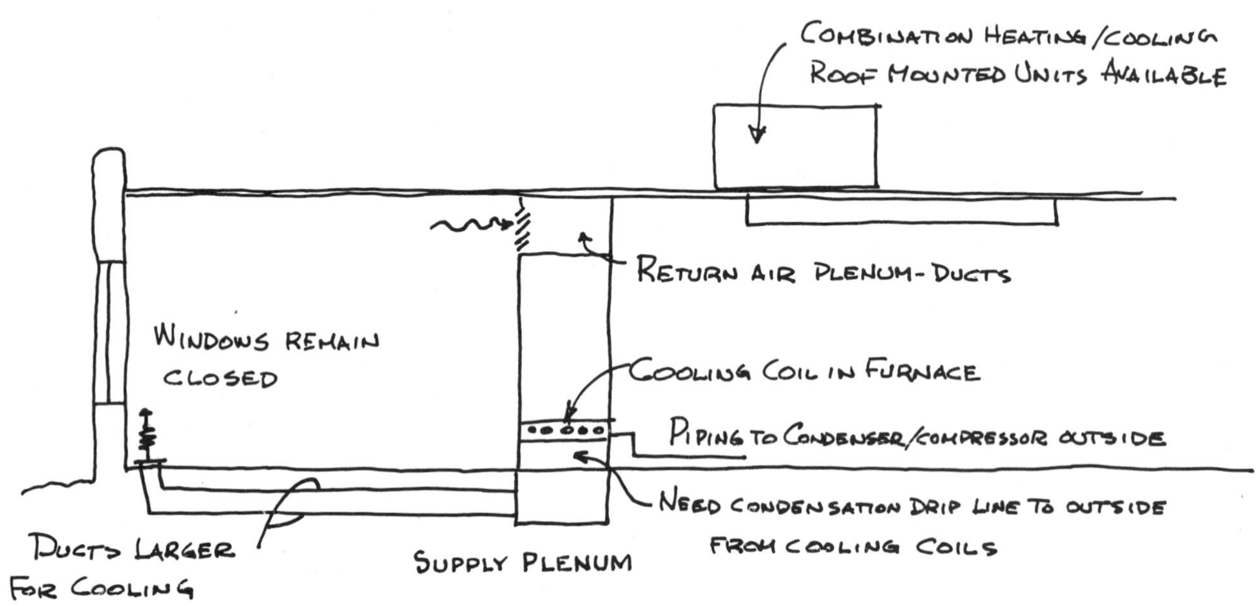

Fig. 12.2 Typical cooling systems.

The cooling coil is normally inserted in a place made for it in the furnace air-handling unit. It requires a compressor and condenser located outside the house, and piping to carry the refrigerant from the compressor to the expansion coil where cooling takes place, then return it to the condenser. Water from natural humidity in the air tends to collect on the cooling coil, just as it forms on a glass of cold water, and this water must be collected in a basin of some sort under the coil and piped outside for disposal. The initial cost of refrigerated air conditioning will be several times that of evaporative cooling and the operating costs considerably higher as well. Refrigerated air, or at least the provision for its future addition, may be a wise investment, even though you do not install the entire system now.

Many new systems are constantly being developed, such as the "heat pump" which, when designed correctly, uses a combined system with maximum economy. Many units are adaptable to several types of fuel. (See Fig. 12.2)

SOLAR HEATING

While this is not a manual on solar heating, adobe and solar work together! Adobe provides thermal mass and heat storage. This means that if the sun warms the adobe wall (directly or indirectly) during the day, the wall will give off that heat at night when the sun is down. If we do nothing to heat or cool the inside of the house, the temperature there will approximate the average of the outside temperature high/low swing in 24 hours. It's not quite that simple but let's go on. Do you want an active or passive system? Adobe works for both.

Active systems can be complicated, expensive, and cranky (ugly, too). A proud owner of a new $19,000 active system told me: "I'll get it back in less than 2 years." His heating bill must have been high! Check costs, savings, and tax credits carefully.

Passive systems can be as simple as orienting windows to the south, maybe adding more, and providing shade for those glass areas in the summer. All that's needed is good design and a slightly larger window budget. No moving parts, keeps on working. Our prehistoric Indians of the Southwest knew it and built this way. One word of warning on solar: There are two seasons... what's it like in the summer?

VENTILATION

Ventilating your home may seem like a minor consideration. However, certain provisions are desirable, and required by most codes. If you have a crawl space under a wood floor, it is necessary that this be ventilated with foundation vents. They usually take the place of several of the foundation stem blocks which are 8″ x 16″. These vents should be placed at least every 16 feet to provide adequate air circulation under your home to prevent dampness and carry off any accumulated gas that may have resulted from a leak.

Ventilation of any attic or joist space is also desirable, although not mandatory in all cases. The reasoning for it is this: the air that is trapped between the roof and a finished ceiling does provide a certain amount of insulation value, but will become overheated in warm summer months far in excess of the temperature outside. Joist vents should be provided on the same basis as foundation vents, and in about the same manner. If a steeply pitched roof is planned, gravity ventilation from louvres or vents may suffice. If a large attic area is involved, it may be desirable to provide mechanical ventilation with a fan. Your heating contractor or supplier should be able to provide valuable advice in your specific case.

Bathrooms that do not have a window on an exterior wall must also be ventilated.

Combustion air must be provided for gas appliances such as furnaces, water heaters, and clothes driers. In certain instances the natural ventilation around doors and windows may be adequate. Gas appliances must have a source of combustion air. Your building inspector will advise you of the requirements. If your home is tightly built and weatherstripped, fireplaces may also have difficulty drawing unless combustion air is provided. Some codes require this.

The cost of installing a heating and air-conditioning system may best be determined by seeking bids on an installed job. Most heating and air-conditioning contractors do their own design work. It is a simple matter for them but will prove rather complicated for you. If you plan to do your own work, it will be necessary for you to design or have designed a system that will be adequate. Many contractors and supply houses will do the design work for you and prefabricate the parts of the system you want them to, allowing you to do your own installation. Insist on an adequate, workable system!

13

The Electrical System

A SUPPLY OF ELECTRIC POWER is the first item you must make sure of in the planning of an electrical system for your home. This may sound like a silly statement, but several problems and/or possibilities may occur. If your building site is in or near the city, the problem is usually simple, but even here certain rules — which can impose unforeseen costs — must be followed.

SERVICE TO THE HOUSE

You must, in the beginning, determine where your electrical service center will be located. This is the point at which power comes in, all circuits terminate, and the circuit breakers are located. It may or may not be the same point at which the electric power lines enter your home.

Most public utility companies have very specific rules and regulations under which electrical power is connected. Most utilities require that a "green tag" indicating an approved installation be obtained from the local inspecting authority before connecting the electrical power to your home. Thus, if you have not had the necessary inspections, which can be obtained only after a permit has been granted, you may encounter serious delay and expense even though your system is completely correct and in accordance with the code.

As a general rule, the utility company will provide power to the corner of the structure that is nearest the power-line pole serving the property. The service line may not pass over any inhabited dwelling or a swimming pool. If your home is located in a rural area, or perhaps even in a new subdivision, you may be required to pay line extension costs for new poles and power lines to bring power within the reach of the normal hookup distance. If the electrical service location is other than at the most convenient point, it may be necessary to extend the supply (you or the electrician must do this) within your home from the point of connection. The whole thing may also be placed underground from the supply pole, at your expense, if you so desire. (See Figure 13.1)

THE SERVICE BOX

We will assume at this point that service to your home is available. Now you will require a service box that will contain the main power supply from its source, the ends of a number of circuits, and circuit breakers for each circuit to prevent them from becoming overheated. The service panel is not too attractive as a wall decoration. Hopefully, you will be able to locate it in a utility room, or perhaps in the garage or carport. Certain locations are prohibited under some codes, such as bathrooms and closets. If no logical locations are available, it may be permissable to locate the box on the outside. Check code requirements.

SAFETY

The first consideration is safety. Adequate service is second, and convenience third. You must have safety above all else. Improperly wired homes can be extremely dangerous since shorting out of a circuit can cause electrical

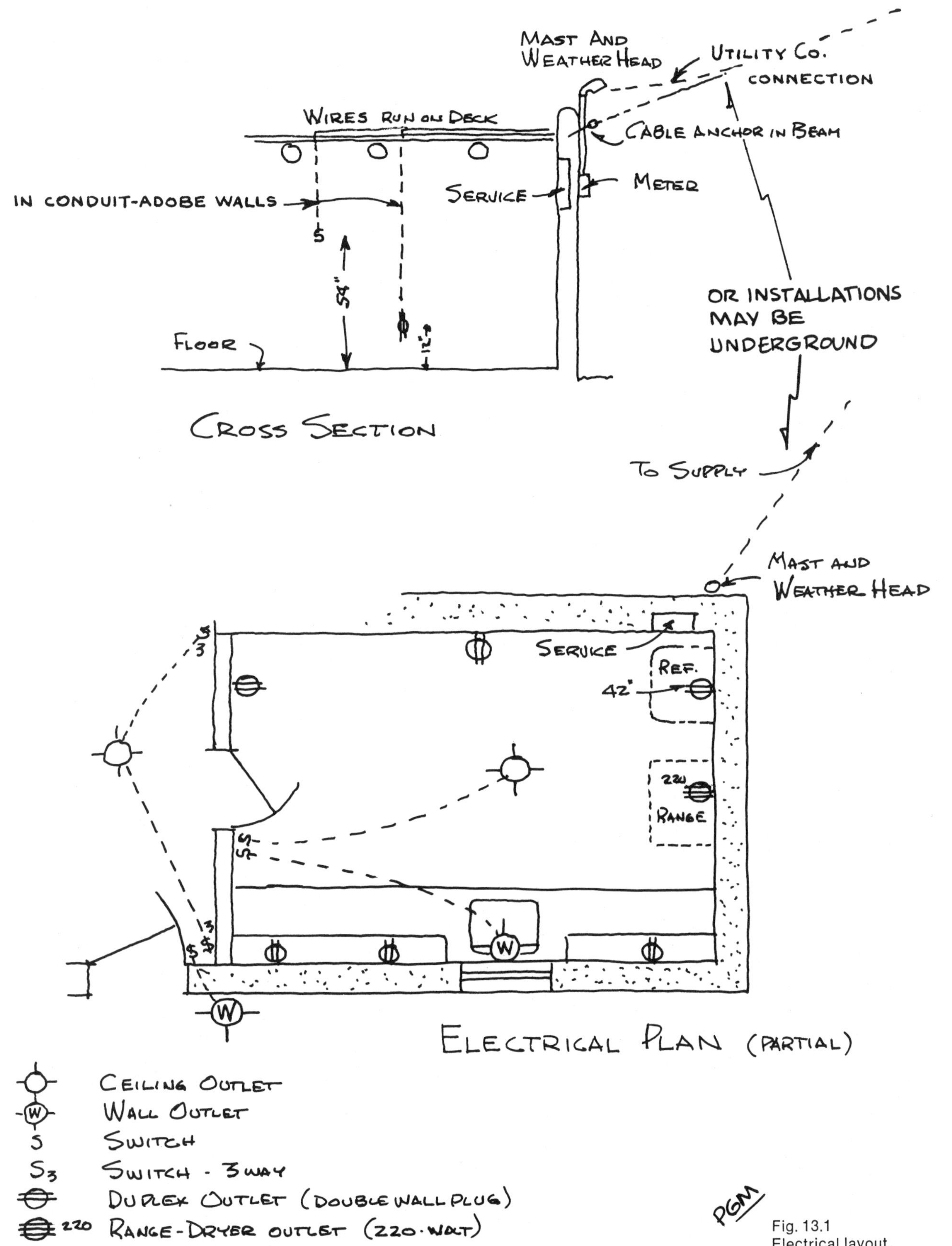

Fig. 13.1
Electrical layout.

shock or fires from overloaded circuits. Your circuit breakers should provide the safety feature to prevent circuits from being overloaded. State and city building codes rigidly prescribe what circuits will be required, the load limit on each, wire sizes, and many other measures to insure maximum safety. All wall plugs (duplex outlet is the correct nomenclature) must be grounded, and have a third slot in the receptacle that is the ground slot. Many older homes built before this requirement do not have this third slot.

Grounding clips from box to ground wire are required at all switches and outlets to prevent accidental shorting to the metal box from a faulty plug or loose wire. It is prohibited, for example, to install a wall switch or receptacle in a shower.

Most safety regulations are just common sense. Some of the other regulations pay dividends not only in safety, but in convenience as well. For example, most states require that each wall have electrical outlets on not more than 12′ centers. This is convenient, and will require fewer extension cords, which often are an additional fire hazard not contemplated in the structure itself.

ADEQUATE WIRING

The need to plan for adequate service and to anticipate future requirements cannot be emphasized enough. We are all constantly being bombarded with new types of electrical appliances that hadn't been thought of a few years ago. Electric clothes driers, toothbrushes, hair driers, and even can openers create new demands on the electrical service system. Better to start with too much capacity now, when the cost of installing additional outlets and capacity is quite nominal, than to require expensive installations at a later date.

The initial installation of wiring for television sets, intercoms, and stereo systems should be considered in your planning. Stereo and intercom systems may call for expert advice because of technical requirements. Incorrectly installed systems may cause unusual problems of feedback, strange noises, and technical complications.

Telephone wiring is best installed in the walls prior to plastering. Private communications systems offer innovations. Specialized advisors can assist you in selecting a system.

CIRCUITS

The circuits must be sized according to the load that will be imposed on them. A heavier load requires heavier wire and a heavier capacity circuit breaker. For example, a wall outlet in most cases will only carry a lamp, or perhaps a lamp and vacuum cleaner, at any one time, and this will be a maximum load of perhaps two or three hundred watts. It would be foolish to set up a circuit to each wall outlet. A number of these outlets can be carried on the same circuit, which is generally rated at 15 amperes at the circuit breaker. Codes require that certain appliances that use large amounts of power may each have to be on a separate circuit. Electric ranges are a good example of this. Electric driers and hot water heaters are another.

Circuit breakers act in this manner: the switch is spring loaded to carry a certain amount of electricity, which is rated in amperes. If an excess demand is made on this circuit, or if a broken or faulty wire is shorted out (grounded, maybe through you), the circuit breaker will trip into the "off" position. If the overload was only momentary, the switch may be reset by throwing it to the "on" position. If the overload is still present, the breaker will trip again and will continue to do so until the overload (short) is corrected. Older houses may have fuse boxes instead of circuit breakers. These are quite adequate, but the breakers are superior. These might be bypassed for some reason in an emergency, but only by a skilled electrician.

A typical list of separate circuits that may be required is listed below, with normal capacities:

Circuit	*Breaker Size*	*Wire Size*
Main	100 AMP	# 2
Range	60 "	# 6
Drier	40 "	# 8
Dishwasher	15 "	#12
Disposal	15 "	#12
Washer	15 "	#12
Freezer	20 "	#12

Bath heaters and lamps	20	”	#12
Air conditioning	20	”	#12
Furnace	20	”	#12
8 outlets/circuit (residential)	15	”	#14
2 outlets/circuit (kitchen)	20	”	#12

A recent innovation and code requirement is the GFI (Ground Fault Interruptor) breaker. This is an especially sensitive breaker that will disconnect before life-safety is threatened. It is used on all bathroom and outdoor power circuits. Check local codes.

Additional circuits do cost money, but the codes must be followed, and safety is beyond price.

SWITCHES

We all take switches so for granted that they may not seem worthy of much consideration. But careful planning should be done in order to put them in the most convenient locations. As in many other areas of your planning, it is most effective to project yourself into the plan and envision typical situations and traffic patterns. Switches are normally located inside the room where they activate a ceiling light or wall outlet, and are best located adjacent to the doorjamb approximately 54″ above the floor. Switches are sometimes inadvertently located behind a door, which means you must open the door, pass through it, and close it again before you can reach the switch. This is most inconvenient.

The light in a hallway should have a switch at each end, either of which will control the light, off or on. This arrangement is called a three-way switch and should be so designated on the plan. If you feel the expense unwarranted, imagine yourself in a dark hallway. You must turn on the light in order to find the bedroom door. Once there, you must turn on the light in the bedroom, and then in order to extinguish the hall light, you must retrace your steps down the hall, turn it off, and return through the dark hall to your bedroom again!

It sometimes is an advantage to control a wall outlet from a switch, so that a ceiling light won't be required. In my own experience, a ceiling light in a bedroom is merely for the purpose of preventing a sore shin until you are able to get a lamp turned on. Then you go back and turn off the ceiling light. Unless you are in love with ceiling fixtures, it may be much more desirable to arrange the wiring so that only half the duplex receptacle is powered by the switch. If this is done, a clock or other appliance can be used from the "hot" side of the receptacle, regardless of the position of the switch.

Lights for closets depend on the type of closet. For walk-in closets they are a necessity. For wardrobe-type closets with wide folding or sliding doors, they are a matter of choice. Each outlet and each switch increases the cost of the electrical system. With ceiling fixtures in closets you may save one step (and thus some costs) by using pull-chain-type fixtures.

RECEPTACLES

These should be located to serve any lamps, clocks, and the like placed near them. Long cords can be eliminated by advance planning of probable furniture placement. Duplex wall outlets are normally located approximately 12″ above the floor. It is quite desirable to arrange for receptacles on the exterior of your home in certain key locations as well. They provide great convenience for grills, mowers, and other garden appliances. If an outlet is to be placed on the exterior of your home, exposed to the weather, a weatherproof cover plate should be provided. Some come with screw-on caps, but more modern ones have a spring-loaded cover plate that stays shut when not in use. It sometimes is desirable to set a receptacle at a different height than the standard mentioned above, as in the case of a refrigerator, for example. Outlets above a counter in the kitchen will, of course, have to be set in accordance with countertop height. Special attention should be given as well to the height of the backsplash above a countertop (if you have one), since it will be easier to set the switch or receptacle either wholly in or wholly out of the backsplash. Where decorative tile is used for a countertop backsplash, it can be particularly trying to have the switch located half in and half out.

ticularly trying to have the switch located half in and half out.

FIXTURES

These can frequently be purchased directly by the owner, either from foreign sources if you are close to the border, or from a lighting supplier. It is customary in most planning budgets to set up a dollar allowance for fixtures. You may not have selected the exact fixture to go in each location, but you can establish an average cost for each, and an overall allowance for the total cost. Bathroom lights normally have a provision for an electric outlet for appliances such as razors and hair dryers, but don't count on it. If this feature is included, it will save the additional cost of another outlet. Make sure you have what you require when you select the fixtures. Some bath fixtures include the mirror, medicine cabinet, lights, receptacle and all. In many cases, a bathroom without a window may require a ventilating fan. Most bathrooms need additional heat as well. Try to combine as many of the requirements into one fixture as you can.

Fixtures and appliances may or may not have an Underwriters Laboratories (UL) label on them. The purpose of the label is to insure maximum safety standards. The wiring of fixtures purchased in foreign countries may be difficult or expensive. Make allowance for this in estimating your costs.

Some fixtures are designed for certain maximum wattage light bulbs. If this limit is exceeded, damage may result to the fixture.

Figure 13.1 provides sketch details of wiring systems and common symbols used on plans that may be helpful.

WIRING ARRANGEMENTS

The wiring arrangements for an adobe home are somewhat different than for the standard frame house. With frame walls you can use Romex cable that can be run between the studs and framing. Wiring in an adobe wall must be run in metal conduit if it is close to the surface of the wall. This conduit is most easily installed by cutting a channel in the adobe wall with a claw hammer to the required location. The conduit, wire, and all is then plastered over.

If you wish to maintain the masonry texture of the wall, you may perhaps run direct burial cable (special wire) in the center of the adobe wall, without conduit, as you lay up the adobes. This is an expensive process, however, is sometimes prohibited by code, and should be avoided or used as little as possible. The main wiring in your home, from the circuit breakers to the various outlets and switches, can usually best be run in a crawlspace, or in a framed area such as an attic. In many cases with adobe construction, however, you won't have a crawlspace under the floor, and you will have a flat roof without open framed areas in which to run wire. The best solution for this seems to be to run the cable (which can be Romex at this point) on top of the deck, prior to placement of the insulation. Drops may then be run to wall outlets, switches, ceiling fixtures, and the like. There is some danger in this system in that it is easy to drive a roofing nail into the cable. Most electricians seem to prefer this method, however, as opposed to running all circuits in the ground under a brick floor. Where a concrete bond beam is used, it will be necessary to provide a channel through this, too, for drops. If the concrete is old, it will be quite hard and very difficult to chip. But if you make the channel shortly after the forms have been stripped, it is quite easy. Another solution is to provide wood knock-out blocks in the concrete bond beam before pouring. They can be left in the bond beam until time to install the wiring.

ESTIMATING COSTS

Most electricians base their estimate of the cost of an electrical plan on the number of outlets, whether they are switches or wall or ceiling outlets, at a flat price per outlet. An additional charge is figured for the service, and for the number of circuits required. It will be necessary for you to make a detailed take-off in order to purchase the necessary individual items, if you plan to do the work yourself. Otherwise you need only to indicate the locations for outlets, fixtures, and switches.

14

Roofing

TRADITIONAL ROOFING for adobe homes was made of a thick layer of earth with a fairly high clay content. As you have undoubtedly discovered by now (or will discover) in making adobes, the clay lumps in the soil seem quite resistant to wetting, and require a period of soaking to wet the clay all the way through. This same drawback in molding bricks turns to an advantage in a roofing material. The arid Southwest usually experiences rainfall of rather limited duration, with extremely dry periods in between rains. It is virtually impossible for the rainwater to penetrate a foot or more of earth that has been packed on the traditional roof. The rain will, however, if channeled by gravity during runoff, erode the roof rapidly in some places, or, lacking a way to run off, will puddle and eventually soak through. In any case, you will find the maintenance of such an arrangement excessive. The early builders didn't have the materials we now have to make the work easier and the maintenance less, but we do, and should take fullest advantage of them.

ASPHALT ROOFING MATERIALS

The best roofing material for your purposes, except some exotic plastic compounds that are quite expensive, would seem to be asphalt products. Asphalt (bitumen) resists water, but is adversely affected by heat and sunlight. Asphalt compounds are composed of light and heavy elements, the lighter ones evaporating under the effects of heat and sunlight. Thus, when an asphaltic surface is exposed to these, the lighter elements evaporate, leaving behind the heavier ones. The remaining material in turn becomes brittle, cracks, and deteriorates to the point that it will admit water through the surface. Asphalt, by itself, has no structural value. It must be reinforced with fibers of some sort, these usually being cellulose fibers (paper), or asbestos fibers that last longer and are more expensive. Paper is made by conventional methods, and then impregnated with asphalts, providing a reasonably strong material, now known as an asphalt roofing felt. This comes in several weights or thicknesses. The asphalt on the surface of this felt is still subject to the deleterious effects of heat and sunlight, and the time that it takes these to penetrate the roofing felt is determined somewhat by the thickness of the felt. Normally you build up the thickness of these felts by using several layers glued together with hot melted asphalt, which hardens when cooled.

To get maximum life out of the roof that you have constructed with several layers of felt, you now should make an effort to protect the layers from the heat and sunlight. This is normally done by flooding the finished surface with additional hot asphalt and embedding gravel or some mineral in this. It serves the purpose of shielding the waterproof surface from heat and sunlight. The felts will continue to deteriorate even though somewhat protected. Asphalt felts can be purchased with an integral mineral surface (mineralized) in a fairly heavy weight that can be used as a one-layer application. The life of this does not, however, seem to be as great as a built-up roof with gravel.

Any pipe, vent, conduit, chimney, or other

projection through the roof must be carefully flashed to prevent water leakage at this point. It is most common to provide a metal "jack" whose wide flange is nailed to the deck, then is covered by the roofing. Joints should be additionally sealed with black plastic roof putty. If the vent is for air circulation into a room, it may require a "rain cap" and insect screen.

CLAY TILE AND SLATE may also be used to protect the asphalt surface. Contrary to popular belief, these materials are not waterproof in themselves, but serve mainly to protect the asphalt felts below them. A roof built in this manner will last indefinitely unless the protecting materials are damaged. The economy of using these heroic materials is more debatable, however. Spanish tile can provide spectacular architectural effects, and is traditional for some forms of design, but is extremely costly. If your design requires it, or you want it, by all means use it, but be prepared to pay the price.

SHINGLES are merely smaller pieces of mineralized felt that are overlapping on a sloping roof to perform a decorative or color function as well as serving as the top layer of the roof. They come in several weights and different mechanical features, such as "lock tabs" and "hurricane." Wood shingles may be used effectively in some nontraditional designs; the same considerations are true of these as were mentioned in roof tiles above. The pitch or slope of your roof must be adequate (3″ vertical to 12″ horizontal) to prevent leakage.

THE COLOR of your roof will affect its heat-absorbing or -reflecting qualities. Dark roofs, of course, absorb more heat, which may be desirable in colder areas, and light-colored roofs reflect it, a desirable feature in warmer areas. With a built-up roof, the amount of reflection is determined by the color of the aggregate that you embed in the final asphalt coating of your roof. White marble chips, for example, are only slightly more expensive than the standard gray roofing gravel. Unfortunately, the public has in many cases been victimized by unscrupulous sales companies that sell a paint or coating of dubious value for a high price. Miracle materials that are represented to be equivalent to a massive thickness of insulation are usually fraudulent. Investigate these carefully with a reputable builder, and perhaps also with the Better Business Bureau of your locality.

THE LIFE OF THE ROOF will depend on the quantity and quality of the material incorporated into its construction. It is common practice to refer to a roofing specification as a "ten-year" roof, a "fifteen-year" roof, for example, without an actual detailing of what will go into the construction. A simple guide follows:

10-year — 3 Ply (15#) + gravel
15-year — 1 Ply (30#) + 2 Ply (15#) + gravel
20-year — 1 Ply (30#) + 3 Ply (15#) + gravel

Surprisingly enough, the roof will last just about that period of time, providing it has been properly installed. If a ten-year roof has been in place for ten years, you can count on trouble at any time. The requirements to achieve a certain life in your roof will vary with the severity of the elements prevailing in a particular geographical or climatic area.

Bonded roofs are almost a thing of the past. At one time, a bond or guarantee against leaks was furnished by the roofing contractor, backed up by the manufacturer. But the paperwork and liability became so burdensome that the roofing contractors have adopted an almost universal policy of guaranteeing the roof against leaks for a period of two years only, regardless of the specifications. Bonds are still provided in some cases on large industrial roofs where the square footage exceeds a certain total. A number of manufacturers have developed new roofing products known as "Single Ply" systems. While details differ, most are a thick single-ply roll of factory assembled layers. The seams are usually heat-sealed in installation, and the entire surface may require an ultra violet protective coating to reduce deterioration. Some systems may require special preparation of the surface before application. Some manufacturers will provide a written guarantee. We have used such a system, are pleased with it (except the cost... double!), and are waiting for the test of time.

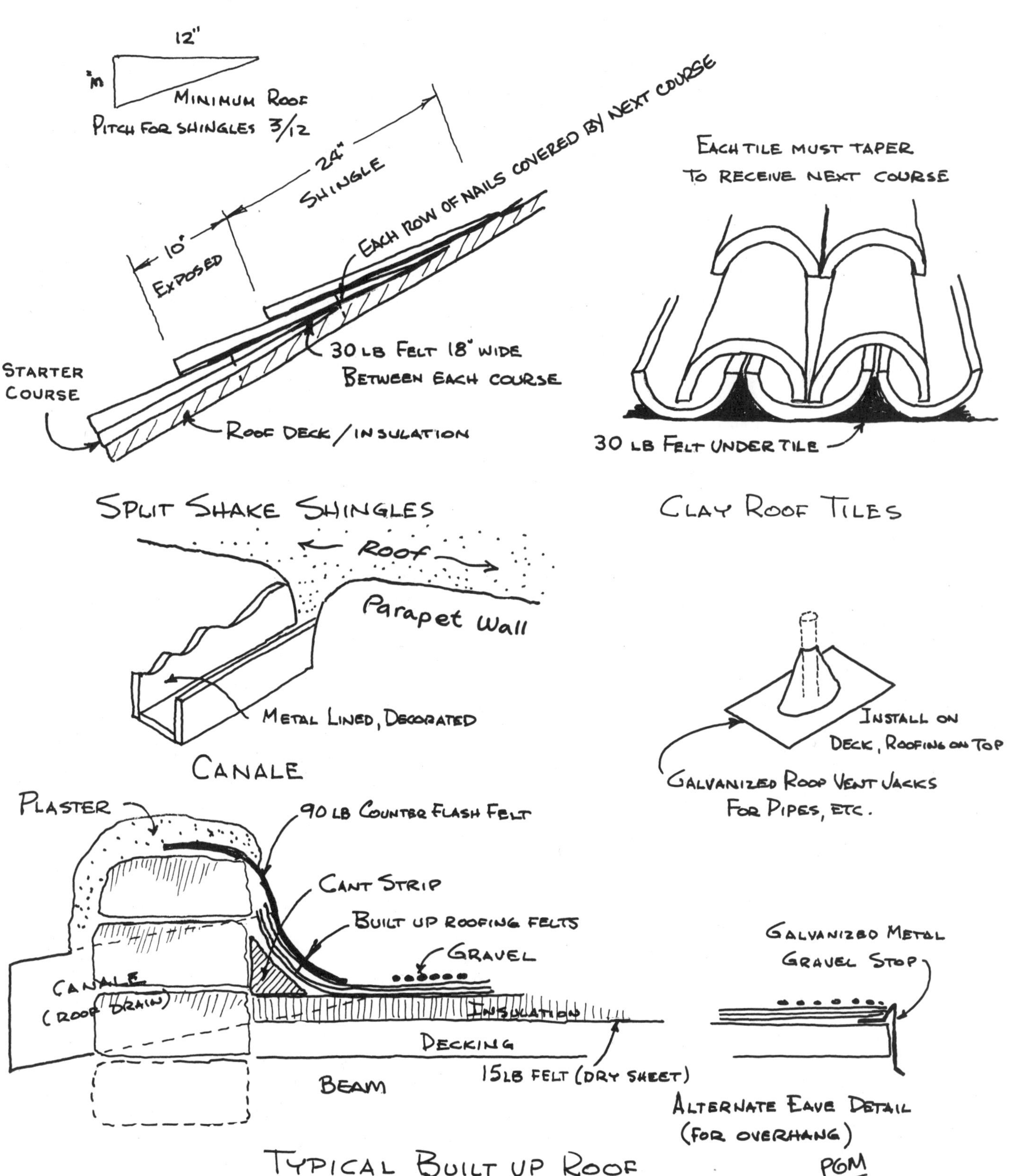

Fig. 14.1 Roofing details.

FLASHING. The final flashing for your roof should be of a more substantial single-sheet material than the base roofing. The flashings are closing strips of metal or heavy, mineralized felt that are applied over the irregular surfaces, joints, and parapets (fire wall). It is essential that a solid surface is provided under any asphalt felt, particularly parapet-wall flashing. If this is not done, felts may be damaged by hail or foot traffic. (See Figure 14.1)

MAINTENANCE

Roofing is normally figured in "squares." One square is 100 square feet, or an area 10 feet by 10 feet. The regular replacement of your roof is an expected maintenance expense that should be counted on. If you use better specifications, the roof will cost more initially, but will have a longer life, and may cost less on a yearly basis than one that must be replaced more frequently.

CANALES

In traditional adobe architecture, the *canales* are the troughs that carry off the water collected on the roof, through the parapet or fire wall. In the traditional design with mud plaster it is of particular importance that the *canales* are long enough (that is, protrude out from the wall far enough) to direct the water well away from the walls. The effect of direct rainfall on the walls is of relative unimportance, but a concentrated flow of water can cause serious damage. The *canales* can be quite simple, or can be in the ornate territorial style. They must, of course, be located on the low side of the roof slope, and some care should be exercised in choosing their locations to prevent them from dripping over a door, window, or patio.

TRAFFIC DECKS

One or more of these may be in your plan. A traffic deck is a roof that will be used as a regular walking surface, such as a sun deck, or porch with a finished room below it. Particular care must be exercised to prevent leakage. The most satisfactory solution perhaps is to pour a concrete slab, which serves as a ceiling for the room below, and as a floor for the deck above. This slab should be strongly reinforced and meshed to reduce the probability of cracking and movement. It should then be flood-coated with hot asphalt, and a solid-wearing surface installed above this. The most satisfactory is brick or stone, set in a cement mortar bed at least 2″ thick, and provided with expansion joints at least every 20′ and at the edges of intersecting vertical walls. If the expansion joints are not provided, movement from expansion may separate even a very strong slab. The entire surface should then be sealed with a penetrating sealer, which should be renewed periodically to prevent leakage.

15

Plastering, Drywall, and Ceramic Tile

PLASTERING is one of the final steps in the construction of your home. The plaster is used to preserve the vulnerable mud structure, make it more attractive, and cover up all the rough work (and mistakes!). Plastering is a skill that can be mastered by the individual with relative ease, except perhaps for the texturing. If you want a special texture, you'd better hire it done. Different materials and mixes and combinations are required for interior and exterior work; these are discussed later in the chapter.

A psychologist once told me that plasterers have fewer mental problems than any other group because they are able to work off their aggressions by slinging plaster in all directions. If you employ a plasterer, be prepared to clean the material off any adjacent surfaces, because plasterers do seem to be messy. If you do your own work, you may not get the aggressive, work-off advantages, but may get the reverse. In the beginning the plaster will suddenly become the slipperiest, most contrary material you've ever encountered, and will tend to slide off your trowel (and the wall) on the floor and your shoes.

EXTERIOR PLASTERING

The plaster on the exterior provides a waterproof covering over the adobe walls. Traditionally this plaster is merely more of the same mud that the adobes are made of, but with a slightly higher clay content. It is placed by hand, and smoothed with a small piece of sheepskin. There is a great beauty in a hand-finished surface using this method, but it has several drawbacks. The main one is that the mud plaster is not as waterproof as cement plaster, and will require more frequent maintenance. Most of the Pueblo Indians still use mud plaster. (It is my understanding that among the Pueblos most of the plastering work is done by women, who seem to have more skill. I tried to sell this program to my wife without much success!) Mud walls (adobe or mud plaster) erode more slowly than you might suspect. One inch per 20 years is average in the Southwest, but concentrated flows from roof drainage can be disastrous. Repair and resurfacing of mud plaster is easier than cement stucco! Just dampen the surface and smooth with a sheepskin; add more dirt as required.

REINFORCING (stucco mesh or "chicken wire") should be used on the exterior. Some codes require that this be of 18 ga. galvanized mesh; other codes require only 20 ga. This mesh is nailed to the adobe with 16d nails and serves as reinforcing to prevent the plaster from coming off in large patches. Any plaster surface will crack eventually, from settling and shrinkage. The bond (adhesive quality) of plaster to an adobe wall is rather fragile under the best circumstances, and as hairline cracks develop, they will admit moisture, further deteriorating the bond between the wall and the plaster; thus, the mesh provides important reinforcement. Re-stuccoing should be counted on as a maintenance chore that must be done at regular intervals, just as painting must be done. It may come as a surprise that re-stuccoing is comparable in cost to painting a wall. If a wall has been painted, it may be difficult to get a new stucco coat to adhere, unless all loose material is removed, and a bonding agent, such as "Stucco Bond," applied before the new stucco is put on. Mud plaster does not require chicken wire.

STUCCO for exterior walls is usually applied in three coats, to a total thickness of approximately ¾″. The first coat is called the "scratch" coat, and provides the primary bond with the adobe wall. It is sometimes "scratched" with a rake or some such instrument just prior to drying, to provide a "key" or tooth for the additional coats. This scratch coat provides the first and toughest waterproof bond with the adobe wall. The second coat is called the "brown" coat, and is a filler to smooth the wall surfaces and fill depressions in the surface.

The reason for several coats is because plaster cannot be applied too thickly in any one application or shrinkage cracks will develop, or it will tend to slump (fall) off the wall. I'm sure all of you have had the experience of trying to patch a hole in a plastered wall. If you try to do this all at one time, the smooth surface you have built up will show cracks several hours later. During hot, dry weather conditions, the scratch and brown coats may be applied on adobe walls shortly after one another in rapid sequence. An area of wall, perhaps 20′ in length, can be scratch coated and then the brown coat applied. The key to how rapidly this may be done is the dryness of the adobe wall, and the speed of drying of the scratch coat. The brown coat should be allowed to dry for at least a week or ten days, depending on the weather, and must be thoroughly cured before applying the final color coat. The brown coat should be wet down with a hose daily for several days while it is curing, and just prior to application of the color coat. The same principles apply to plaster curing as do to concrete. (See Figure 15.1)

The color coat is of stucco and is very thin, seldom more than ⅛″. Ready-mixed colors are available in many attractive shades, but I prefer to use a basic color mix and then temper it with stucco color to achieve the color desired. Many ready-mixed colors are rather harsh, just as ready-mixed paint colors are. When you feel you have the color you want, spread a small patch on the wall and let it dry. It *must* be dry to determine what the final color will be. Usually, a small thin section of this will dry in a few minutes, so that it won't delay the job. It is my personal preference to achieve a color which echoes the adjacent earth color.

INTERIOR PLASTERING

The procedure for plastering the interior is about the same, except that you will not need the stucco mesh for reinforcing, and you may omit the "scratch" coat. You will, however, need to apply the brown coat, let it dry, and then apply a finish coat (which is not oriental stucco, however, but merely plaster and sand). If you want a smooth finish (usually for bathrooms and kitchens), you will use a special Keene's cement plaster. The smooth finish is achieved by careful troweling as the plaster sets, much as in smooth finishing of concrete. The Keene's cement and gauging plaster mix will set up very rapidly, so don't undertake too large an area at first. Experiment!

If you wish a textured finish, a thin mix of plaster material may be "dashed" on and smoothed with a trowel, creating swirl patterns or whatever effect you want to create. You may also use a sand finish. To achieve this, you must wait until the final coat is almost set up (dry). Rub out the surface with a wet sponge-rubber "float" until a smooth sandy surface is achieved. Timing is critical. Too late is too late; keep the float wet. This technique is also valuable in matching a patch to an existing wall, adding sand to the patching plaster mix.

If any of the plaster coats sets too fast, it will be soft and chalky. This may also happen near fireplaces or furnaces in the winter. This condition may be corrected by the addition of more water to the surface, even after it has dried.

THE MASONRY TEXTURE of the adobe wall may be retained by the following method. The adobe wall must be first water-brushed adequately to smooth away trowel marks, fill small holes and voids, and remove any loose sand or grit that might prevent your finish coat from bonding. After enough brushing and drying, check the surface of the wall with your hand to see if the surface has a tendency to "chalk" or show a dusty coating on your hand. If it does not do this, and the wall's appearance is to your satisfaction, you may then apply the finish.

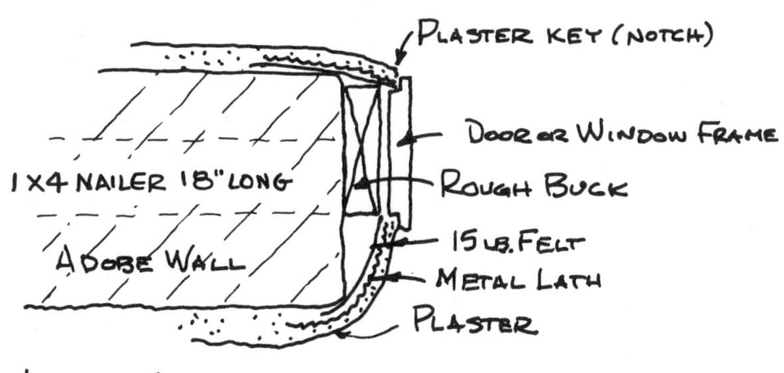

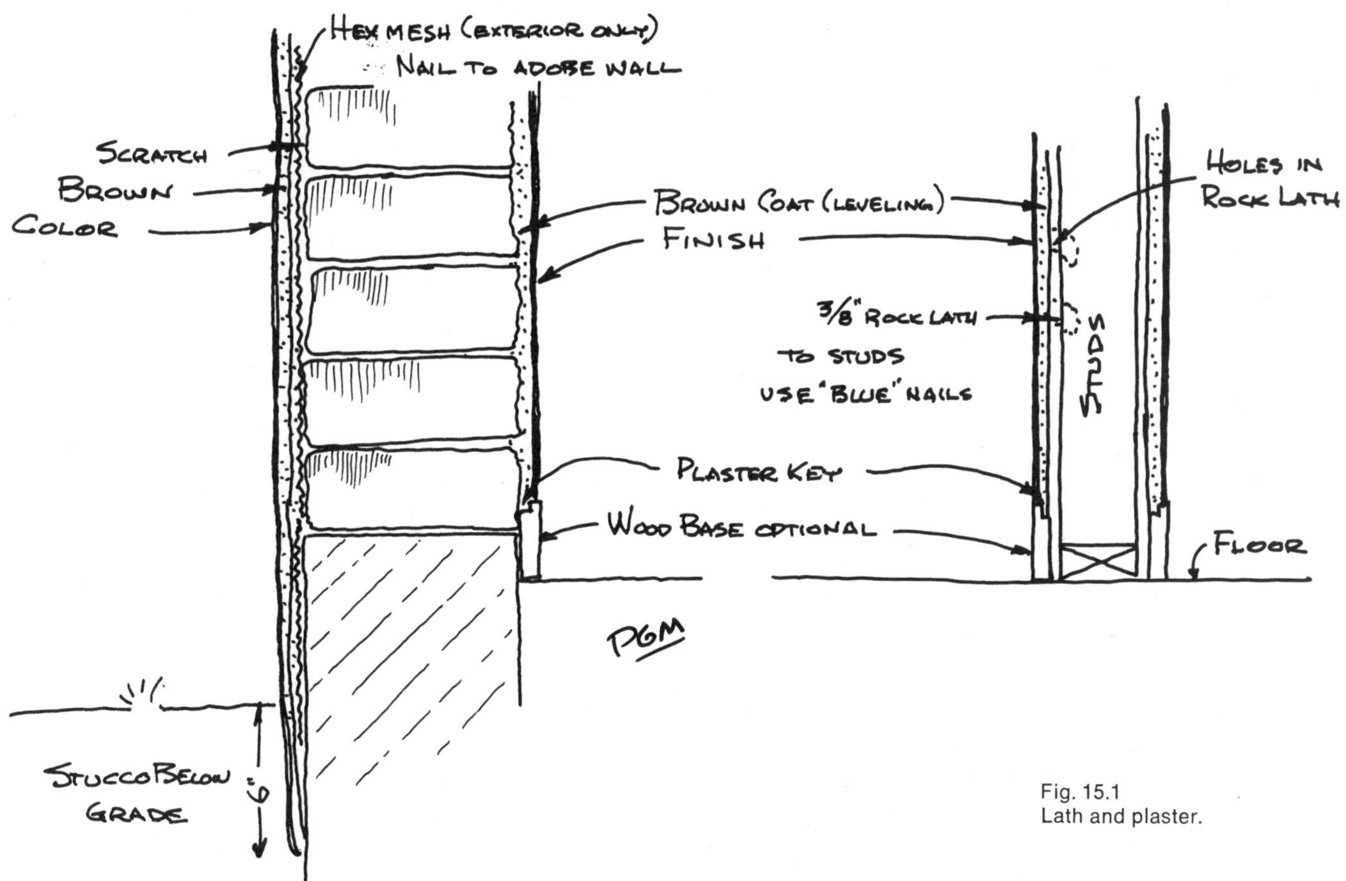

Fig. 15.1
Lath and plaster.

The surface should be sealed (sized) with a penetrating sealer if you plan to paint it, otherwise the paint will not cover. The same sealing is required for mud plaster to be painted. The oil base varnish for floors, diluted 50 percent with mineral spirits, will work, as will other commercial sealers. The resulting surface will be fragile, so children beware!

LATHING of frame walls and wood surfaces that are to be covered with plaster is a necessary but not too demanding job if you follow the rules. The first rule is that no wood surface may be covered with a coat of plaster without first protecting it from the moisture in the plaster. The moisture will cause the wood to swell, and then subsequently shrink, causing cracks in the plaster, or separation, and frequently the plaster will come off at this area. Use one layer of 15# asphalt felt for this purpose and then overlay it with a strip of metal lath.

The most common material for lathing of frame walls is rock lath. This is a gypsum-board

EXTERIOR

	Material	*Coverage*
Scratch Coat:	1 sack Portland cement ½ sack lime 25 scoops (#8 coal shovel) sand (richer with Portland on metal lath)	10-12 sq. yds.
Brown Coat:	Same, plus 15 scoops sand	10-12 sq. yds.
Color:	4 sacks colored stucco ½ sack lime (No sand. Add water until trowelable)	40–48 sq. yds.

INTERIOR

Brown Coat:	1 sack fibered plaster 20 scoops sand	10 sq. yds.
Finish:	1 sack unfibered plaster 10 scoops sand	12 sq. yds.
Smooth:	1 sack Keene's cement 2 sacks lime 1 scoop gauging plaster	30 sq. yds.

Fig. 15.2 Plaster mixes.

material with holes in it to hold the plaster. It is purchased in bundles of sheets 16″ x 48″ x ⅜″, each bundle containing 32 square feet (6 sheets). It can be cut and trimmed easily with a knife. One side is scored and then the sheet is broken, and the other side cut. It is generally applied with blued lathing nails, which are more resistant to rust and are not so likely to bleed rust stains through the plaster as it dries. There are different coefficients of expansion with transitions from wood to adobe, to rock lath, and so forth, and these are normally best bridged over by expanded metal lath. This metal lath can be purchased in large sheets that can be cut to size with a pair of tin snips (wear gloves because it is vicious), or it can be obtained in narrow strips already bent for corners and the like.

It is particularly important to reinforce bullnose corners with felt and metal lath, where an adobe wall meets with a wood frame or surface. The frame is best "plaster keyed" (a continuous rabbet at the intersecting edge). If the door frame should loosen from vibration, the plaster will tend to crack off in long strips at this point if not reinforced.

MIXES

The mixes for your various plastering operations are detailed in Figure 15.2.

Don't be afraid to experiment. Try different textures in different small areas, perhaps in a closet or some area that won't be exposed readily to view.

DRYWALL

Drywall may be your choice for covering interior frame walls. I prefer plaster, but drywall provides a smoother, more level surface, if it is properly installed and finished. Inasmuch as you must have a plasterer on the job, for the exterior at least, the economy of drywall may not be as great, since its installation requires a different craft, or at least different tools if you plan to do it yourself.

Drywall material provides a smooth paintable surface in itself. The sheets are nailed on the studs, with as smooth a joint as you can manage. It is sometimes better to apply these sheets to the wall in a horizontal position rather than vertical to reduce the number of vertical joints. Badly finished horizontal joints are less noticeable. If you have followed your stud layout, 16″ o.c., the ends of the drywall sheets (4′ or 8′) will fall at the center of a stud. If not, you must cut the sheet so that it will. You cannot leave loose ends unsupported. The edges should be nailed on approximately 8″ centers and the intermediate studs nailed at about 16″. After the board material is in place, the joints must then be taped and bedded. A smooth layer of drywall bedding compound is applied to the joint with a "broad knife" (6″) and a layer of perforated drywall tape is bedded in this joint with the same knife. Do not press too hard with the knife, or you may cause bubbles later from stretching the wet tape, or voids from forcing too much joint cement out with your knife. The nails and hammer marks (nails should be embedded slightly below the surface) are also smoothed over with this compound and the broad knife. This compound must then be allowed to dry, at least overnight. The room should be at least 65 degrees, since the mud will be slower in setting and may even freeze at a lower temperature.

The next step is to "float" the joints, with a slightly curved drywall trowel. This smooths up the rougher surfaces and depressions left by the broad knife to spread irregularities over a wide area. This should be allowed to dry overnight as well. After drying, the joints should be sanded smooth. If you have done a rough job with the broad knife and trowel, it will require a lot of hard sanding; less sanding if smoother.

Texturing is then done if you wish. It is merely the application of an additional coat of the same bedding compound, but applied with a paint roller, brush, or trowel. Thin the mix with water to obtain the best consistency for your texture. Remember while sanding that the texture won't cover uneven, badly floated joints. A badly floated joint will still be visible under a rough texture.

A waterproof type of sheetrock should be used behind areas that are to receive ceramic tile. This is called "tile backer board" and is almost identical to standard gypsum board except that it is resistant to moisture.

CERAMIC TILE

Installing ceramic tile is one of the fun parts of the job for most people. Good ceramic tile is manufactured to unbelievably precise standards. These standards will be more important to the tile mechanic than to you; however, you should recognize the problems. If you are to stack a series of tiles one on top of another, as you must for any sizeable area of shower stall or tub splash, you must keep the vertical lines straight or the appearance will be sloppy. The accumulated difference of a few thousandths of an inch on each tile can create quite a curve by the time you get six feet high. Consequently, you want to start with a plumb vertical line (and horizontal too), as determined by a long level (don't count on the tub or floor being a guide). The tile will be about ¼″ thick and you will have to finish this off at the edges, go around corners, both inside and out, and cut pieces to fit. For this purpose there are a large number of trim pieces available. Familiarize yourself with the various shapes so that you will be able to order what you need. They fall, generally, into two categories, one for "surface" mounting (to a flat surface) and the other for "radius" or "mud bed" type application. The "field" tile will be the same in either case. Radius trim covers the additional thickness of a "mud bed" projection out from the wall.

CUTTING ceramic tile can be a nasty job if you don't have the right tools. Many tile suppliers will loan or rent these to you. Simple cutting may be done with a tile cutter (very similar to the glass cutter), where the tile is just scored and snapped. The more complicated cuts will require a diamond-blade tub saw. You will find this useful throughout the job for cutting bricks, stone, and other hard materials. It may be wise to try to rent or even buy one for your job, with the intention of selling it later. The market for used tub saws is quite good. A pair of tile "nippers" is a good addition to your toolbox. These are used to "nibble" corners and irregular cuts, split tile, and "nibble" holes for pipes. Circular-blade hacksaws are useful for curved cuts.

Smooth the cut edges with a carborundum stone.

SURFACE MOUNTING is the easier of the two application methods. Once a flat surface has been prepared, of either cement plaster and metal lath, or of drywall (tile backer board is better), the tile is glued into place with either an organic mastic, or by "thin set," which is a portland-latex mixture. The layout here, as in most phases of construction, is of the utmost importance. At typical layout is shown in Figure 15.3. The layout will be the same whether you use the surface or radius type, except for the thickness. It cannot be emphasized too much that the surface to which the tile will be applied MUST be plumb, level, and smooth. It takes a longer distance to go around a curve than to follow a straight line. If the surface is not flat, level, and plumb, the joints on the tile will tend to creep, and will not match. In small areas of tile, this is not too important, but for big areas it is vital.

THE MUD-BED method merely provides approximately an additional ⅜″ thickness where the field tile will occur, with radius trim reaching to the main wall surface. This may be built up by the use of metal lath. (The perforations have an up-and-down angle. If you install the lath upside down, the mud will slide off.) Screed strips should be applied absolutely dead plumb and level, and the rich portland-cement plaster screeded from these. After the preliminary set, the screed strips may be removed and the voids filled with more plaster. It is easiest to provide such a bed one day, and apply the tile the next, with thin-set mortar. Follow the directions on the package for mixing.

FASTENING the tile to the prepared surface is quite simple. Place a temporary level strip of wood at the bottom, less than one full tile above the starting point. This is because, in 99 cases out of 100, the bathtub or surface from which you start the tile is not level. It is easier to attach the level strip, work upwards from that, and then cut the bottom row of tile in to fit. By using less than a full tile for the bottom cut row, you will avoid unsightly gaps of grout, or irregular tile in the wall higher up.

Buy or borrow a notched trowel (⅜″ x ⅜″ notches) and spread the thin-set mortar over a fairly small area. Don't spread the mortar over a larger area than you will be able to apply the tile to quickly, for it sets rapidly. Start at the bottom and merely stack the tile in place, following your center guidelines previously established. Start on the line and then build out from there. Take care in your layout so that you won't require just a sliver at either end, since slivers are difficult to place. It may be best, for your early efforts at least, to use an "ashlar" pattern that staggers all vertical joints.

GROUTING your tile is the final step. This involves making a mix of grout powder (almost pure white kaolin clay) and water. It should be mixed to the consistency of thick whipping cream and spread on the surface of the tile with a rubber squeegee, which helps force it down in the cracks and crevices between the tile. After it takes an initial set, it is wiped off with a wet sponge, allowed to dry more, and wiped again. The final glazed surface of the tile is wiped with a dry rag. Be careful during the cleanup with the sponge not to leave too much in the joints or wipe out too much. You will be able to tell the correct amount as you do this.

Caution: When using thin-set mortars and grout, it is important that you wear rubber gloves or coat your hands with a protective cream of some sort. This wet mix is extremely alkaline, caustic, and will damage the skin on your hands almost like acid. Take precautions to protect your skin.

MEXICAN DECORATIVE TILE can be an attractive addition to your adobe home. Several comments might be made on this. First, this tile is quite intense in color, and a little of it goes a long way. It will be difficult to match the trim pieces that will be required. This tile is not as precise in size as you can expect in good domestic tile, so large areas will be difficult to deal with. You may wish to embed individual pieces of the tile in wall and in fireplace surfaces. If you plan to do this, apply them at the completion of the brown plaster coat, with thin-set mortar. The brown coat may have to be chipped to accommodate the tile thickness. The finish plaster coat will enclose the tiles smoothly. Adding the tiles

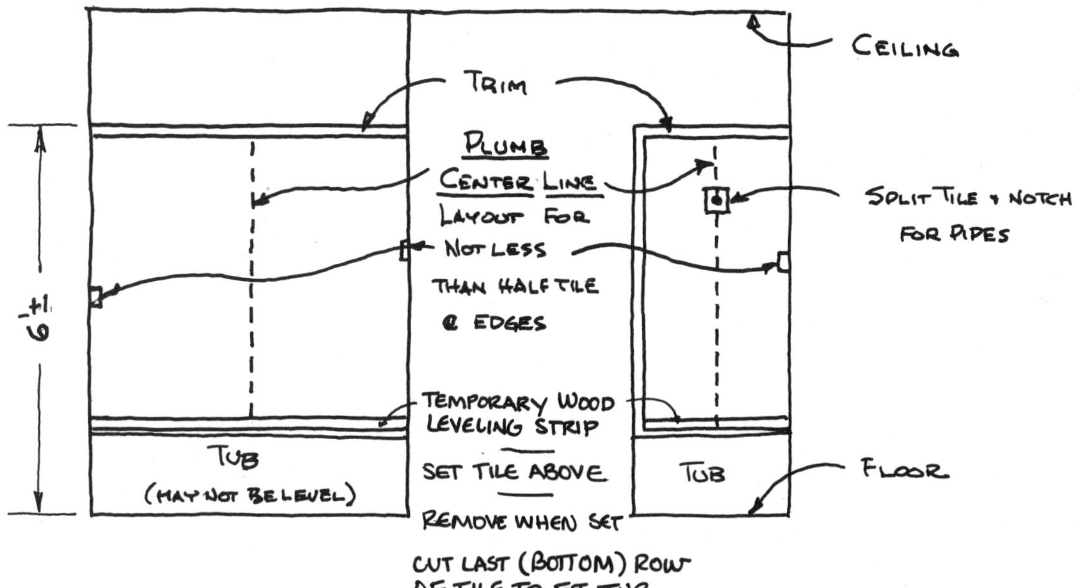

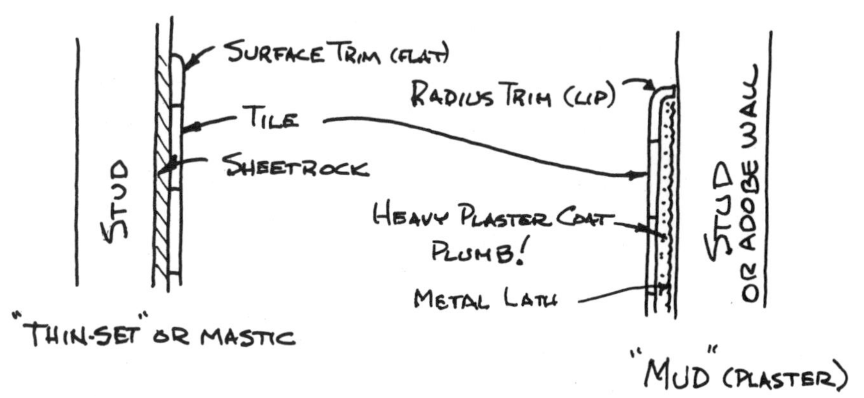

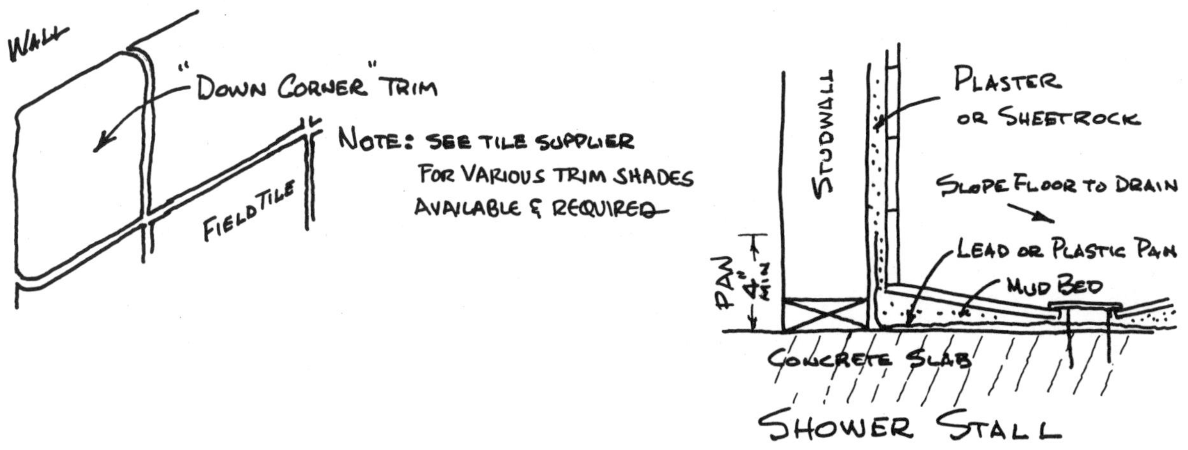

Fig. 15.3 Ceramic tile installation.

can be done after finish plastering, but the end result will not be as smooth, since you will have to patch the edges.

SHOWER PANS need some special treatment. The drain in the floor will not carry off the water from the shower rapidly enough to prevent a "head" of water from building up in the bottom of the shower. The corners must be absolutely water tight, or the resulting leakage will damage plaster and walls, even in adjacent rooms. The cement bed and the grout between the tiles cannot be counted upon to stay completely water tight. Thus, you must provide a separate "pan" right at the beginning. This is best made of seamless sheet lead. This can be easily shaped, with the corners and edges folded and bent up to at least a distance of 4″. If a sheet-rock backing is to be used on the walls, it should be clear of the shower pan, and not extend down into it since a wick action will result, letting the water creep up into the vulnerable walls. The drain on the shower floor must extend slightly above the rough concrete slab, in order to have room for the tile. The floor of the shower is filled with a rich cement mortar that is only damp, not wet, and sloped to the drain, allowing enough for the thickness of the tile. The tile is then placed with thin-set mortar, and allowed to dry. Then the walls may be covered as previously outlined (see Fig. 15.3).

FLOOR TILE of the thick Mexican variety, or quarry tile, must be set in the same manner as the shower floor, using a rich, damp mix of portland and sand, leveling and placing tile as you go, or you may use a thin-set type of mortar if your slab is quite accurate. The thickness of Mexican tile will vary considerably, and some allowance must be made to level up even in the thin-set method. This may be accomplished by adding sand to the thin-set mortar mix. Up to 50 percent sand may be added, or you may buy a premixed material. Using a ½″ notched trowel, and a stiff mix, you then gently tap the tiles into a level position with a rubber mallet. The tile should be soaked in water overnight prior to application over a damp mortar bed. Soaking need not be done using "thin set" mortars. Try a small area first before attempting a big one.

16

Cabinets and Countertops

CABINETS AND COUNTERTOPS for your home should be selected with even more care than you take with the furnishings. You will have to live with them for a long time, for they cannot easily be changed. They must be thoughtfully planned for convenience, durably built to give many years of trouble-free service, and at the same time provide an attractive decorative touch.

CABINETS

You will have three general types from which to choose: job-built, custom-built, or prefabricated stock units. The first two are self-explanatory, and the last ones work quite well, since many modular ranges of sizes and arrangements are available. If you wish to do the work yourself, you must be prepared, with tools, to do some very exacting carpentry. If you plan on a rough motif, the work will not be so critical. Shop-made cabinets can be made economically with power tools, in a fraction of the time and probably of better quality than they can be made on the job. The prefab units can be economical and quite satisfactory as well. The finishing of cabinets can be done by you, or your painter if you hire one, but if they are to be stained, lacquer-finished cabinets, it is perhaps advisable to have this shop-done by the cabinet manufacturer. A better and more economical job may result.

THE ANATOMY OF A CABINET may re-require a little explanation. A cabinet is basically a frame, covered with plywood or finished material on any side that will be exposed to view.

The front-finished face frame must be arranged with openings to receive the doors and hinges. Base cabinets must have a toe space at the bottom so you can stand against the cabinet without bumping your toes. There must be finished sides where exposed and perhaps even a back, depending on the basic wall material against which the cabinet will be placed. The finished countertop height should be of a standard dimension (36″), unless of course you have some good reason for changing it. The type and thickness of the top material determines exactly how high the frame should be. As a general rule, the countertops are fabricated separately from the cabinets, and installed after the base cabinets have been set. A typical cross section of base and wall units is shown in Figure 16.1.

If you stay with standard sizes and dimensions, you will increase the number of possible accessories that are available, such as dishwashers. They are made to fit in standard dimensions. The sink size will determine part of the layout that you must make. The space directly under the countertop is lost at the sink area, so the most desirable arrangement of doors and shelves should be planned in advance. Most cabinet shops will not undertake to build cabinets until shop drawings showing major details have been approved by you. This helps prevent any misunderstandings.

DOORS for your cabinets come in a wide variety. You may choose flush doors, which fit level with the face frames. Most doors, however, are ⅜″ offset, so that the door has a lip on all sides that fits around the opening in the face frame,

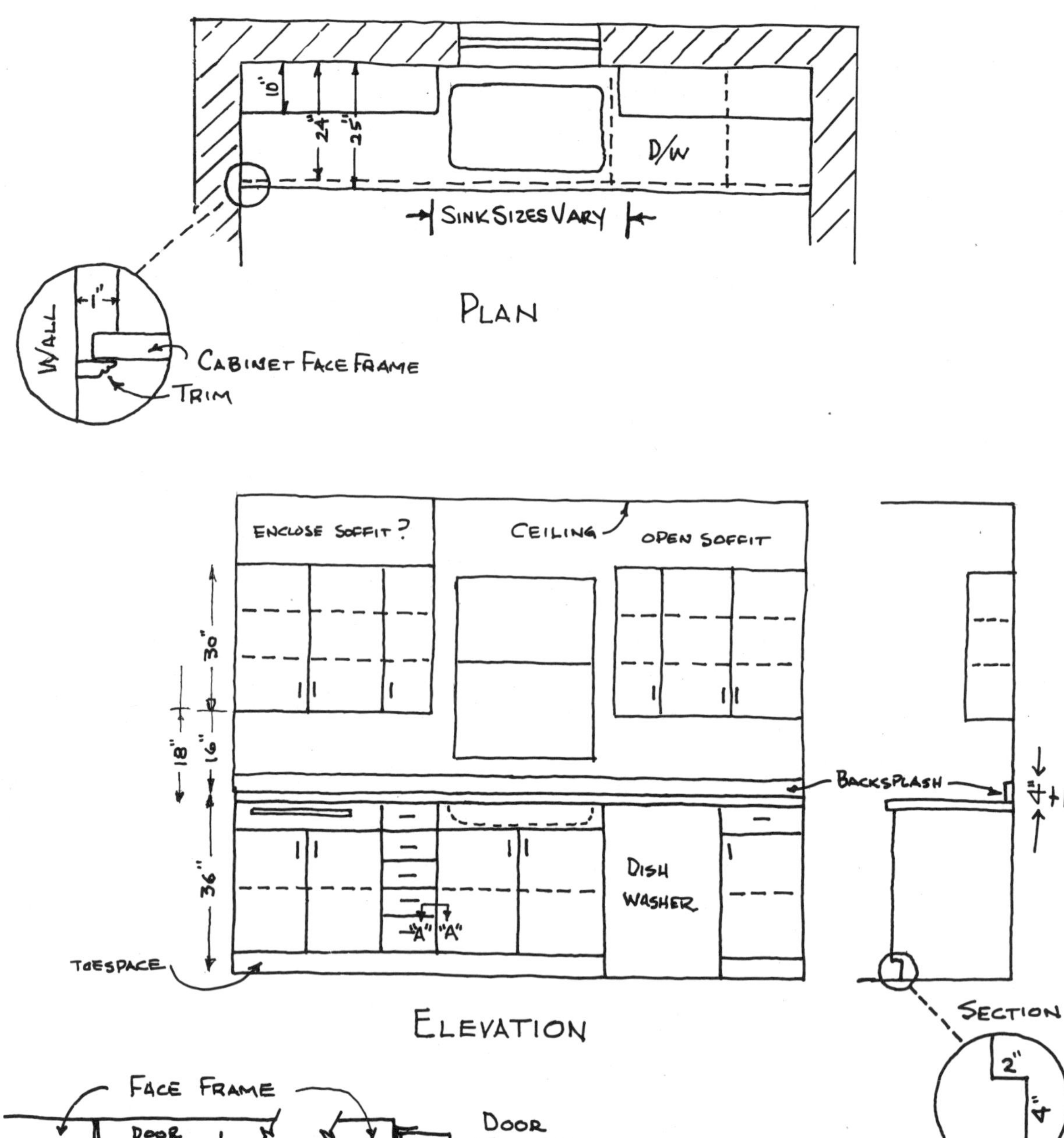

Fig. 16.1 Cabinets.

and helps conceal minor irregularities that would be very apparent in flush doors. The doors themselves can be made of a plain sheet of plywood that is routed and patterned for the edge lip, or of special veneer plywoods for flush doors, or even of pressed hardboard that needs only painting. Incidentally, there is a difference between paint-grade plywood and plywood that is intended to be stained. Sound paint-grade plywood may have plugs that will provide a smooth surface but would be unsightly with a clear stain. Specify!

Panel doors can be of virtually any pattern. Most cabinet manufacturers have samples of each type they are set up to manufacture, and may charge a higher price per door for patterns that differ from these. The cabinets are generally figured at so much per lineal foot, which includes standard doors. If you specify premium doors, there is an additional price per door, regardless of size, since the labor in fabricating a small door is the same as a large one. Extremely large cabinet doors have a tendency to warp; thus, such doors should be only as large as is absolutely necessary. If one must be large enough to approach the size of a regular door, use the regular door, cut down if necessary.

ACCESSORIES for your cabinets are almost endless, and include built-in cutting boards or "butcher" tops that slide into the base cabinets; pull-out shelves; electric-mixer stands that pop out and up to convenient height like a typewriter in a desk; cup and silver racks; vertical dividers for serving trays; and countless more. Other more sophisticated accessories include "power tops" that provide spindles to operate such appliances as mixers, blenders, and juicers. The "Lazy Susan" arrangement of a corner often provides usable space that might be largely lost otherwise. I suggest that you visit a large kitchen-cabinet supplier and see what he has to offer. You'll see many good ideas and you may want to incorporate at least some of them in your design.

FITTING the cabinets to a given wall space is a little tricky, but if the cabinets are properly made, they will provide enough room for the necessary scribing (cutting to an irregular surface) to be done. Very few walls are exactly plumb and square; plastered surfaces are particularly uneven. The face frame of a cabinet usually protrudes at least 1″ on each side more than the cabinet frame itself, so the face frame can be scribed to the existing wall. If there are any resulting gaps, they are usually closed with a piece of millwork trim, finished in the same manner as the cabinets themselves. Anchoring wall cabinets in an adobe wall can be troublesome. The simplest method is to provide nailer strips in between the adobes as they are laid up. If you have not done this, sizeable wood dowels may be inserted, in holes drilled in the adobe wall, after being coated with casein glue; the cabinets are then attached with sheet-metal screws. Do not figure cabinets to fit too tightly in a given space. Plan on some method for a little adjustment, which may be closed with a molding.

FINISHING of your cabinets is best done in the shop where they are made. The cost of finishing them in the field, in place, will usually far exceed shop finishing where spray equipment and ideal controlled conditions can be obtained. Many cabinet makers will charge approximately 15 percent additional for finishing, which is more economical than a painter on the job.

Special effects can be economically achieved, particularly on a do-it-yourself basis. Very plain cabinets can be transformed by several methods ranging from the use of shotgun pellets for worm holes (be careful!), to "antiquing" with a short length of chain, wallpaper, or even shellacked newsprint. Plain cabinets can be panelized by the addition of millwork moldings. Sometimes decorative Mexican tile can be added either flush or appliqued with a molding finish.

It would seem desirable to use old wood to make antique cabinets. But, in the main, this is perhaps the most expensive route you can take, since the wood will be warped in most cases, and all but impossible to make fit smoothly. The same is true of rough-sawn wood. This, and any solid lumber, is quite difficult to work because of existing or potential warpage. Plywood is much more stable.

COUNTERTOPS

Tops for your cabinets must have two main features, durability and beauty. A wide selection of materials is available, each having its own advantages and drawbacks, and cost. Some of these are discussed below.

PLASTIC LAMINATE tops (such as Formica and Micarta) are perhaps the most versatile. They are stain resistant, reasonably economical, and available in an endless number of patterns and colors to fit any decor. Their main drawback is that they can be damaged by hot pans, knives, and sharp instruments. A popular misconception is that Formica-type material is resistant to heat; this is not true with standard material. It will discolor (brown) if the article is hot enough, or may bubble (separate from the plywood top) even under moderate heat. When this type of top is used, provision should be made for an area adjacent to the stove to place hot pans. This can be of ceramic tile, or marble in a relatively small panel. If not desirable full width, a section can be routed out deep enough to receive the thickness of your heat-resistant panel.

The plastic laminate tops are attached to a ¾″ sheet of "shop"-grade plywood with contact cement. This cement is a rubber-base type that is brushed on the pieces to be glued, allowed to dry, and then the two pieces are pressed together. Contact cement is rather tricky to work with, because when the two glued surfaces touch, they are permanently attached and cannot be shifted. It is best to have the plastic-laminate sheet slightly oversize, and then place waxed paper or some sort of spacers between the two surfaces you are laminating, to allow for final positioning. The waxed paper or spacers can be carefully removed as the sheet of laminate is lowered to make contact with the other coated surface. If this lowering is begun without having perfect alignment of the two surfaces, *disaster!* To make this alignment process easier, you can cut the plastic sheet a bit oversize, so that it protrudes slightly beyond the edge of the surface to which you are laminating it. The excess can then be cut off with a router, or a file.

CERAMIC TILE makes an attractive top for base cabinets, but has several serious disadvantages. The first, of course, is cost. Tiles are expensive, even when you install them yourself. Secondly, the joints between the tiles have a tendency to collect dirt and grease, and are difficult to keep clean. Thirdly, the surface is quite hard, and anything dropped on it will either shatter the dropped object or chip the surface of the tile.

The ceramic tile top must be built in place. The common wood top from which you must work is ¾″ plywood attached to the cabinet. This must be protected with a layer of 15# asphalt felt, and then with a sheet of expanded metal lath. A plaster bed with a thickness of at least ½″ must then be troweled on to provide a smooth, flat surface onto which the ceramic tile can be cemented.

The tile is then applied as detailed earlier, either by providing a true surface which can be worked after it is hard and dry with thin set, or by the "mud-set" wet method, where the tile is soaked, and tapped into position in a bed of soft mortar. For this application, trim is extremely important at the edges. The most suitable type is called a "sink rail." If the edge trim is not attached securely, it will repeatedly come loose or get broken, and be almost impossible to fix without retiling the whole top. A decorative wood strip may be used in place of the sink rail-trim more easily.

SIMULATED MARBLE tops of epoxy resins are available in many places at a price that is competitive with plastic laminates. The material is heat resistant and comes in a variety of colors. Frequently the manufacturer will have molds whereby lavatory sinks can be made of the same material, cast integrally with the top. The fabrication of these tops should be left to the professional manufacturers.

LINOLEUM tops need hardly be considered, because they are vulnerable to heat, abrasion, and moisture, and are not particularly economical after you have bought special metal trim shapes to trim out the edges.

A BACKSPLASH is a necessary part of your top structure, to finish out the work, and to prevent liquids from running down any void that may exist between the top and the wall. It may be made integrally with the top, or you may wish to use decorative colored tile that enhances the "hand-made" appearance of your home.

CUTTING BOARDS are a nice addition to kitchen countertops, providing a cutting surface (which will also take hot pans), and a change of texture and color in the room. To be completely satisfactory these must be made of a thick, laminated hardwood (maple is the most common). These can be purchased prefabricated from most kitchen-supply establishments in several sizes.

17

Paints and Stains

WOOD SURFACES that are exposed to the weather are normally protected from the elements by a protective coating of some sort — most commonly paint. If the paint idea does not appeal to you, it is quite in keeping with the adobe motif to let the wood weather naturally and turn the silver gray that is attractive in "old" adobe homes. The main drawback is the fact that it takes a number of years to achieve this effect naturally, and in the meantime, the wood will have a new raw look.

The selection of surfaces that will be treated must be made with some care. The sun in the Southwest seriously affects any surface that is exposed to it. If the wood members are sufficiently large, a natural weathering will result. If they are not, as in the case of window mullions, and slender trim, the continued, unprotected exposure may cause dry rot, warping, and failure of the purpose of the wood. Thus, perhaps we can make the statement that windows, doors, and the like should be protected, but you need not give as much concern to vigas, beams, and lintels.

You may choose to let an exposed surface weather naturally whether it is wood, concrete, or whatever. However, if you paint a surface, you must count on the continuing need to paint it at regular intervals.

It makes sense, therefore, to choose materials that will require as little maintenance as possible. Choose a good grade of paint for this purpose. Many new chemical discoveries have outdated traditional materials so that you now have a wider choice of coatings. The preparation of the surface for the paint is probably as much work as the painting itself. You must have a smooth, dry, tight surface, or the paint will separate from the surface long before it has actually deteriorated itself. Provide a well-prepared surface, use good material, and you won't have to paint so often. The application of the next required coat of paint should be done prior to the time that the surface and old paint need extensive preparation. Ask the advice of a reputable paint store for the best possible material for your particular application. The priming of wood moldings that are to be painted can be done before installation, which will speed up the hand work considerably. Repainting of existing surfaces can be a problem where incompatible earlier paints or surfaces will not accept some of the new coatings. Check with a qualified paint dealer for possible problems.

RE-STUCCOING of exterior masonry or plaster surfaces usually makes more sense than painting them. It may come as a surprise that the cost of re-stucco may be only slightly more than painting. First of all, you must recognize that paint will not fill cracks, on any surface. If you paint a stucco surface, you may be creating new problems, in that if the paint doesn't bond properly (and it frequently doesn't because of dust, chemical incompatibility, and so on) it may not last as long as you had expected. Then, at that point, you decide to re-stucco. Bad news! The old paint is loose in places and it must be removed by sandblasting, with a wire brush, or with some such method that may cost more than the paint job in the first place. In most cases, it is necessary to apply a bonding agent such as Stucco Bond to seal and size the old paint surface before you can re-stucco.

Exterior colored stucco will not do for interior finish work in place of paint. The colored stucco will not cure evenly indoors, creating odd-colored spots.

INTERIOR PAINT is not quite as critical as the exterior, because it won't be subjected to the same abuse from wind and sun. Again, though, you must carefully prepare the surface. Paint for walls and woodwork can be oil, latex, acrylic, or others of a wide choice. A frequent error, however, is to try to use a "flat" (not shiny) paint on doors, windows, and other wood surfaces. Flat paint on wood surfaces will show grime much more readily, and will not present as pleasing an appearance. The full "gloss" finish can be objectionable, too. There is a middle ground that seems to be most satisfactory. This is the semi-gloss or "satin" finish. This type of finish will look seasoned without the glossy glare.

COLORS for your home can pose difficult choices. Most factory-mixed colors do not appeal to me. They always seem too harsh or raw, or too intense. It will simplify matters if you are able to settle on one color for walls (flat paint) and trim (satin-finish enamel) to be used throughout. A few simple experiments with a color wheel will help educate you in the mixing of colors. It is amazing what a little dab of black or red can do to a can of "white" paint. Painted surfaces will pick up the colors that are adjacent to them. And the same paint will look different on the north, south, in shadow, and so forth. *Experiment!*

A color that is warm and may be entirely satisfactory on the rooms having a south exposure, may look like prison gray on the north side. The color will be different under artificial light, as compared to natural sunlight, direct or indirect. It is possible to coordinate your wall colors so that they will complement drapes, carpeting, and other major color items in the room. This may be accomplished by the addition of minute amounts of the color of the accessories to the basic wall paint.

STAINS are the area where you can let your imagination run wild! Many attractive stains can be purchased ready mixed, and which work beautifully. They come clear or opaque, and will vary in color depending on the surface to which they are applied. Stains can further be broken down into two types, one which must be wiped off after application, and the other which can be sprayed, and left alone with no further treatment. I prefer the latter, if the proper effect can be achieved.

Ever since an old painter explained to me how stains are made, my Scottish ancestry seems to urge me to make my own. A stain is made up mostly of very economical materials. The main ingredient is mineral spirits. To this you must add a small amount of linseed oil to give a little more body, and some drier (clear varnish will do) to insure that it won't stay tacky. The stain is colored, of course, by oil-base pigment. My procedure for making stain is as follows:

Put a gallon of mineral spirits in a large bucket. Then, in a smaller can, mix small quantities of mineral spirits, linseed oil, varnish, and the color pigments of your choice. You may find that the pigment doesn't want to dissolve in the thin liquid; if so, add a touch of lacquer thinner, which seems to break this down into a mixable solution. Spread this mixture on a test board of the same material and finish as the wood on which you will be applying the stain and adjust the colors as necessary. *Note:* keep track of how many teaspoons of what pigment you have used so that you can mix a larger quantity if necessary. Add varnish and clear linseed oil in whatever proportion seems to give you a usable mixture. Very simple!

The resulting mix can be sprayed on a ceiling or wood area without further treatment. If you spray, make sure you use a mask of some sort, and protect all surfaces in the room that might be damaged or discolored by the overspray. It works out best to spray the ceilings prior to the painting of the walls. That way, you can be as sloppy as you like. If the room has been plastered, and wood surfaces to be stained are adjacent to the plaster, make sure that all the excess plaster has been cleaned off the wood prior to spraying, or it will mask the area where you want stain.

If you use a wiped stain, it is generally better to do the staining prior to erection of the beams and deck. You can do this work on the ground on a couple of sawhorses. This is much easier than having the stain run down your arm, working from a ladder. You won't be able to do a perfect job this way, and there will be some touch-up required, but certainly it is much easier than doing it all up in the air.

ANTIQUE FINISHES can be achieved, but the process is difficult. I have never found one that satisfied me completely. Some builders and painters have such a finish, but in most cases it is a closely guarded secret. The application of a single stain or pigment will not do. It will require several coats or treatments, with widely differing materials or colors. The wood may be "distressed" by the application of acid — which will give it a sort of rotted look — that is then neutralized with soda. Next, a background color, dark gray, almost black, must be applied. Then comes the artistry of wiping or brushing on a lighter color. This can sometimes be done with a clay "grounding" material that is used as a base for treating canvases for oil painting. Paint is generally not suitable for this because it flows too much and covers too completely. Experiment with a large enough piece to get a variety of wood textures and absorption rates. One prominent stain manufacturer advertises an exterior "bleached" stain that will acquire a weathered look within one year. I haven't tried it, but it may work!

18

Fireplaces

BUILD AS MANY FIREPLACES as you can afford! They will give a sense of warmth and solidity to your home that can't be achieved in any other way. The trend to modern motifs and our more sophisticated heating and air-conditioning systems have caused a decline in their popularity. Some fussy housekeepers object to the dirt and mess that they create, and they do cause dirt, but I feel that they are well worth the trouble. They are also a great comfort when the electric power goes out and a picnic effect can be enjoyed as a change of pace. One of the most enjoyable breakfasts I ever had was the first house we ever moved into, a day ahead of the power company's hookup, and we had to fix breakfast in the fireplace. *Great!*

Practical considerations do almost rule out the fireplace as the sole method of heating our homes, however. It is an inefficient way, and the cutting (or buying) of enough firewood would be most uneconomical. Let your imagination run wild then, and make your fireplaces as decorative as possible, but still workable with the least amount of effort and discomfort.

A fireplace is a delicate piece of work, in spite of its great weight and size. The proportions of its anatomy must be carefully planned to get the right combination that will draw well, without smoking, and without burning too fast. I remember one in Michigan, without a damper, that ate logs like a boiler on a ship, and it was almost a full-time job to stand in front of it and feed wood into it. This situation was finally corrected by modifying the opening in the face with a glass screen to control the draft. The manufacturers of fireplace dampers and accessories will gladly provide you with charts and tables showing the proper relationship between firebox size (opening), flue size, and height.

If these are not correct, your fireplace will not draw properly, and either will smoke up the place, blackening the face and mantel, or will burn too rapidly, requiring too much wood. Most masons who specialize in fireplace construction are artists of a sort, and are almost all rather cantankerous. They are always proud of their work and resent any criticism, however well meant, and sometimes even any questions. If you employ a mason for this, treat him with great diplomacy. If you do your own, then you can be cantankerous.

Circulating fireplaces are sometimes a wise choice, particularly for the amateur builder, since most of the hard part of cutting and fitting firebrick is unnecessary. The pre-built units can provide an excellent source of heat, which may be of great value in climatic zones where heating need only be nominal. These units are discussed at greater length later in the chapter.

ANATOMY OF A FIREPLACE

The various parts of a typical fireplace are shown in Figure 18.1. These are:

FOUNDATION. This is a thick, concrete slab normally at least 12″ thick and 4″ larger than the basic fireplace structure. The foundation is better overbuilt than underbuilt, since there

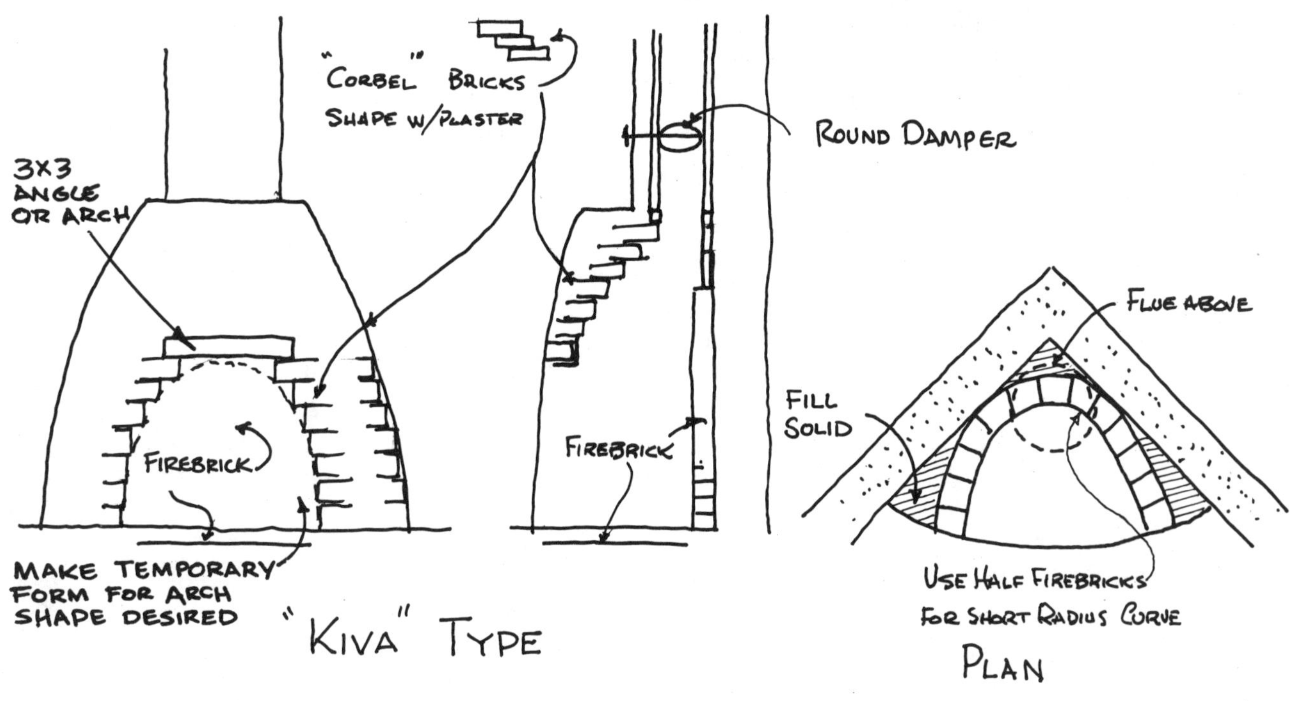

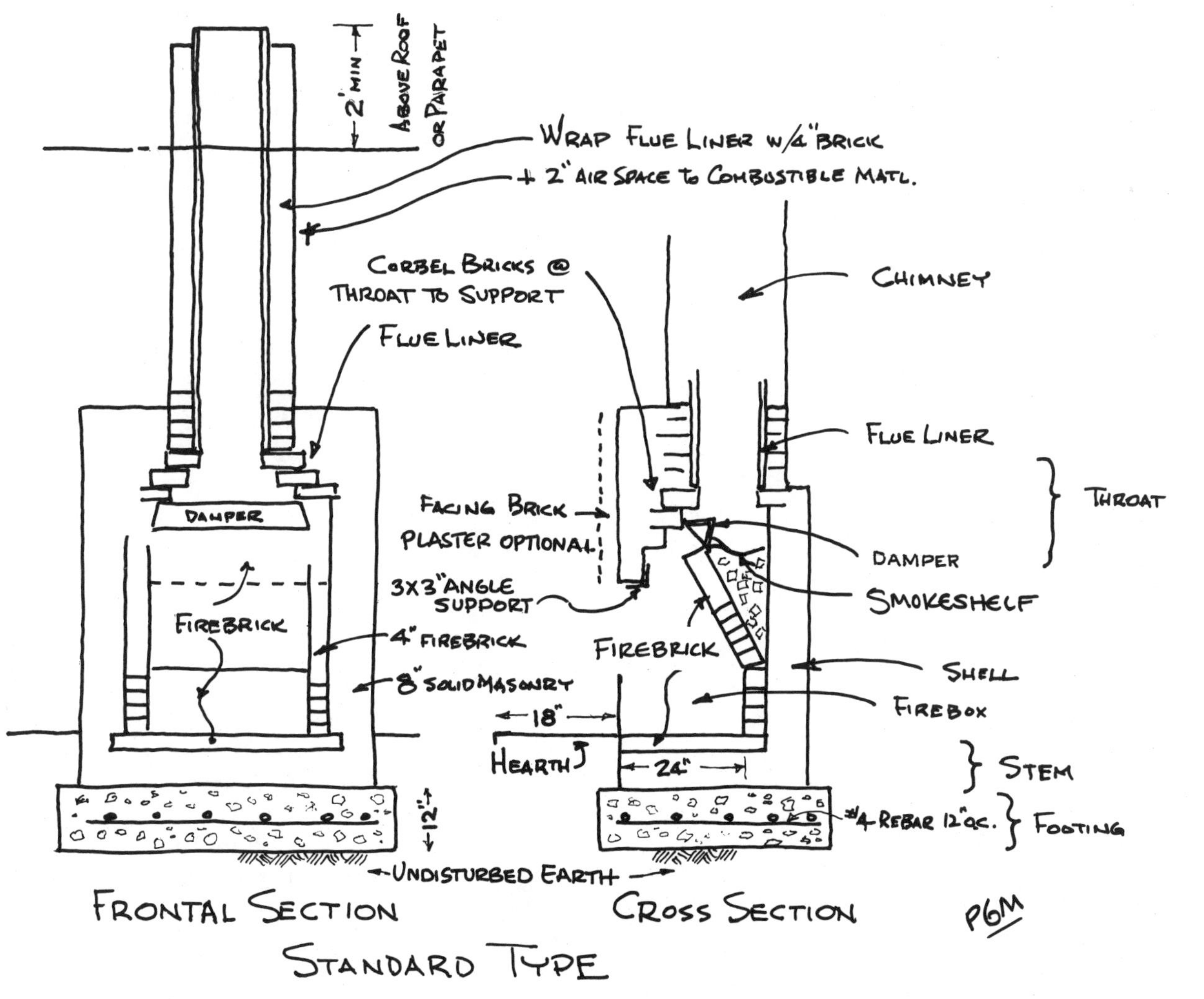

Fig. 18.1 Fireplaces.

will be a great deal of concentrated weight on it. It should be on undisturbed soil, and be strongly reinforced with #4 rebar, on 12″ centers, running both ways. If it starts to tip over ten years later, you've got big problems. Don't skimp on the foundation. If you have any suspicion that you later might want fireplaces in additional locations in your home, put the foundations in as you build.

STEM: A masonry structure that is between the foundation and the firebox. Where you have a basement, it can be quite tall. In a slab floor with monolithic foundation it will be nonexistent unless you have a raised hearth. The stem is normally solid construction, and a good place to get rid of all the rubble and old masonry scrap that seems to be in the way. All crevices should be filled with mortar. This job seems to require a quantity of mortar, and if you don't have a helper, you will wish for one at this point. The same principles for help prevail on this as in any masonry work; namely, it is aggravating to have to change hats from laborer and mixer to master mason. The ash dump, if you want one, is a hollow place in this stem. Patented devices allow the ashes to drop into the ash pit from the bottom of the firebox. An outside clean-out door can be provided if in a suitable location.

FIREBOX: This is the combustion area where most of the heat occurs. It is normally built of firebrick, which is laid up with fireclay, or special ready-mixed refractory cement, such as Saraset or Hueco Bond. The mortar joints between the firebrick should be as thin as possible. Many traditional fireplaces in adobe houses have no firebrick, but merely use adobe mud for plaster on the inside of the firebox. This will work just fine, where firebrick is not required by code, and where you don't mind the labor of replastering the inside every year. The adobe mud will bake hard just like a clay pot, but has a tendency to separate in large chunks from the wall.

The back wall of the firebox should be vertical for approximately 12″ and then slant in towards the room at an angle that will provide adequate room for the damper. This angled surface reflects the heat and provides most of the warmth the fireplace will produce. The side walls of the firebox are also angled to the back to provide a reflecting surface.

SHELL: This is the masonry wall that surrounds the firebox. The firebox will have been built to a precise size, and the shell makes up the main structure, which can be any size that appearance dictates. The shell is usually built of "solids" adjacent to the firebox, which do not have holes as do common bricks. Most codes require that a total solid masonry thickness of 12″ be installed between the inside of the firebox and the exterior of the shell. If an adobe wall is adjacent, it will serve as part of the total requirement, because it is masonry too. The shell extends upwards to the damper, which is placed in the "throat."

THROAT: The throat is a "corbelled" (each brick extends beyond the one below it) treatment of the masonry stack at the top of the firebox, which tapers in to support the damper. In the prefab unit, this is made of metal, and although you don't have to build masonry to support the damper, you do have to enclose it by corbelling bricks in a taper inwards to roughly follow the shape of the unit. It is extremely important that metal surfaces close to the brick be insulated with fiberglass or similar insulation, and that the brick does not touch the metal at any point. The expanding metal would push and crack the brick.

SMOKE SHELF: This is the feature that prevents your fireplace from backfiring from downdrafts in the chimney flue (see Fig. 18.1). If there is only a straight passage from the firebox upwards through the flue, the heat will go straight up and the occasional downdraft (and they do occur!) will blow ashes (maybe hot?) out onto your floor. The traditional New Mexico corner fireplace does not have a smoke shelf, and the damper, if any, is a "butterfly"-type stovepipe damper inserted in the flue. This type will work, but it is not as efficient as the other type, and has an inherent hazard of downdrafts.

FLUE: This may be made of brick, but clay-tile flue liner of the proper size is easier, more

Albuquerque Journal *photograph.*

Fig. 18.2 Residence, Placitas, New Mexico. P. G. McHenry, Jr., architect-builder. New bricks antiqued by tumbling in a concrete mixer soften the sometimes harsh lines of a brick-faced fireplace.

economical, and safer, since it doesn't have as many joints that the fire or heat could leak through. The flue should be encased in brick and should extend at least two feet above the adjacent roof area. Odd wind currents or conditions such as parapet walls, trees, and the like, may require that you extend it even further than this. It is wise to make tentative provision to extend the flue if required, and the fireplace should be used and tested prior to the application of the finished exterior plaster or brick coping, to make sure that it will perform as expected under most conditions (see Fig. 18.1).

FACE: The facing for the fireplace is usually built as a distinctly separate item from the fire-

Fig. 18.3 Residence, Albuquerque, New Mexico. P. G. McHenry, Jr., architect-builder. Sculptured plaster for fireplace facing creates an old world atmosphere. Stone slab for hearth allows for wood storage below.

Fig. 18.4 Residence, Albuquerque, New Mexico. P. G. McHenry, Jr., architect-builder. Native stone facing for fireplace relates to its surroundings.

place "rough," which we have so far discussed. It can be of brick, marble, stone, plaster or whatever. In many cases it won't matter too greatly at what point you decide on the face material, since it won't affect the rough, unless dimensions are critical. Be sure and allow enough room for the thickness of the face so that the areas adjacent to the fireplace will fit.

Rock makes an attractive face, and is fun, but frustrating to lay. If you make your face of native local rock, which may give it the "at home" look that we all strive for, it will be economical to gather your rock, a few at a time if necessary, in your car trunk if you haven't got a truck, and stockpile the rock for future use. The most common mistake in laying up such a face is to start too narrow at the bottom. This is slow work and must be carefully done. Buy a rock chisel and a small hand sledge if you plan to do this. You can only lay up a row or two at a time and then must let the mortar set. Wet the rock and use a rich portland-cement mortar in place of the lime mortar. To insure a good bond, sometimes it is necessary to hold the rocks in place temporarily with wire until they are dry. After the face is all up, the wires can then be cut off and the joints pointed up with more mortar. Keep the work as clean as possible from mortar stains by wiping and brushing with water. The rock face should be anchored with brick ties or wire to the rough.

Brick can also be used, if you're not in too much hurry; however, it may not turn out to be as professional a looking job as you want. *Plan ahead!*

Careful layout is the key to good bricklaying. Water-brush and clean your work before it dries so that mortar stains are at a minimum. The finished job can be cleaned with a dilute solution of muriatic acid (one part muriatic to 8 to 10 parts water). The difference between a professional job and an amateur one frequently is the mortar stains. A professional doesn't have to do much cleaning up because he doesn't waste and splash the mortar around. Probably you will, so it will take you longer to clean up.

A HEARTH is required by most codes to prevent the sparks that pop out from landing on a combustible surface. The hearth is normally 16″ to 18″ wide and needs to be only directly in front of the firebox. If you have brick floors, you have a built-in hearth and the codes require nothing further. A raised hearth makes handy seating and may be combined with a *banco* (wall seat).

PREFABRICATED CIRCULATING FIREPLACES

These make the amateur builder's job somewhat easier, because they consist of a double-walled metal firebox, damper, throat and all, in one package. Nearly all of these do require that you provide a floor of firebrick larger than the unit; the prefabricated unit merely rests on this. It must then be further encased by the shell, with provision for grilles for the air circulation. Instruction sheets are normally enclosed with each unit giving necessary dimensions. There is little difference in total cost between the two systems. What you pay for a prefabricated unit will be offset by materials and labor for the more conventional. As a general rule, the prefab firebox will require a larger shell and structure, because of the room required for air ducts and the like. Additional accessories are also available for fan circulation of the air.

FREE-STANDING FIREPLACES

Metal free-standing fireplaces and custom metal hoods can add startling and attractive effects to your general decor. They are not as traditional as the more conventional types, but can be effective. If you want something like this, by all means don't be bound by tradition, but do check carefully on the cost. By the time you buy the necessary accessories for a modernistic free-standing metal fireplace (not the air-circulation type) you may spend as much as you would for a conventional one. A custom-fabricated metal hood can frequently cost as much as the entire fireplace done by an expert mason. Investigate your costs completely.

FINISHING TOUCHES

MANTELS can be formed from the fireplace shape or can be purely decorative. If yours is not going to be formed from the basic structure, make sure that you have provided anchorage for the mantel supports.

Plaster is probably the most economical face

Fig. 18.5 Residence, Albuquerque, New Mexico. P. G. McHenry, Jr., architect-builder. Raised hearth and combined charcoal grille give an old-fashioned look.

Fig. 18.6 Residence, Placitas, New Mexico. P.G. McHenry, Jr., architect-builder. Traditional *kiva* corner fireplace is improved by the addition of a damper and a hidden smoke shelf.

that you can use. Many striking effects can be obtained from sculpted plaster. The major drawback is that most fireplaces expand with heat, and a plastered face will show even the slightest movement in the form of a crack. This may be alleviated somewhat by the following treatment. After the application of the brown coat of plaster is well dried, a slow but hot fire should be gradually built up in the fireplace until it is quite hot. Cracks will appear in the brown coat at expansion points. Now, drive cut nails (masonry nails) into the cracks on about 6″ centers while the fireplace is hot; this will tend to wedge the masonry in the expanded position. The final plaster coat will then have less tendency to crack at these natural expansion points.

WOOD STORAGE should be provided. Sometimes this can be done by using a cantilevered projecting hearth with storage space beneath. A woodpile for a fireplace is a dusty, unattractive area at best, but you've got to have one, so hide it as conveniently as possible. Exterior wall hatches are also available as accessories, so that wood can be loaded directly from the outside if the location is suitable.

ACCESSORIES include ash dumps, grates, pot hooks, screens, and so on. See a material supplier who sells brick and fireplace accessories. Browse through his stock and his literature. Most contractors can't take the time (and are afraid to spend their client's money) to do much more than provide the bare essentials. *You* aren't under that restraint.

PLACEMENT of your fireplace is quite important. Plan the dimensions of the fireplace you want first, and then make sure there is enough room to put it where you have planned. It will take a surprising amount of room. For example, if you have a narrow room (10 feet), there isn't room enough to build the fireplace inside that wall. The fireplace in most instances will be a minimum of 3 feet wide by 6 feet long. Subtracting 3 from 10 leaves a room width of only 7 feet, less the hearth if one is to be included. In some cases you can save space (providing the fireplace is on an outside wall) by putting the main structure of the fireplace on the outside of the building line, or straddling it part way. Sometimes closet space will serve the same purpose. A corner fireplace with smoke shelf and conventional damper requires a minimum radius at the corner of 3′ 6″, plus the hearth. It may interfere with locations of doors or windows.

PADERCITAS (little walls) are clever architectural devices whereby you create a corner where you do not have one. This is accomplished by building a little wing wall out perpendicularly to the main wall, but only as high as the fireplace itself, thus creating a corner. These *padercitas* are traditional, charming, and quite functional. They also serve as area dividers so that you can make two rooms or activity areas from one larger space and still retain the illusion of the larger area.

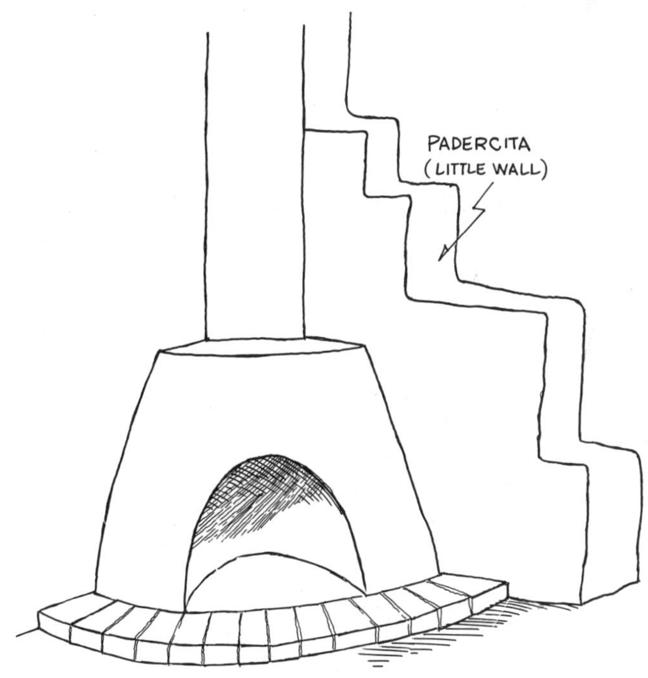

Fig. 18.7 Fireplace and *padercita.*

SAFETY

Caution! A fireplace is a potentially dangerous fire hazard if improperly constructed. Most codes prohibit any structural item, such as roof beams, lintels, and the like from resting on the fireplace structure. The latter should be planned to be free standing, totally independent of any other part of the building, except perhaps the adobe wall. It should be separated from combustible materials by brick and air space, with tightly sealed joints where fire and extreme heat will occur. The following checklist emphasizes the more important points:

Foundation: Level, on undisturbed earth, minimum 12″ thick, reinforced on 12″ centers.

Firebox: Use fire-resistant materials that will withstand severe heat and direct flame (most common brick will disintegrate under such severe conditions). Make sure that corners and joints are tightly sealed to prevent the spread of flames to combustible materials. Provide 12″ of solid masonry.

Damper: This will prevent drafts, dirt, varmints, and the like from using the chimney as an entry when the fireplace is not in use.

Flue: An adequate size for the opening dimensions of the firebox, damper, and height that will be required to raise it a minimum of 2′ above adjacent construction. The flue liner should be vitreous tile, cemented at the joints, and surrounded by at least 4″ of masonry (one brick thick), and the brick should be further separated from any wood framing by a 2″ air space.

PLANNING

One of the best books on fireplaces is published by the Lane Magazine and Book Company, Menlo Park, California, in the "Sunset Books" series. The title is *How To Plan and Build Your Fireplace.* It gives accurate, clear, technical information on the actual construction of a fireplace, with nearly all the possible variations of building conditions, and a bewildering array of pictures of every conceivable style of fireplace arrangement and facing. Picture books such as this (and this particular one is more than just a picture book) are useful, perhaps more for general ideas than for specific details. The details never seem to quite fit with what I'm trying to do, but they do provide inspiration. *Get inspired!*

FIREPLACES: REEVALUATION 1984

Attitudes towards fireplaces have changed since this book was written in 1970. While the original concepts and emotions are still valid, rising energy costs make us take a deeper look. The "standard" fireplace we know from the past can be inefficient, and may need to be modified if we are to enjoy the pleasures a burning fire provides, without major energy cost.

Today's homes are being built much tighter than before so that special provision for combustion air must be made. Some of these provisions are as follows:

The firebox construction systems with draft controls can easily be incorporated into the design, so that the handsome fireplace doesn't act as a drain for heating systems.

The fireplace can actually be a heat exchanger and contribute to the overall heating system, rather than serving primarily as an attractive decoration.

Two new names (old ideas) have surfaced in the past five years. One is the "RUSSIAN" fireplace, and the other is the "COUNT RUMFORD" design. Both of these designs extract the heat in the exhaust gases to add heat to a masonry mass that can radiate this heat into a living space over a longer period of time. The "Russian" design uses a small firebox which can be closed after combustion is underway (like an "airtight" stove), and the masonry flue may follow a circuitous path so that most of the heat is used to heat up masonry mass within the living space. The final flue gases are barely warm. Problems of soot collection and cleanouts must be recognized and dealt with in the design. The "Rumford" does somewhat the same, mainly employing a massive "throat" to absorb the heat. While we are not able here to go into specifics in the design, reference works are available on both designs. See Bibliography.

In summary, we must also conclude that, while efficiency of thermal design is an important factor, economics may deny that the ideal design be used, and we must use what is necessary. Fireplaces work for heating and all kinds of enjoyment!

19

Landscaping and Yard Planning

IN ALL of our architectural considerations, we have stressed the importance of a natural, "at home" look that is compatible with the surroundings. The landscaping you choose provides the final decoration that can add to or detract from the appearance of your home.

LANDSCAPING

The first and foremost requirement of any planting is that it will grow in the particular climate in which you live. We tend perhaps to go back to previous experiences where certain plants, trees, and flowers did well, perhaps in another area or climatic zone. You must investigate carefully what will do well, or at least survive in the climate in which you live. Especially in the Southwest, each particular area, even though perhaps separated from another by only a short distance, may support a different type of vegetation. Palo verde trees and saguaro cactus that are native to the warm desert areas of the Southwest would not begin to survive in northern Arizona or New Mexico, or in any of the higher altitudes of the mountains of the desert areas. Certain species of palm trees may do well in low desert regions of California and in more tropical climates, but are marginal at higher elevations and may be destroyed by occasional severe winter conditions.

Choose plants that are native to, or that have proved they flourish in, your particular locale. This is especially true of trees, shrubs, and hedge plants. The transplanting of wild plants is frequently disappointing unless special care and precautions are taken (and sometimes even then!). Certain types of grasses do better in certain localities than others, if you plan to plant a lawn. Make a careful survey of what looks good on established, landscaped yards in your area. You can gain valuable information by merely stopping and asking the advice of the owners. They will be delighted that you like their yard and should be most helpful. The advice of a local nurseryman is also invaluable.

Rocks and natural physical features of your lot can help keep a natural look, if they haven't been bulldozed down in the construction, or covered with splashed plaster or paint. I once built a home in a natural rock setting, and after many months of careful protection of a rock garden under a porch was dismayed to find the plasterer dumping the leftover plaster over it. If you use large areas of stone or gravel for more formal themes where you don't want any vegetation, cover the area first with plastic sheeting to prevent plant growth from coming up through the gravel. The size and character of the rock or gravel can be important. Check with the local gravel supplier on what better kind might be available for a little additional cost.

Hardy perennials should be the basis of your main theme of natural color. Here you may depart somewhat from the idea of using only what you see around you, since there are certain flowering plants or trees that do well even though they are not native to a certain area. The "Sunset Books" series has an authoritative book on Western gardening. The Arizona-Sonora Desert Museum at Tucson has excellent living examples of the flora native to the southern Arizona-Sonoran Desert region. Try to determine the time of year that each particular plant or tree comes into bloom. If you look carefully at the desert, hot or cold, you will find that it is a blaze of color nearly all year round. As one kind of plant fades, another seems to take its place. Caution should be used in watering these native plants, since they sometimes do better under natural rain conditions (or the lack of it) than with encouragement.

Annuals can be selected from regular nurseries and seed catalogs to reinforce and regulate areas of color in the garden.

Trees, if you have any on your property to start with, should be carefully protected. If you buy some, select the size carefully. If you buy small, young trees that are more economical, it may take years to achieve the effect you want. But if you buy mature ones, they may keep on growing and may overpower the house you were trying to decorate. A happy medium and careful placement, allowing for growth, is best. Trees with shallow, wide-spreading roots, such as eucalyptus, should not be near a house, swimming pool, or sewer line. The transplanting of large trees requires special equipment and knowledge. Let the nurseryman do this.

WATERING SYSTEMS

The watering of your garden and lawn (if you have one) should also be planned in advance. If you are to be successful at growing grass in desert areas, sprinkler systems (or irrigation) are virtually a must. Bubblers are useful for trees and planters. Plan these watering or sprinkler systems in advance. If you haven't decided what will go exactly where, at least make some provision for extending a water line from the house so that the system can be added later without tearing out walls or tunneling under the house to tie into a water line. If it will be some time before you are able to extend the irrigation system, mark the locations of the tie-ins carefully on a "map," and put it in a safe place where you can find it easily when needed.

An adequate number of outside faucets (hose bib is the proper term) should also be included in your water system.

ZONING THE YARD

It makes sense to zone your yard, but zoning is one of the most frequently ignored aspects of planning. You must have some sort of access to your home. It may take the form of a path from which most of the larger items of vegetation have been removed, or it may need to be a concrete paved driveway, depending on a number of things, including climate. Everyone in your home will generate a certain amount of trash that must be carried out and disposed of, either by you or the garbage people. If at all possible, plan a place for trash cans that is reasonably close to the source of the trash, and also where they may be picked up or disposed of easily.

PLAY YARDS. When there are children, certain other items seem to come into view. There are always bicycles, broken toys, and other items for their play that may be somewhat offensive to the eye of the more particular. Why not plan a play yard where the children can do what they please? A swing set is extremely hard on grass, and it doesn't make sense to locate one in a spot where it will do damage to the landscaping.

SERVICE YARDS. Woodpiles for fireplaces, wheelbarrows, gardening tools and supplies must all be stored somewhere. Frequently a small yard or enclosure behind an economical screening fence or wall is an ideal answer. This same area is also a suitable spot for a clothesline.

DRIVEWAYS, or at least the space for them, must be provided. Most people don't realize how big an automobile is and how much room it takes to park or turn one around. The most serious, and most common error is an awkward driveway. If you have a sloping site, make sure that the access grade is gentle enough for normal use without having to resort to four-wheel drive. The cost of constructing such a road can be far greater than you might anticipate. In colder climates, winter conditions may cause extra hazards in the form of snow or ice, particularly on the north side of a house or slope. You can minimize mud or puddles by a little grading or the addition of gravel or "base course" to the dirt. Base course is a mixture of crushed rock and sand that packs down with traffic and will ultimately provide a firm surface.

Circular driveways are particularly troublesome. Usually they are too narrow. Haven't you ever experienced the aggravation of driving into a curved driveway, only to discover that a car is parked there and that you must back all the way out into the street? Double driveways should be at least 20 feet wide, in spite of the fact that the average automobile is less than 8 feet wide. If you curve the driveway, make it at least 30 feet wide. The width required will increase with the narrowing of the radius of the curve. Prior to doing any grading of a driveway, set some little wood stakes along the course where you think the driveway should go. Then drive along it and see how it feels. If a turnaround will be required, stake that out too, and drive on it. Chances are that you will widen it considerably!

WALLS AND FENCES

Often a wall or fence for the garden or patio is necessary or at least desirable. All of us have a natural tendency to define "our property" lines with some sort of marker. Certain localities seem to follow certain customs, and you may feel left out if you don't go along with the local customs. Albuquerque, for example, uses cinderblock walls almost exclusively. El Paso is given to rock walls. Tucson and Phoenix go in for grapestake fences and masonry walls. Each of these local customs has a reason behind it. Many ranch houses on working cattle ranches have walls or fences enclosing the more formal gardens so that the cows or sheep (or wildlife) can't get in.

It may be wise to contain and protect only a small portion of your yard, for a more formal garden, with a low wall to protect it from encroaching natural vegetation, rattlesnakes, or whatever. I recall a beautiful green lawn out in the desert where the rabbits came to feed each evening. It was delightful to watch the rabbits, but they sure were hard on the grass. Rabbits and other small wildlife are the reason so many homes in desert areas have walls or fences around their patios or gardens.

Plan your yard as carefully as you do any other part of your home. *Think about it!* Then plan it and think about it again.

20

Estimating and Tools

ESTIMATING THE COST of your building project is not really as awesome a task as you might imagine. It does seem to bug some people because of its complexity, but if you break it down into its smaller pieces it is quite simple. As was pointed out in the beginning, the building of a home is a complicated task in its entirety, but really is just a large number of very small and not so complicated tasks.

HOW TO ESTIMATE

You must first have your plans complete, with details of exactly how you hope to accomplish each phase of construction, from excavations for foundations through the installation of cabinets and bathroom accessories. You must also accept the fact that no matter how detailed you make your plans, some of the details won't work out when you get to the point of installation. It is all but impossible to visualize all the details in a three-dimensional situation and how they will relate to or fit in with other parts of the construction. It is important that you try your very best to do this on paper, however, because without a starting plan you will be completely lost.

There are an incredible number of items that must be considered in your estimate. So don't trust to memory but, like the pilots and space scientists, use a checklist to try and make your estimate as complete as possible. You must also bear in mind that even the best checklist in the world may not fit this particular building project exactly. Some items will not be required and others will be added. You must allow for extra expense, also. Each item on your list will have three possibilities — materials, labor, and subcontractor work. All are interrelated, and sometimes overlapping. Your job as the general contractor is to keep them sorted out and in the correct sequence.

The following list is a guide, with columns for quantities, material, labor and subcontractor costs. Use a columnar pad:

Permits
Plans and blueprints
Survey
Layout and stake
Landscape removal, site clearing
Excavation:
- Primary grading
- Footings
- Backfills
- Piers and pads
- Roads, other
- Fine grading on completion
- Rock removal — blasting

Concrete:
- Footings
- Stem, stem fill
- Piers and pads
- Steps and stoops
- Slabs
- Curb cuts and removal
- Sidewalks (city)
- Curb and gutter (city)
- Column fill
- Bond beams

Accessories:
- Form rental
- Rebar
- Mesh
- Miscellaneous

Masonry:
- Stem block
- Adobe walls
- Fireplaces
- Fireplace facings
- Roloks, door and window sills
- Brick floors
  - Sand and plastic
- Rock walls
- Flagstone
- Stoops and steps
- Porch floors
- Copings

Carpentry, rough:
- Beams and girders (*vigas*)
- Posts
- Joists, box sills, bridging
- Stud walls and plates
- Parapets
- Floor decking
- Roof decking
- Porch framing
- Porch decking, railings
- Wall sheathing
- Dry sheeting (roof)
- Wall insulation
- Roof insulation
- Stairways
- Rough bucks

Carpentry, finish:
- Doors (make schedule)
  - Frames, trim*
  - Hardware
- Windows (make schedule)
  - Frames, trim*
  - Hardware
- Shelves
- Stairway treads, railings
- Millwork
  - Base shoe
  - Stops and trim*
- Paneling
- Bath accessories, medicine cabinets
- Cabinet work
  - Base cabinets
  - Wall cabinets
  - Vanities
  - Broom closets
  - Wall-oven cabinets
  - Bookshelves
  - Other
- Nails, shingles, caulking, miscellaneous

Roofing

Plumbing System
- Gaslines
- Water-line extensions, yard lines, wells, meters
- Septic tanks, street cuts
- Bathtubs and trim* (faucets and controls)
- Water closets (toilets)
- Lavatories and trim*
- Kitchen sink and trim*
- Shower rough, trim*
- Washer rough-in
- Hose bibs (freezeproof?)
- Water heaters

Heating System
- Gas line extensions, yard lines

Air conditioning

Electrical System
- Line extensions
- Fixtures

Lathing

Plaster

Dry wall

Painting

Resilient flooring, base

Glazing

Mirrors

Ceramic tile

Clean up

General items:
- Ornamental iron
- Hardware
- Skylights
- Appliances
- Toilet rental
- Construction Utilities
  - Water
  - Gas
  - Electricity
  - Phone
- Insurance
  - Workmen's Compensation
  - Builder's risk
  - Public liability
- Finance charges:
  - Discounts on loans
  - Closing costs
  - Interest on construction loan
- Scaffold rental
- Trucking expense

Miscellaneous

---

* The "trim" should be specified, since it will vary widely in quality and price.

It really looks like a formidable task, doesn't it? But instead of being overcome, examine each item, use a separate page for each if necessary, make a schedule, or do whatever is needed to break each item down into its individual parts. Use columnar pads, be systematic, plan your estimate as carefully as you do your home itself.

The list could be almost endless. Include as much as will apply to your particular project, until you have the feeling that nothing of major importance has been left out. You are bound to miss some items; this is what the miscellaneous is for. Some of your items will be over, some will be under, tending to balance each other out. A careful material take-off and comparison of material suppliers' quotations will reduce the material-cost error to minor importance. The labor is another matter. Inasmuch as you are not contracting to supply the labor for a fixed figure, and probably will do much of it yourself, your real need is for an estimate of how many hours will be required so that you can budget your time and scheduling for the job. The hours can then be translated into dollars if necessary.

The best help I can recommend in this direction is the *Building Estimator's Reference Book* by Frank R. Walker (see Bibliography). This is as accurate as any guide you can use. It is available at most libraries, and gives such diverse information as how many hours it takes a laborer to load eight yards of dirt on a truck with a shovel, to how many square feet of tile roofing a crew can put on in one day. Your own experience is, of course, the best guide, but if you haven't done this particular type of job before, try to visualize.

Let us now run down just a few of the items included on the estimate form, and I will make comments that may prove useful in completing each item in detail. We'll try to cover the main items, and give you a clue as to how to proceed.

Permits: What permits will be required? Perhaps in your locale none are. A telephone call or two should answer most of your questions regarding requirements and charges that will be incurred.

Survey: Was a survey made on the property when you purchased it? Are the stakes still intact? Will the organization providing financing require a certificate?

Layout and stake: Are the dimensions and placement of your building critical with regard to lot lines? If so, perhaps it will be economical to employ a surveyor who will set the stakes and furnish the foundation certificate.

Site clearing: Are there trees on the building site that must be removed? Rocks, boulders? Are access roads needed?

Excavations: Main lot leveling? Heavy equipment work? Is the site level enough to use a trenching machine, or must a backhoe be used? By hand? What are the various sizes of footing that must be dug? Make a schedule.

Concrete: This is figured in cubic yards; figure enough quantity to pour at one time to get maximum economy. If in a remote location must you mix your own? What does it cost to get gravel and sand delivered, to rent or buy a mixer?

Forms: A good tip is to order all of your rough framing lumber early, use it for forms, and then take the forms apart and use it for your structure (concealed).

Masonry: What will it cost to get an adequate supply of adobes, brick, block, mud, sharp sand, cement, and lime? Try to combine deliveries. Frequently the brick seller can deliver these on the same load as the masonry.

Rock: Look around the site and adjacent roads and along streams and washes. The rock may be right there *free!*

Carpentry: Make a detailed take-off of all the dimension lumber, well labeled on your take-off sheet so that if changes are made you'll be able to easily identify what items aren't required, without having to take it all off again. Figure the lengths of boards required. When purchasing, it may make sense to pay a few pennies more for some items and get them delivered by the same supplier rather than make a special trip. Schedule your requirements for material with the progress schedule so that lumber won't be in the way or subject to weather damage until you're ready to use it.

Doors and windows: These may require several weeks for delivery. Make a careful schedule with all items identified by number or letter showing all details for frames, swing, hardware, and so on. Millwork can be determined in advance in a general sense, as far as quantity goes, but you may run over or short. Plan to buy additional as required, and return any surplus in good condition. Cabinets can't be finally measured (usually) until the interior is complete as far as partitions and plaster or wallboard.

Roofing: Has the roofer included all the necessary metal, flashings, cant strip, gravel stop, *canales,* and the like in his bid? Perhaps he can apply the insulation as well. Make sure the bid is clearly spelled out.

Plumbing: Many plumbing bids (if you plan to use a plumber) only include piping to 5 feet from the house. Establish the distance precisely, and for what unit prices the necessary yard lines will be installed. Specify fixture quality.

Appliances: If you buy these from a builders' supply, they don't come installed. Someone has to install them.

Subcontractors: Although each subcontractor may furnish a complete bid for his portion of the work, they all will depend on a certain amount of direction from you to get a satisfactory job. These people make mistakes too! Although you may be able to get them to correct any gross errors they have made, at their expense, the trouble and problems are better avoided by a little good supervision on your part. Include some lost time to cover this, and also for the time that will be lost waiting for material deliveries and subcontractors.

Miscellaneous: This item may sometimes be expressed as a percentage of the above totals. If the estimate has been carefully made, it may be quite small, but if carelessly made it can be real big. I would include everything you can think of, and then add a lump sum figure for the totals of each item of somewhere between 5 and 10 percent.

TOOLS

Although all through the ages, our ancestors have accomplished miracles with a minimum amount of very primitive tools, you will discover that having the right tools for the job will reduce the work and the frustrations, and will usually result in a better finished job. One rule to remember is this: *Buy only the tools you have a specific need for!*

When you have decided what you need, buy the best you can afford for your own use. Good tools, properly cared for, will last a lifetime. There is a wide range in quality and price. For example, you can pay anywhere from $2 to $8 for a hammer. The cheap one will not do as satisfactory a job and may not even last out the day. The thing to look for is a store that sells craftsman or mechanic tools, as opposed to do-it-yourself tools. If in doubt, ask the advice of a reputable supplier.

The following is a list of tools that will be indispensable in building and maintaining your own home:

Shovel, long handle, round point
Shovel, long handle, square point
Wheelbarrow, contractors' heavy duty, 3-ply inflatable tires, with a practical (not rated) capacity of 2½ to 3 cu. ft. Bigger than this will be too heavy to handle unless you're really in shape.
Mattock. This is like a pick but has one flat end. Great for truing footings and chopping adobe walls.
Saw, hand, finish 10 pt. for cross-grain sawing
Saw, rip 5 pt. for sawing with the grain
Saw, electric, heavy duty, with at least 7″ blade
Hammer, framing, straight claw, 20 oz.
Hammer, finish, curve claw, 12 oz.
Hammer, sledge, 3# short handle, for driving stakes and chipping concrete. Very useful!
Hammer, mason's brick
Square, framing
Square, try
Level, 48″, brass bound or metal
Level, 24″, brass bound or metal
Brace, and various bits. Several expandable bits will cover a wide range.
Hatchet (Boy Scout type)
Chisels, wood, set, various widths
Chisels, cold, various widths, lengths
Planes, small block plane and medium-size smoothing plane.
Trowels:
- Block
- Pointer
- Flat point
- Cement finishing
- Plaster

Hawk, for holding plaster if you do your own
Nylon cord, and mason's line
Catspaw (for removing embedded nails)
Chalk line (plumb-bob type)

21

Restoring Old Adobes

THE RESTORATION of an old adobe structure begins with a difficult choice to make. "Paste" the house together so that it will look livable, and will require a lot of maintenance to keep it looking that way, or restore it soundly, which will probably cost more than if you tore it down and started fresh.

If the structure has some historical significance, by all means it should be preserved, but be prepared for disappointment, in that the old floorplans were not designed for modern living, and the addition of "necessary" conveniences such as plumbing and heating is a big challenge. Nothing is impossible in the construction business if you are prepared to spend enough money. If you go this route, bring lots of money!

About the only thing salvageable in a restoration are the adobe walls, and sometimes the roof timbers. This may involve only a small portion of your total construction budget. Assuming that you will be able to live with the floor plan and traffic pattern, let's start at the bottom and work up:

Foundations: If the building is truly old, it will most likely have rock foundations, without benefit of cement mortar. The mere fact that the walls are still standing may testify to the fact that the foundations are sound. Just as we all have experienced ground build-up in our lawns, from the blowing in of airborne soil, so we may expect this in old adobes. Frequently the floor level is below exterior grade, leaving the adobe walls subject to any stray groundwater that may occur. These walls must be protected from moisture at all costs, or they may fail, bringing down the rest of the structure. To correct such a condition may require underpinning, or replacement of the foundation or wall to a point above exterior grade. Damp adobe has no strength at all. I've seen old adobe walls, apparently intact, start to squeeze out from the weight above or start to tip over. This kind of trouble you don't need.

Windows and doors: Although it is a simple matter to cut a hole in an adobe wall, it can be difficult to anchor it against a vibration unless anchors are laid up in the wall as it is built.

Old walls seldom were installed with proper bond beams, frequently resulting in cracked corners, and tipped walls, which usually continue to cause trouble. (See Figure 21.3)

Roof framing is frequently inadequate, rotted, and unsafe. If you try to add insulation to this it may cause further structural problems. In any event, to restore the building soundly, you may have to remove and then re-lay the roof structure. (See Figure 21.2)

The charming details in an old adobe, such as hand-carved beams, door and window casings, *latillas,* and decking, if sound, can be more easily incorporated in a new structure, leaving behind most of the all-but-impossible problems. Fixing an old adobe is like eating peanuts, or trying to rejuvenate a worn-out automobile. It's hard to know when to stop. You replace the engine, and find that the clutch is gone, replace the clutch, and the transmission is faulty, and so on ad infinitum, until the whole thing has been replaced anyway and you may not achieve your desired result.

Many people fondly dream of buying an old adobe house and "fixing it up" on weekends at relatively small cost. This is a myth. Restoration can be accomplished, but it requires considerably more skill and knowledge to "restore" an old adobe than to build one from scratch. The soundest advice I can offer is to be extremely wary of any such efforts, and plan the restoration details and estimated costs as carefully as you would for a new house.

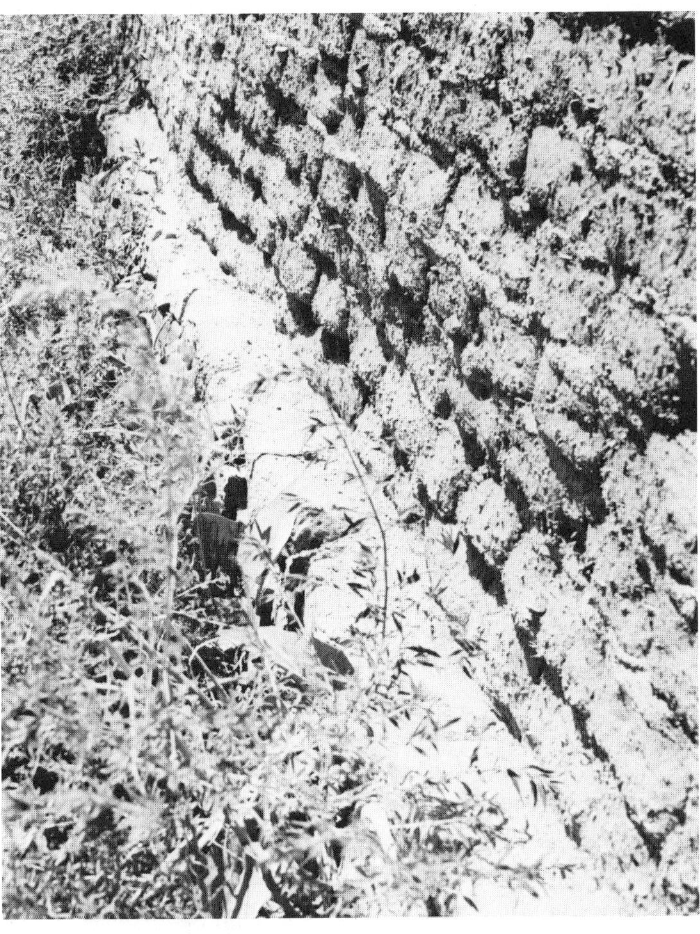

Fig. 21.1 Adobe restoration problems. In spite of a rock foundation, mud adobes have been badly eroded by drip and splash from the roof.

Fig. 21.3 Old adobe. Wall has begun to tip, due to eroded bottom portion and the lack of a bond beam to tie it to intersecting walls. Note wood nailer inserted between courses for some forgotten purpose.

Fig. 21.2 Old adobe. Collapse of wall is being hastened by the concentration of water flow off roof at point where roofing has disappeared.

22

Conclusions

THE CREATION OF A HOME, from earliest design concepts to successful completion, is one of the most rewarding experiences you can ever have. It seems to satisfy some primitive urge in all of us to create a snug shelter. We see this expressed simply by children, who love to build playhouses from boxes, blankets, or whatever is at hand.

Expect also a somewhat traumatic experience. It is impossible for you to perceive, at this point, what a complex task you have undertaken. Don't be discouraged, however, because one day you will look up from your labors and it will be done.

Building can be a lonely business. The ultimate responsibility must rest with one person who makes the decisions. It takes a considerable amount of courage to dig the first shovel of dirt, cut the first board, or pour the first wheelbarrow of concrete. A husband and wife who undertake the task of building a home will discover new areas of interest and capacities in each other that they never knew existed. The doubts and worries that attack the amateur builder create severe pressures on the soundest marriage. One must make the decision (certainly only after due conferences and deliberation) and be responsible for it.

A word must be said about working alone. It is not good for people to work alone. Problems seem to magnify themselves all out of proportion. The material you are working with seems to get more contrary, the weather seems much colder or warmer than it really is, and the job seems impossible. I have found in the contracting business that it is usually best to send two men on a job, even if only one is really required. The company of your wife, a friend, or even a small child seems to help, even if the person doesn't do anything but make sympathetic noises, and hand you a tool now and then.

Problems and errors will occur. Expect it! Forbearance, understanding, and tact must prevail. You do not have the years of experience that make old builders secure in their knowledge that every problem has its solution, usually quite simple. You must bear in mind constantly that the world will not come to an end if you do something wrong. It may take only a few minutes thought, only one dollar, or only a gallon of sweat to correct the error. It frequently turns out that what you had planned won't work, and the new solution is much better than the original idea. When an expensive beam is cut too short, a large blue cloud of profanity sometimes helps. On the part of the helper, silence may be golden, but sympathetic noises may be even better. Recriminations may lead to bloodshed.

Try for perfection, but don't be too disappointed when you don't get it. You will only destroy your enthusiasm in an impossible effort. Every plan and every building has its mistakes, no matter how competent the architect or the builder. Why should you fare better than they do? At times the job may seem endless, and incapable of completion. There will be times when the crooked board you cut just won't quite fit and you finally say the hell with it and nail it up anyway. Expect this to happen and forgive yourself. Chances are that when the project is all finished, you will be the only one to be aware of it anyway.

Realistic analysis is the key to your project. At every step of the way you will have, and must make, a choice of what you plan to actually do yourself. You should examine each phase closely enough, in detail, to find out what it will entail, and then decide whether you have time, or if you really want to do this. To start with, for example, you must have some definite plans and details on precisely what you intend to build. You can do the entire job yourself, buying a few tools, and learning a little bit yourself about drafting in the process. You can have a fairly precise idea of what you want and have a draftsman or an architectural student do the actual drafting. If you don't feel up to this, engage an architect, who can provide complete working drawings, with specifications, and even supervision to see that the contractor does it the way it was planned. If you engage an architect, help him, and yourself, by making some sketches of how you feel the rooms should be arranged, and the general scheme of things. Include specific favorite details and strong feelings about the most important part of the house to *you*. He will then be able to blend your ideas with a sense of beauty and integrity, and sort out the technical problems on how it must fit together. He may further help you avoid many of the more common pitfalls that beginners sometimes overlook, such as the bathroom door opening into the dining room, or not enough space for the refrigerator. Most architects will effect savings in materials and arrangements that will more than offset their fee, and you get the bonus of professional help.

So . . . in reviewing the foregoing paragraph, we find that you have three choices: do it all yourself, compromise with a combined effort, or have it all done for you. The same three choices will be available at each phase of your project. If you hire expert help, get the best available, and don't rely on price as the ultimate measure. Be careful of the apparent cheap price. Analyze it as carefully as you can, make a choice, and have confidence in the people you select.

There is a real thrill in building. Most people who are engaged in the construction business for any length of time either never leave it or eventually return to it. Perhaps they don't even know why. They may curse the problems and the business, but everybody involved from the architect to the lowliest laborer feels a sense of pride in what has been accomplished, and he feels he had a part in creating it. Let yourself get caught up in the romance of this, plus the fact that you are carrying on the tradition of the pioneers and early explorers who built their homes, railroads, and empires with their bare hands. It is hard to maintain your enthusiasm when the sweat drips in your eyes as you dig a trench, or lay adobes in the hot sun. Why not leave at least some of the hard parts to someone else, and save the fun parts for yourself?

When all is done and you sit back in your favorite chair on a cold winter night in front of a flickering fire, you get your reward. The afterglow from building a home is the greatest sensation on earth. Compare yourself to the caveman with his family, fire, and haunch of venison, or the lonely rancher, completely dependent on his own resources, snug behind thick adobe walls with the portals barred, a meal on the table, family and possessions safe inside.

Plaque by Jan and Denis Cummings, Albuquerque, New Mexico.

Fig. 22.1 The above saying is what the man of the household tells his wife as he leaves for work: "While you're resting, make some adobes!"

Bibliography

BDM Corporation. *Adobe Brick Manufacturing Feasibility Study.* Albuquerque, N.M., 1979.

Boudreau, E. H. *Making the Adobe Brick.* Berkeley; Fifth Street Press, 1971.

Bunting, Bainbridge. *Early Architecture in New Mexico.* Albuquerque: University of New Mexico Press, 1976.

__________. *Of Earth and Timbers Made.* Albuquerque: University of New Mexico Press, 1974.

__________. *TAOS ADOBES.* Fort Burgwin Research Center. Santa Fe: Museum of New Mexico Press, 1964.

California State University. *Manufacturer of Asphalt-Emulsion-Stabilized-Soils Brick and Brick-makers' Manual.* Fresno, California, 1972

Clark, K. N. and Patricia Paylore. *Desert Housing.* Tucson: University of Arizona Arid Lands Studies, 1979.

Clough, Richard H. *A Qualitative Comparison of Rammed Earth and Sun-Dried Adobe Brick.* Albuquerque, University of New Mexico Press, 1950.

Fathy, Hassan. *Architecture for the Poor.* Chicago: University of Chicago Press, 1973.

Four Corners Regional Commission. *A Study of the Feasibility of Mechanized Adobe Production.* University of New Mexico Center for Environmental Research and Development, 1971.

Gallagher, D. L. Stabilization Processes of Existing Adobe Structures. Ph.D. dissertation. School of Architecture, University of New Mexico, Albuquerque, 1972.

Golaney, Gideon, ed. *Housing in Arid Lands: Design and Planning.* London: Architectural Press, 1980.

Gray, Macrae, and McCall. *Mud Space and Spirit.* Santa Barbara, California: Capra Press, 1976.

Harrington, M. R. *How to Build a California Adobe.* Los Angeles, Ward Ritchie Press, 1948.

International Workshop, Earthen Buildings in Seismic Areas. Conference Proceedings, University of New Mexico, 1981.

Iowa, J. *Learning From Las Cruces.* Privately printed. Santa Fe, 1982.

Lumpkins, William. *Casa Adobe.* Santa Fe: Santa Fe Publishing Co., 1950.

__________. *Casa del Sol.* Santa Fe: Santa Fe Publishing Co., 1981.

__________. *Modern Spanish Pueblo Homes.* Santa Fe: Santa Fe Publishing Co., 1947.

Mazria, E. *The Passive Solar Energy Book.* Emmaus, Pennsylvania: Rodale Press, 1979.

McHenry, P. G. Jr. *Adobe... Build It Yourself.* First edition, Tucson: University of Arizona Press, 1973. Second Edition, 1985.

__________. A Manual for Simple Housing. Albuquerque, New Mexico.

__________. An Examination of Mud Brick Architectural Forms in Iran With Experimental Applications in the Southwestern United States. Master's thesis, School of Architecture, University of New Mexico, 1974.

__________. Report on Research and Investigations, Conclusions and Recommendations for Tumacacori National Monument Stabilization. Washington, D.C.; National Park Service, 1978.

__________. Shelter in the Harsh Land. Albuquerque, 1976.

Museum of New Mexico. *Adobe, Past and Present.* Santa Fe, 1972.

Nabakov, Peter. *Adobe: Pueblo and Hispanic Traditions of the Southwest.* Washington, D.C.: The Smithsonian Institution Press, 1981.

National Bureau of Standards. Factors Affecting the Durability of Adobe Structures. Washington, D.C. NBSIR 78-1405.

__________. Mechanical Properties of Adobe. Washington, D.C.: Technical Note 996, 1979.

__________. Methods for Characterizing Adobe Building Materials. Washington, D.C. Technical Note 977, 1978.

__________. Preservation of Historic Adobe Structures. Washington, D.C., Technical Note 934, 1977.

__________. Protecting Adobe Walls From Ground Water. Washington, D.C., NBSIR 79-1730, 1979.

Neubauer, L. W. *Adobe Construction Methods.* University of California Experiment Station, 1979.

New Mexico Energy and Minerals Dept. *The New Mexico Home Cooling Guide.* Santa Fe, 1981.

Robertson, David K. Expanded Revision of Effective U Values. New Mexico Energy Research and Development, University of New Mexico, 1981.

Schultz, K. *Adobe Craft.* Castro Valley, California: Adobe Craft, 1977.

Scoggins, Howard. *The Portalab Manual.* New Mexico Appropriate Technical Program, Alamogordo: 1981.

Shelter Publications. *Shelter II.* Bolinas, California: 1978.

Smith, Edward. *Adobe Bricks in New Mexico.* Socorro: New Mexico Institute of Mining and Technology, 1982.

Stedman, Myrtle. *Adobe Architecture.* Santa Fe: Sunstone Press, 1973.

__________. *Adobe Remodeling.* Santa Fe: Sunstone Press, 1973.

U.S. Department of Agriculture. Building with Adobe and Stabilized Earth Blocks. Leaflet #535. U.S. Department of Agriculture. Washington, D.C., 1965. Revised 1972. U.S.

U.S. Department of Housing and Urban Development. "Adobe as a Socially Appropriate Technology for the Southwest." *Papers in Housing and Community Affairs.* Washington, D.C., 1980.

National Park Service. *Preservation Briefs #5.* Department of the Interior, Washington, D.C., 1979.

Wiley & Sons. *Architectural Graphic Standards.* PP 246, 247, 248. New York, 1982.

Wolfskill, Dunlop, and Callaway. *Handbook for Building Homes of Earth.* Reprint Series, Chamisa Books. College Station: Texas A & M University Press, 1979.

Worldwatch Institute. *Global Housing Prospects: The Resource Constraints.* Worldwatch Paper #46, 1981.

Illustrations

Index